CLEM BASTOW'S [...] OF BRILLIANT WIT AND ASTUTE OBSERVATION. THIS STORY IS ONE OF AGENCY, AND SELF-POSSESSION. GENEROUSLY TOLD, IT ALLOWS US TO WITNESS HER EXPERIENCE OF 'STEPPING OUT OF THE SHADOWS, AND INTO THE LIGHT'.
CLARE BOWDITCH

LATE BLOOMER AUTHENTICALLY ILLUSTRATES THE IMPORTANCE OF UNDERSTANDING OUR AUTISTIC IDENTITY AND LOVING WHO WE TRULY ARE. CLEM'S CLEVER AND HEARTFELT STORYTELLING WALKS US GENTLY THROUGH THE JOURNEY SHE HAS TAKEN SINCE HER LIFE-CHANGING DIAGNOSIS. AN IMPORTANT READ FOR EVERY PARENT, TEACHER, THERAPIST, OR INDIVIDUAL WANTING TO LEARN MORE FROM THE #ACTUALLYAUTISTIC COMMUNITY.
KATIE KOULLAS, YELLOW LADYBUGS

For Mum, my hero ♥

LATE BLOOMER

BLOOMER

HOW AN
AUTISM
DIAGNOSIS
CHANGED
MY LIFE

CLEM
BASTOW

Hardie Grant

BOOKS

Published in 2021 by Hardie Grant Books, an imprint of Hardie Grant Publishing

Hardie Grant Books (Melbourne)
Wurundjeri Country
Building 1, 658 Church Street
Richmond, Victoria 3121

Hardie Grant Books (London)
5th & 6th Floors
52–54 Southwark Street
London SE1 1UN

hardiegrantbooks.com

 A catalogue record for this
book is available from the
National Library of Australia

Late Bloomer
ISBN 978 1 74379 600 9

10 9 8 7 6 5 4 3 2 1

Cover design by Ella Egidy
Typeset in 10.75/16 pt Sabon by Cannon Typesetting
Cover image courtesy of Stocksy/Pixel Stories

Printed in Australia by Griffin Press, part of Ovato, an Accredited ISO AS/NZS
14001 Environmental Management System printer.

 The paper this book is printed on is certified against the Forest
Stewardship Council® Standards. Griffin Press holds chain of
custody certification SGSHK-COC-005088. FSC® promotes
environmentally responsible, socially beneficial and economically
viable management of the world's forests.

Hardie Grant acknowledges the Traditional Owners of the country on which we
work, the Wurundjeri people of the Kulin nation and the Gadigal people of the
Eora nation, and recognises their continuing connection to the land, waters and
culture. We pay our respects to their Elders past, present and emerging.

CONTENTS

AUTHOR'S NOTE

You will notice that, outside of direct quotes from other writers, I capitalise the 'a' in Autism. This is a personal choice, reflecting the importance of Autism to my identity and sense of community, though it's a choice that many others make also. In capitalising Autistic and Autism, I am recognising that this is not just a 'condition', but a community and a culture.

I also use identity-first language rather than person-first (except where it would clash with someone's personal preference, or where an alternative is used within a quotation): 'Autistic person' rather than 'person *with* Autism'. Again, this is a personal choice, though it is also one that is increasingly prevalent among Autistic people. I use identity-first language to reflect the fact that Autism is an important part of my identity. I may have been recently 'diagnosed with Autism', but I have been Autistic since birth.

Person-first language is often preferred by parents of Autistic children, and by some clinicians and therapists who work with Autistic people, due to concerns that their child or charge will be unduly stigmatised by identity-first language. I understand that this comes from a place of care, and from a desire to protect. However, while the intention is to affirm the person, the separation of their 'condition' suggests there is nothing about Autism that could contribute to that person's worth. Identity-first language, on the other hand, believes that a person has worth *because of* their Autistic identity, not in spite of it.

Any use of functioning labels – 'high functioning' and 'low functioning' – outside of direct historical quotes will be placed in inverted commas. To many in the Autistic community, functioning labels are unhelpful at best and slurs at worst. 'Low functioning' denies agency (such as the notion that a person is incapable of communication simply by virtue of being unable to speak), and 'high functioning' prevents access to supports. Some Autistic people choose to self-identify as 'high functioning' as a point of pride, or to distance themselves from Autistic people with higher or more complex support needs; this book is probably not for them. Similarly, 'nonspeaking' is used where 'nonverbal' might once have been expected. This is because nonverbal implies that a person has no forms of symbolic language, whereas nonspeaking simply means they do not use speech to communicate. The vocalisations that a nonspeaking person may make, while they are not 'words', are still vibrant and valid forms of intentional communication.

The neologism 'neurotypical' is used to refer to people who experience, as queer Autistic scholar Dr Nick Walker puts it, 'a style of neurocognitive functioning that falls within the dominant societal standards of "normal"'. It doesn't mean 'non-Autistic', but rather, is the opposite of 'neurodivergent'. While humanity as a whole is neurodiverse, a person is neurodivergent. There are multiple types of innate neurodivergence, such as dyslexia and ADHD; my experience of neurodivergence is one of Autism. There is a lot of overlap between the Neurodiversity Movement and the Autism Rights Movement, but they are not quite the same thing.

Where I have mentioned a study of Autism, I have provided citations in endnotes. This is an act of academic accountability, but it is also political: it is a way to demonstrate, however subtly, that the

Autistic person is so often viewed as an object, not a subject. There is a reference list at the end of the book, which provides both broader context and further reading for anyone who is keen to go deeper, but I have tried to avoid extensive endnotes, if only to pretend, for one brief, shining moment, that I'm not a complete nerd. My reading of any studies (etc.) was based on what was current during the writing process, but Autism research is a dynamic field.

I could never hope to address every possible way Autism has manifested in my life (nor how it might manifest in others'), so there may be some 'typical' Autistic experiences, behaviours or 'symptoms' that you are surprised to find don't get a look-in here. It may be that you read this book and think, 'Hey, what gives? I thought this was a book about Autism?' Well, it is and it isn't: it's the story of an Autistic person's life, written by that Autistic person. Some of it may be hard to read; indeed, some of it was hard to write. But I have been honest in my account of my life's ups and downs as they intersect with my Autism because, as Autistic Self Advocacy Network co-founder Ari Ne'eman has put it, 'By being proudly Autistic in our moments of excellence as well as our moments of struggle, we help to change the public image of Autism and tell the world that we have much to offer.'

Online reviews of so-called 'Autism memoirs' often seem perplexed that these books do not involve the experiences of others throughout, as though one might pick up the memoirs of Noël Coward and come away disappointed that the book didn't go into great depths about the life of Gertrude Lawrence. For the most part, *Late Bloomer* concerns my own experience, though I have included the voices of other Autistic people to convey a sense of the diversity of experiences within the Autism spectrum. Some readers may see echoes of their own experience in mine – indeed, I hope they do! That's the nature of Autism; sometimes our Venn diagrams collide – but I can only speak for myself. To give some sense of this diversity, I have included a chapter of short interviews that offer some insight into the lived experiences of a number of Autistic people I know. Some of their experiences are very similar to mine, and some are very different.

Every day I am inspired by and learn from the young Autistic people around me. Their self-actualisation astounds me; not having had that roadmap of earlier diagnosis and support, I can only look back on my life and consider the ways in which my strengths and challenges were intertwined with my Autism. In this way, *Late Bloomer* is not a memoir in a traditional sense, nor is it always chronological; to write and remember in neat order would be to deny the nature of my Autistic personhood.

Now get in my spaceship and let's go back in time.

INTRODUCTION

'Fucking *asps*.'

Even though it takes, on average, probably about fifteen seconds to ascend from the Melbourne Central food court to Hoyts Cinemas, this might be the longest escalator ride I've ever taken; it's like someone has welded me to the step. I can see his words floating in the air before me, like they're in a speech bubble: 'Fucking asps.'

It's 25 July 2018, and I'm here to see a movie

on a date?

just catching up??

being friends???

with a guy

I like?

who had subpar sex with me once so thus should probably be the recipient of my other free ticket to *Mission: Impossible – Fallout*???

I'm not sure I do actually like but now it's too late oh god I want to go home

and he's just gone on a tear about his painful day at work, because I asked – as I have been led to believe a good Human Woman should ask, on a date or otherwise – how his day was. His store was not, in case you were wondering, overrun by small snakes: 'asps' is how he refers to 'Aspies', or people with Asperger syndrome, or Autism Spectrum Disorder, or Autism, who are evidently overrepresented in the clientele of the pop culture store he works at.

These 'fucking *asps*' evidently had the temerity to ask for ... things they wanted to buy? From a shop where things are available to buy? (I'm trying to keep up.) At this point it's becoming clear that I, too, have been confused about the rules of engagement in pop-cultural retail for some time. 'Ha ha,' I laugh, 'yeah ...'. I stare somewhere off into the distance at a smear of bain-marie lemon chicken on the floor of the food court, wishing that Tom Cruise would come crashing through the Shot Tower and hold this dude down while I roundhouse kick him in the face (the dude, not Tom; I'd never do that to Tom).

I wonder how long it takes for Tom to start running in this movie?
he's so good at running
I wish running didn't hurt my knees

As the escalator grinds skywards I start wondering what I'm doing here: why did I give this guy my +1 to see the film that one of my favourite critics described as 'like watching the most intense man on Earth compete in a relentless foot race against his own demons' when I could have brought literally anyone else? Why, in fact, did we have sex in 2013 in my suite at the Town & Country San Diego, where there are 'beautiful roses everywhere you look!' (©TripAdvisor), when I would have been better off looking at said roses or visiting the ice machine or ordering room service or doing literally anything other than having ho hum sex with a guy I'm pretty sure had mistaken my bumhole for my vagina and who I will discover, six years later, refers to Autistic people as 'asps' with acridity so cutting it takes my breath away?

Speaking of acridity, whenever he speaks I can smell bile on his breath, and I'm not sure if the smell is actually coming out of his mouth (he's still talking), or if my brain is doing that thing where it can't understand a particularly *live* metaphor as anything other than scientific reality; ergo, to say something with bile; ergo, to literally smell bile when someone says something mean. Then *I* feel mean for thinking this. Be more empathetic, Clem, maybe he vomited from nerves before he got here; maybe he has an eating disorder; maybe he has one of those rare stomach issues that typically appear around the midpoint of an *ER* episode when a guest character presents with hiccups that won't go away and it turns out they have a one in a million type of fatal diverticulitis.

> in Year 8 I became so obsessed with *ER* that I decided I wanted to be a doctor
>
>> in Year 8 I was so bad at maths that my teacher asked my parents if there had been a death in the family; she couldn't comprehend how else a student could be both so catastrophically bad at maths and so evidently uninterested in improving this situation
>>
>>> later in Year 8 I discovered that you had to be good at maths to study medicine

Dating has always been difficult for me – the small talk, the existential confusion, the looming threat of post-coital Cronenbergian body horror – but I'm struck at this moment by how paralysed I feel, as though I'm being sucked into the escalator, living out my vivid childhood fear of being vacuumed into the gap at the top where the steps disappear into the void. But this is different. 'Fucking *asps*,' he says, and the rest of his words go all fuzzy, like those trombone noises the grown-ups make in *Charlie Brown*, because at that very moment I am in the process of investigating whether I, myself, am also an 'asp'.

WELL, HOW DID I
GET HERE?

After being assessed for Autism Spectrum Disorder shortly before my thirty-sixth birthday, in 2018, everything moved in slow motion while I waited for the 'results'. The journey to receive my diagnostic report – or, as I feared at the time, lack thereof – took one hour and thirty-eight minutes. Across the course of that journey, on 3 September 2018, I listened to Queen's 'Now I'm Here' approximately twenty-three times. Getting ahead of myself, I had already picked out the image that would articulate, on social media, my feelings if I *was* diagnosed as Autistic: a monster truck slamming over a giant mud pile, its livery daubed with the slogan 'AUTISM: IT'S NOT FOR WIMPS'.

> monster trucks are *extremely sick*
>> did you know there's a monster truck called Higher Education
>> that's made from a school bus?
>>> one of the happiest moments of my life was when we went
>>> as a family to the Monster Truck Madness × Supercross
>>> Masters spectacular at Rod Laver Arena

The monster truck image served a number of purposes: I was touched by the story behind the picture (the truck's driver was a down-home bloke whose Autistic nephew inspired him to raise Autism awareness by mowing down car carcasses in mud-daubed arenas while heavy metal played), but it also served as a pre-emptive show of confidence. I knew that my being Autistic would be a surprise to some, and that their reaction would likely be one of incredulity. By assuming the persona of the Autism monster truck, I could do a burnout so loud it would drown out any critical voices – including my own. Diagnosis: it's also not for wimps.

A year or so earlier, I had been in a script development meeting, discussing a screenplay I'd been writing. The general tone of the meeting was, as was often the case with my screenwriting, that the script was structured well (thank you) and very funny (oh, thank you), but there seemed to be consensus that my protagonist was confusing the reader. Nobody really seemed to know what was driving her actions.

It seemed perfectly clear to me: it's a romantic comedy, so the expectations of genre and plot dictate that the protagonist must start the script *thinking* she wants something in particular, but *learning* that she needs something else. It's my job as screenwriter to deliver this in a Fresh And Entertaining Way. Apparently, this was not the correct answer, because this character's emotional motivation was, according to the experts assembled before me, utterly opaque. As soon as this topic arose, I grasped the moulded plastic arms of my office chair with a white-knuckled grip; I knew what was coming. It was the same question that's always coming in any discussion of screenwriting, the one about the protagonist's *emotional journey*. What's her *problem*? And I knew it would be utterly unprofessional to respond in the way I felt compelled to, which is to yell 'I DON'T FUCKING KNOW!' before throwing my office chair through the window and rappelling down the outside of the building.

I didn't know what my protagonist was feeling because I barely knew about my own emotional state at any given moment. I only perceived the broad brushstrokes of vivid 'primary colour' emotions 'happy', 'sad', 'angry', at best

maybe 'hungry'?

no, that one is often a mystery, too

that I was generally the last to recognise. You know those moments in movies, where robots become self-aware and cry for the first time, and reach up in amazement to touch the tears rolling down their cheeks? That's me, every time my body has an emotional response to something.

I mean, I *did* know what the protagonist's problem was, at least to a certain extent: I had recently decided that she was 'on the spectrum'. Up until that point, it had never really occurred to me that the female protagonist of the very loosely autobiographical screenplay I'd been working on for a while might be Autistic, even when I had a minor character yell at her 'Jesus, are you on the spectrum or something?' That is, until I consulted *The Emotional Wound Thesaurus: A Writer's Guide to Emotional Trauma*[1], a popular text that aims to assist screenwriters in '[rooting] your characters in reality by giving them an authentic wound that causes difficulties and prompts them to strive for inner growth to overcome it'. My script editor had recommended I look through it to consider some different approaches that might liven up the next draft, given the issues I was having in communicating the protagonist's emotional state.

Skimming over the entry for 'Social Difficulties', I noticed that one of the examples given was that a character may struggle socially as the result of Autism. Intrigued, I read on. As I read the words 'BASIC NEEDS OFTEN COMPROMISED BY THIS WOUND: Love and belonging, esteem and recognition, self-actualization', Peter Gabriel's 'Solsbury Hill' started playing as I gazed skyward in a moment of realisation.

Shortly after, I googled terms I had never thought to look up in tandem before: 'female + Autism', and entered a research hole that was, in its intensity, not unlike Leeloo[minaï Lekatariba Lamina-Tchaï Ekbat De Sebat] in *The Fifth Element*, learning about all of human history while eating microwave roast chicken. You've seen those 'galaxy brain' memes? That was me.

I read about how boys are diagnosed with Autism Spectrum Disorder at a rate roughly three times that of girls. I read about how girls and women may be misdiagnosed with other conditions (such as Obsessive Compulsive Disorder or Attention Deficit Hyperactivity Disorder) while their Autism is missed because its presentation is different. I read about how Autistic girls are more likely to camouflage or 'mask' their Autistic behaviours. Across dozens of tabs and hundreds of hours, I read absolutely everything I could find on the topic. After exclaiming 'Oh my god, that's me' for the twentieth time, I texted an Autistic friend and asked if she thought I might be, as they say, on the spectrum myself. Her response was one of delighted relief: 'lol we have had our suspicions about you!' I returned to my screenplay and realised what I'd been missing: not only was the protagonist Autistic, it seemed that I might be, too.

My family, to me, had always seemed pretty normal, or perhaps more correctly, I seemed normal in the context of them, but then I suppose that's the way family works. There was my mum, Helen, the original 'slashie': formerly a model/actress who used to run with the Melbourne new wave scene. She had a keen interest in psychoanalytic theory and turned to creative writing and academia later in life, returning to uni at thirty and later inspiring me to do the same. There was my dad, John, an architect who'd been the original lead singer for The Wild Cherries only to be summarily kicked out and replaced by Lobby Loyde. (Don't believe anything you've read about John Bastow 'returning to his studies'!)

Dad's mum, Perle – 'Mumple' to us – was the local grandparent (Mum's parents lived in South Australia), a very English matriarch with a habit of marching out of the bathroom stark naked to answer a ringing phone, and who would stay up watching *rage* until 6 am in case a Midnight Oil song came on. She once tripped and fell on me, and her enormous bull terrier, Jenny, thought it was a game and jumped on top of her. (I thought I was going to die face-down on the scratchy coir carpet of my nightmares.)

My older sister, Blazey, Dad's daughter, lived in Sydney with her mum and stepdad. The distance added to the degree to which I hero-worshipped her, so much so that, for example, a letter she wrote me about O-week took on the significance of the Rosetta Stone ('There are lots of clubs with names like The Hamster Appreciation Society, whose activities include bulk masking tape distribution …'). And then there was my younger brother, Atticus, the funniest person on earth; I once returned from the bathroom to discover he'd nailed my breakfast croissant to the ceiling.

We lived in Port Melbourne, back before it became Melbourne's own Miami Beach. The real Port Melbourne is still there, of course, if you know where to look for it. It's like that school science experiment where you use a red cellophane filter to reveal secret messages written in different colours. I stand on the shoreline and hold my red cellophane, looking north, and see Dugga Beazley's fishing boat parked on the corner of Dow Street and Rouse Street. I hold it over The Anchorage apartments and I see the Swallow and Ariell factory, and smell the baking biscuits on the breeze. I hold it over Bay Street and I see Coles New World and Scrooges. I see the old Lagoon factory and its giant oddment jars of Sherbet Bombs for $2. I see Circus Oz trapeze artists on their way home from rehearsal dodging the rat-arsed revellers chundering rivers of green beer in the gutters outside Molly Bloom's on St Patrick's Day. Brucey's giant tin shed. The sky-blue door of the old Port Melbourne Lifesaving Club.

Mum's parents had expressed their concern in no uncertain terms: in moving to Port Melbourne in the early 1980s, young Helen was absolutely in mortal danger of being killed by the painters and dockers. (The Federated Ship Painters and Dockers Union, that is, not the band, though given they had a song called 'Die Yuppie Die', they probably would've shanked Mum, too.) Undeterred by the certainty of a violent end, Helen and John moved to a little weatherboard house on the corner of Esplanade East, and I was born not long after, on 21 June 1982. A few years later, we moved to an old pub on Rouse Street opposite the Transport Workers Union HQ.

Our household was filled with music – Tabu Ley Rochereau, Aretha Franklin, Jonathan Richman, Franciscus Henri – and, frequently, also with Mum and Dad's friends. Dinner parties would stretch long into the night; I have fond memories of wandering, blinking, from my bedroom into the kitchen to witness sights like Dad's friend Chris dancing to ABBA on the dining table, wearing a wig. For my bedtime stories, I was read *The Iliad*, *David Copperfield*, and the *real* Grimm's fairy tales.

My early childhood was one of blissful routine. We would go for family dinners at the Wong Shing Kee on Russell Street, where the ancient patriarch greeted customers by intoning 'Only cash', and I'd spend the evening tracing patterns in the red flocked wallpaper over a dinner of short soup and Fanta. Afterwards, we'd head over the road for a few rounds of pinball (good hand–eye coordination training), and the drive home would be punctuated by a visit to 'the fish lighting up', which was what I called the old Allen's Sweets 'skyline spectacu-lar' neon sign in South Melbourne, because to my mind, the wrapped lolly looked like a fish.

But the most beloved routine of all would come on 24 December each year, when we'd gather in front of the Christmas tree to watch *Meet Me In St. Louis*. My love of Christmas is a dense potpourri of family memories and pop-cultural references, and sometimes – like so many things in my life – it's hard to tell where one ends and the other begins. Decorating the Christmas tree was always an exercise in replicating *Pluto's Christmas Tree* – the 1952 Disney short that had bewitched my parents and now me – and shoving lights, blown glass baubles and tinsel deep into the branches of the tree to create magical little caves of light and sparkle, just like Mickey's tree. Mum's family tradition brought the booming voice of Mario Lanza to the Christmas vernacular (to this day, when I see a particularly traditional Christmas display, I can't help quoting Lanza: 'THEN BALTHAZAR SPOKE!').

After Atticus arrived in 1988 (himself a Christmas gift of sorts, being born on 21 December), a new tradition was established: a gift of a packet of Garden Wafers with a note, hand-drawn by Dad, imploring 'EAT ME FIRST'; yes, he wanted us to eat the entire packet – all the better to delay the two of us charging into Mum and Dad's room to yell them awake. And, thanks to repeated hirings of the VHS master-piece *Santa Claus: The Movie*, every year I would empty a packet of green glitter over a plate of cucumber peel in order to replicate the 'reindeer food' from that film. I still believe in Father Christmas and I will never, ever, give up tinsel and glitter.

For all our struggles – and they have been manifest – we were, as far as I could tell, a perfectly ordinary, slightly eccentric family: loving, reasonably functional, nothing to write home about (other than to sing our praises). Mum and Dad split up when I was twenty-four, but even that experience was, at least compared to some Terrible Family Break-ups I had heard about, not as bad as it could have been.

I mean, it was also clear that we were eccentric by any standard – Dad's habit of commanding rapt dinner table attention with his 'poo stories of Africa', the tales of his tribulations with dysentery and paratyphoid during his youthful travels, ending with him in the London Infectious Diseases Hospital; the constant quoting of lines from movies and plays as conversation; Atti's archive of recordings of his farts; our collective habit of addressing Puss (cat) and Coco (dog) as though they were people. But at home, I was always in a safe space; perhaps this was why it didn't become clear to me that I might be *significantly* different from those around me until I had well and truly left the nest (at twenty-three). At home, my own eccentricities were only ever viewed in the context of everyone else's.

Even then, there were things that I can now say, looking back, were 'signs'. Take, for example, literal thinking. As a child (and even, in some cases, to this day), I was incredibly literal. I had learned our phone number as 'six four five *two double-oh one*'; when Mumple rang and I picked up the phone, awaiting the caller's voice, and she asked 'is that six four five *two-thousand and one*?' I replied, sunnily, 'No!' and hung up. Similarly, Mum once told me not to drink the bath water. I nodded – the bath taps must be hooked up to a separate water system, I figured – and never again filled a water glass from the bath taps. It took some time (okay, I was twenty-nine) before I realised she meant don't drink the bath water *you are sitting in*.

When I *wasn't* at home, it was a very different story. From an early age, it had become apparent to me that the simple act of socialising was something that came naturally to most. They implicitly understood the unwritten and unspoken rules of engagement, like 'don't try to corral the other seven-year-olds at your birthday party into a rehearsed interpretive performance of *The Wizard of Oz* when they'd rather just play pass the parcel'. Existence seemed like a riddle I couldn't decipher. Why was I hyperlexic, miles ahead of my peers in written expression, but unable to make a phone call? How could I quickly learn how to dismantle my computer, or make royal icing, or mimic celebrities' voices to an uncanny degree, but not understand my times tables? These questions followed me into adulthood. Friends didn't understand why I didn't like the single-page orientation of my Kindle. Didn't anybody else need to read both pages of the book at once, like the robot Johnny 5 from *Short Circuit*? I had started to get the feeling, by my mid-twenties, that it was both unusual and probably bad to pick my nose to the point of self-harm, and to think nothing of collecting my 'findings' underneath my office chair. My fantasies were highly active, almost places I could visit, but I'd forget the essentials (phone numbers, names, birthdays), as though I'd tuned them out in order to focus on the things that really interested me.

So many things started to flood back during my diagnostic 'journey'. The way I spent my early school years mimicking cool girls and TV characters in an occasionally vain attempt to make friends. The two years I spent echoing everything I just said under my breath. The social anxiety. The crushing homesickness that made sleepovers and school camps so fraught. The laissez-faire approach to deodorant. The merciless bullying at school. The rampant anxiety and depression. The unfinished university courses. The way I felt confused and dizzy in busily decorated public spaces, and shied away from certain sounds that others couldn't hear. And the 'tantrums'. Oh, the tantrums.

It's nearly impossible for me to recall a time in my life where I didn't feel, to some degree, alien to the people around me. Sometimes this was a point of pride (teenagers are like that), sometimes it was a wellspring of existential agony, but most of the time it was like an itchy clothing tag or a distant, irritating noise that keeps waking you up at night; eventually, through sheer persistence, it starts to wear you down.

By the time I sought diagnosis, the notion of being Autistic was, to me, something of a last resort. Other suggested diagnoses had been off the mark; at this point, if it wasn't Autism, I was surely just a lost cause. But that thought – *what if I wasn't?* – continued to gnaw at my psyche. In the period between my assessment (15 August 2018) and the follow-up appointment on 3 September, an acquaintance asked me, with a stony expression, what I would do if the clinician told me I wasn't Autistic. I drew a blank.

Happily, I never had to find the answer: on 3 September, I received my diagnosis. It would go down in the history of great things to have happened on that date, including Richard the Lionheart's coronation in 1189, the *Viking 2* landing at Utopia Planitia on Mars in 1976, and Sir Malcolm Campbell becoming the first person to drive an automobile at over 300 miles per hour in 1935.

It's hard to qualify just how life-changing it is to receive an Autism diagnosis well into adulthood. Suddenly, it was as though I had a road map, translator and code-breaker all in one. Social interaction wasn't hard because I was a weirdo or defective; I literally lacked the neurotype for it. I wasn't 'losing it' when I thought the room was too hot, or a noise was too loud, or a texture was revolting. My legendary childhood 'tantrums' were, in fact, meltdowns, unstoppable reactions to sensory overload and anxiety. Most strikingly, my toughest challenges *and* my brightest talents suddenly had a root in something concrete: they weren't just things that had happened *to* me, they had happened *because* of me. This was as thrilling as it was bittersweet. And yet, part of me found being newly diagnosed an incredibly fragile state, like it was a precious object that might slip from my hands at any moment and shatter across the ground beneath me.

As it turned out, there were not many incredulous reactions when I revealed the news of my diagnosis, first to family and then to friends. There were lots of 'we've always suspected as much', and plenty of 'welcome to the club'. My extended family contains a number of Autistic people, in both the officially diagnosed sense and the sense of diagnosis being almost a moot point. Academia, it will not surprise you to hear, tends to be overpopulated by Autists.

My immediate post-diagnosis 'journey' was similar to many who've finally found clarity: I was VERY POSITIVE!!! about it, which was possibly a subconscious way of heading off any naysayers at the pass. I was determined to frame it as a good thing: both the fact of being diagnosed and the fact of being Autistic. (Both of which I still absolutely believe, I must stress.)

A few months after receiving my Autism licence (otherwise known as a diagnostic report), I was asked by Katie Koullas from Yellow Ladybugs, the fantastic Autism advocacy group who work with young Autistic girls and gender diverse kids, to give a speech at a mental health symposium they were running in February 2019. It wasn't the first time I had been 'out', professionally speaking, as Autistic – I'd written a short reflective piece for *The Age* in late 2018 – but it was my first involvement in an Autistic-led event; my first time with 'my people' (explicitly, at least), and my excitement was palpable. I was asked to reflect on what I wish I'd known about myself when I was younger. The answer was, clear as day, **I WISH I HAD KNOWN I WAS AUTISTIC.** (Which I wrote just like that, in caps and bolded, in my notes for the speech.)

Friends and family of people who they suspect are 'on the spectrum' often ask me, 'But won't they be labelled?' It's true that growing up is difficult for everyone (except for maybe one school friend of mine who was a junior ballroom dancing champion), and a label like 'Autistic' or 'on the spectrum' might seem scary to consider. But when you're well aware of the fact that you're very different from your peers, sometimes a label is the very thing you need. And besides, there are worse ones.

Some of the 'labels' that were applied to me included 'difficult', 'angry', 'selfish', 'remedial', 'incompetent', 'weird', and the evergreen Australian playground slur 'spastic'. One day I looked at my sports teacher's notes and discovered that I, who until that moment had enjoyed running, had 'inappropriate arm swing'. Cue: fifteen straight years of avoiding sports and exercise. If someone had taken me aside at ten or fifteen and said something like 'your brain is so good at some things (like art and performing) that it doesn't have much room left for others (like maths or socialising)', a huge weight would have been lifted from my shoulders.

Looking back at the speech I gave that day, I can see I was leaning heavily on the positives, partly in defence against the response I feared from friends and colleagues: oh no, how do you feel, now you know the terrible truth? Often, when Autistic people 'focus on the positives', we're accused of having a rose-tinted view of the world. I won't lie to you: there are many challenges that I continue to face on a daily basis, even as an Autistic woman with relatively low support needs. In the privacy of my own room, I am still prone to meltdowns – RIP the DVD cover that I couldn't open, which I attacked with a chisel and hammer shortly before jumping on it like Donald Duck having a spin-out. (It still didn't open.) There are some behaviours and tics I just don't talk about with non-Autistic people, because I know that, to them, they are utterly abject.

It's interesting to return to that speech now, as a snapshot of my headspace in the immediate afterglow of the vindication that diagnosis offered me. I hadn't yet gone deep into the world of Autistic self-advocacy, and so much of the Autistic experience – although I'd lived it my whole life – felt new to me. It was a constant process of 'Whoa, is *that* why I did/said/thought that?!' I was still learning the ropes.

To discover, or to be reassured, that you are Autistic when you are well into adulthood is to be pitched headfirst into paradoxical thinking. In one breath I longed for the interventions and therapies that I missed, while in the other I wished for all Autistic children to be allowed to simply *be*, as I was, more or less. This is the positionality of late-life diagnosis: I was simultaneously subject and object, feeling things anew even as I was on the outside, looking in. It took me a long time to stop questioning my own experience

is that *really* 'an Autism thing'?

surely everyone goes through that

what if I'm not really Autistic?

and to start trusting that the things I now understood as uniquely Autistic (and even then, unique to my own experience) were, in fact, happening – and had happened my entire life. Even though I was a latecomer, I was still a valid member of the club.

There is a tendency, in some quarters, to characterise accounts of later-life diagnosis as being simply the end result of little more than 'feeling a bit different' one's whole life. Surely, this thinking runs, these people are not *truly* Autistic – after all, they managed to make it this far without being diagnosed. Many people are diagnosed later in life precisely because they've managed to do such an expert job of masking their Autistic behaviours; for women and gender diverse people, this is often doubly true. What this misunderstanding of late-life diagnosis misses, however, is the fact that diagnosis is usually sought because whatever facade the person has managed to maintain until that point has in fact begun to crumble.

In the time leading up to my diagnosis, my experience of being in the world was becoming increasingly fraught in a way that went beyond merely being a bit awkward at parties: human interaction, and my inability to navigate it, was wearing me down. At the same time, I had taken on so much work – frantically trying to maintain my productivity as a measure of my worth – that I was coming apart at the seams. In November 2016, I experienced such a profound physical and emotional exhaustion that my GP ordered me to stay in bed for a week; even watching TV was deemed too taxing. Now, I understand that as Autistic burnout; at the time, it was a terrifying mystery.

Occasionally I wonder what might have been different had more time passed before deciding to pursue diagnosis – and, thus, learning what aspects of my life might be relevant to the clinician. As it stood, I was aware of some of the emerging thought regarding how Autism can manifest in girls and women, but other aspects of my understanding were based on what I 'knew' about the condition. I was only looking for the most obviously 'Autistic' behaviours in myself, in order to report them.

I think this is mostly because there's a part of me that knows how hard I've worked (not always consciously) to minimise and avoid so many of what I now recognise to be Autistic behaviours, interests and ways of being; in a way, the mask was still firmly affixed when I stepped into the consulting rooms. It is, of course, a psychologist's job to be able to see beneath that facade, but when you're thirty-six they don't sit you in a room and observe you playing with dolls or model trucks. How many of my truly Autistic behaviours were so innate, hidden or repressed that I wouldn't even think to mention them? Not long after my diagnosis, I recall seeing the Autistic comedian Hannah Gadsby discussing her own experience, explaining that at home – free of the pressures of the world at large – she 'wasn't Autistic'. In a way, my experience was the opposite: I only felt safe to be truly myself in the safety of my own home. If only the clinician could have seen me plummeting into an internet hole, going deep on one of my special interests at the expense of things like rational thought or food. But there was another problem, too: as Gadsby says in her stand-up special, *Douglas*, 'My issue was I didn't understand enough about Autism to understand how I could have Autism.'

A BRIEF HISTORY

For a condition that was only named in the early twentieth century, the clinical definition of Autism has shifted so many times it's like trying to keep track of who's married to whom on *The Bold and the Beautiful* – and just as dramatic.

Reading about the history of Autism is a little like undergoing a virtual reality experiment in which you instantly develop the symptoms of Autism: you may begin to see giant, free-floating Venn diagrams colliding in the air above you as differing definitions crash into each other and mutate; you may feel confused, even a little gaslit. It is difficult to know who to trust, which theory to stick with, who is right and who is wrong. Eminent researchers are revealed to have toxic sociopolitical views. Previously popular diagnostic criteria are relegated to the scrapheap of history. Labels become slurs. As soon as you think you've grasped some aspect of the clinical understanding of Autism, the goal posts are moved again. They're probably moving right now.

None of this is helped by the fact that the history of Autism – like so much of history – is typically written by those who are not directly affected by it. This subtle but powerful positionality means that our understanding of Autism is filtered through a lens that is almost exclusively white, male, neurotypical, classist and with a tendency towards pathologising; what Autistic scholar Melanie Yergeau refers to as

18

'non-Autistic Autism discourse'. No overview of Autism will ever be perfect, nor complete, due to both the heterogeneity of its presentation and the constantly shifting sands of both diagnostic criteria and understanding of Autistic experience.

Today, a diagnosis of Autism Spectrum Disorder necessitates two features: persistent impairment in reciprocal social communication and social interaction, and restricted, repetitive patterns of behaviour. This is according to the American Psychiatric Association's *Diagnostic and Statistical Manual of Mental Disorders (DSM)*. To grasp Autism in a modern context, it's impossible to avoid mentioning that tome, a taxonomic and diagnostic tool that many specialists use to guide their work.

In terms of these two features, in the former there must be difficulties with social-emotional reciprocity (what we might call the 'back and forth' of communication), issues with nonverbal communication (difficulties with gestures, or problems making and maintaining eye contact, for example), and issues developing and maintaining relationships. In the latter, the person must demonstrate at least two of the following: stereotyped or repetitive speech (such as using an odd turn of phrase, using stock phrases, robotic or 'sing song' manners of speaking); excessive adherence to routines, ritualised patterns of verbal or nonverbal behaviour, or excessive resistance to change; restricted, fixated interests that are abnormal in their intensity (such as needing to 'know everything' about a particular public transport system); and hyper- or hypo-reactivity to sensory input (either a heightened sensitivity to certain sounds, temperatures and textures, or a lack thereof that means they don't notice if they're getting cold or hot, for example) or unusual interest in sensory aspects of their environment.

The *DSM* isn't the sole diagnostic text on the matter, but like many aspects of American cultural hegemony, it looms large in the discourse, and has plenty of internal prejudices regarding gender, race and class. The World Health Organization's International Classification of

Diseases 11th edition, on the other hand, has a less culturally specific approach; it allows clinicians to assess the individual based on a list of Autistic traits. (This is not to position the ICD as 'good cop'; it has its own shortcomings.) Don't let the *DSM*'s clinical title fool you into thinking of it as a neutral object. In an edited collection of philosophical reflections on the *DSM*, Steeves Demazeux and Patrick Singy characterised it not as 'The Psychiatric Bible', but as the psychiatric Tower of Babel. 'A monument that was originally built to celebrate the new unity of clinical psychiatric discourse, but that ended up creating, as a result of its hubris, ever more profound practical divisions and theoretical difficulties.'[2] Nowhere is this more evident than in the ever-shifting sands of the definitions and diagnoses of Autism.

Released in 2013, the fifth edition of the *DSM* was the first significant edition of the manual in two decades. Known both colloquially and professionally by an epithet that makes it sound like either a megalomaniac artificial intelligence system or a Starfleet spaceship, *DSM-5* radically revised multiple diagnostic definitions. The two most notable changes were the removal of the previously defined subtypes of schizophrenia, and the deletion of subsets of Autism. Asperger syndrome, classic autism, Rett syndrome, childhood disintegrative disorder (CDD) and pervasive developmental disorder (PDD-NOS) were removed as discrete diagnoses and instead folded into the broader umbrella of Autism Spectrum Disorders. *DSM-5* arranged Autism Spectrum Disorders in levels of severity: those requiring 'very substantial support', 'substantial support', or 'support'. (These are often referred to by clinicians and other services by descending numbers: ASD-1, or Level 1, for 'support', and so on.)

The 2013 revision wasn't the first time that the *DSM*'s definition of Autism had undergone a major renovation, however. Both the *DSM-III-R*, published in 1987, and the *DSM-IV* in 1994 had expanded the diagnostic definition of Autism and included those who – due to their inability to fit into the rigid diagnostic categories of Autistic presentation as previously defined – had been either misdiagnosed or were bereft of a diagnosis altogether. *DSM-III*, published in 1980, established Autism as a psychiatric condition separate to schizophrenia (references to 'autistic' behaviour appeared in the context of schizophrenia in *DSM-II*, published in 1968). To the uninitiated, this constant revising of Autism's diagnostic framework must seem like psychiatric flip-flopping (and no doubt provides naysayers with fuel for the fires of their belief that Autism is a 'made-up epidemic', or 'not as bad as you say it is'). In that case, let's restart this contextual overview from the beginning and work back to the present day.

In his seminal 1943 paper, 'Autistic Disturbances of Affective Contact', the Ukrainian–Austrian–American psychiatrist Leo Kanner studied eleven children (eight boys and three girls) whose behaviour and symptoms Kanner attributed to 'infantile autism'. Though this is often credited as the first time Autism was recognised, in 1938 Austrian paediatrician Hans Asperger had recognised the behaviour of what he termed 'autistic psychopaths'. A popular view of Asperger has long focused on his recognising of 'little professors', the so-called 'high-functioning' children who could expound upon their special interests, and the type of kids who would – decades in the future – be given the diagnosis bearing his name. Yet Asperger was also working under National Socialism. In that paper, 'The Mentally Abnormal Child', he wrote, 'The central idea of the new Reich – that the whole is more than its parts, and that the *Volk* is more important than the individual – had to bring about fundamental changes in our whole attitude, since this regards the nation's most precious asset, its health.'

Herwig Czech's 2018 investigation[3] into Asperger's work reveals that Asperger 'joined several organizations affiliated with the NSDAP (although not the Nazi party itself), publicly legitimized race hygiene policies including forced sterilizations and, on several occasions, actively cooperated with the child "euthanasia" program'. That is to say, although he worked at the Vienna University Children's Clinic's

Heilpädagogische Station (Therapeutic Pedagogy Ward), Asperger actively referred children to Vienna's Am Spiegelgrund clinic, the centre for 'child euthanasia' programs later known as Aktion T-4, where from 1940 to 1945, 789 children were killed by methods including lethal injection, gas poisoning and physical abuse.

It became *de rigueur* for a while, thanks largely to the 2015 publication of Steve Silberman's engaging popular history of Autism, *NeuroTribes*, to think of Asperger as an unsung hero of Autistic people. Silberman writes that Asperger 'intentionally highlighted his "most promising" cases to deflect the wrath of the Nazis', in essence saving Autistic kids from being murdered by demonstrating their value to the Reich as future code-breakers. Asperger's focus on skill, rather than defect, may well have prevented the murder of *some* Autistic children – his 'little professors' – but what is unspoken in these heroic depictions is the fate of the children deemed 'low functioning'. 'In the context of the "euthanasia" killing programmes, psychiatrists and other physicians had to determine who would live and who would be murdered,' the prominent Autism specialist Simon Baron-Cohen wrote. 'It is in this context that diagnostic labels such as "autistic psychopathy" (coined by Asperger) were created.'

In his poem 'Dog Fox Field', the Autistic poet Les Murray reflects on the Nazi test for 'feeblemindedness', which was to ask an individual to construct a sentence using the words 'dog', 'fox' and 'field'. Many people with disabilities who failed the 'test' were murdered using the exhaust of the trucks that transported them. Murray describes as 'sentries' the people with disabilities whose treatment to this day (whether societally, bureaucratically, medically or otherwise) alert us that we have not strayed far from Dog Fox Field.

To be Autistic, and to identify as a self-advocate, means reckoning with the fact that our contemporary understanding of Autism – and, indeed, the notion of 'functioning' – has its roots in humanity's darkest moment.

Many people diagnosed and self-identified as 'Aspies' decried the *DSM-5*'s removal of a discrete Asperger syndrome as an affront to their identity. I couldn't think of anything worse than self-identifying with the affectionate name for someone who sent children to the gas chambers. There are some terms that can never be 'reclaimed'.

To return to 'Autistic Disturbances of Affective Contact', Kanner's paper provided a framework with which to diagnose children whose challenges might previously have been attributed to schizophrenia, or to being 'feebleminded'. Kanner noted in these children 'extreme autistic aloneness', 'delayed echolalia' (a tendency to repeat stock phrases, words and sounds, seemingly free of context or meaning) and an 'anxiously obsessive desire for the maintenance of sameness', as well as – in some cases – higher than average intelligence and a particularly impressive memory. The paper also, crucially, made more than passing comment on the possibility that the Autistic child's parents' emotional warmth – or lack thereof – might be responsible for the child's condition.

Later, in the fifties and sixties, emerging psychoanalytic theory posited that Autism in children was a result of their upbringing at the hands of cold and uncaring mothers; the 'refrigerator mother' later popularised by psychologist Bruno Bettelheim. Though Kanner himself later retracted the notion, the damage had been done. In his 1967 book, *The Empty Fortress: Infantile Autism and the Birth of the Self*, Bettelheim compared the mothers of Autistic children to Nazi prison guards, describing their children as 'dehumanized' (by their mother's wish that they were dead) in the same way that prison camp internees were.

While we can comprehend Bettelheim's work through the prism of his own experience as a survivor of both Dachau and Buchenwald concentration camps, it is difficult to convey just how devastating this position on the role of the mother in the development of the under-standing of Autism was. The idea that mothers 'caused' their children's Autism had been absorbed at a cellular level by many. Indeed, in the midst of my own journey to diagnosis, my own mum – my sweet, caring mother who has survived more trauma than any ordinary person should bear – reacted with angry tears during one argument we had, terrified that were I to be diagnosed as Autistic, people would think it was her 'fault'.

In his 1964 book, *The Etiology of Infantile Autism: The Problem of Biological versus Psychological Causation*, research psychologist Bernard Rimland argued against the notion that so-called infantile Autism was entirely psychogenic in its cause; there was the clear possibility that Autism, instead, had stronger ties to biology, and thus neurological (rather than psychological) development.

From the mid-twentieth century, the understanding of Autism began to shift and develop at an exponential rate. British psychiatrist Lorna Wing, along with her collaborator Judith Gould, was the first to expand the notion of Autism as a spectrum rather than a collection of discrete and differentiated disorders, and to coin the term Asperger syndrome. Wing's work in the late seventies and early eighties, such as the 1981 paper 'Asperger's Syndrome: A Clinical Account'[4], popularised both the work of Asperger and the understanding of the now eponymous syndrome.

> 'The children may be mercilessly bullied at school, becoming, in consequence, anxious and afraid.'

> 'Their social behaviour is naive and peculiar. They may be aware of their difficulties and even strive to overcome them, but in inappropriate ways and with signal lack of success.'

> 'Pedantic speech and a tendency to take things literally can also be found in normal people.'

It's not clear what, if anything, Wing knew of the specifics of Asperger's work under National Socialism; nevertheless, Asperger syndrome – colloquially 'Asperger's' – was eventually presented as a separate diagnosis from Autism in the *DSM-IV* (1994). Like many aspects of Autistic history, there was some conjecture as to whether Asperger's was separate to so-called High-Functioning Autism, or whether the two terms essentially referred to the same presentation. In order to necessitate a diagnosis of Asperger's, the individual would display some Autistic behaviours (what University College London Institute of Cognitive Neuroscience professor Uta Frith describes as 'having a dash of autism'), but their most significant challenges would be in the areas of social and communication skills; they would also be unlikely to have experienced delays in language development.

In the eighties, the concept of 'theory of mind' emerged as a possible key issue of Autism. Theory of mind, or the ability to attribute mental states to others as well as ourselves, is a cornerstone of empathy. Uta Frith and Simon Baron-Cohen's 1985 investigation[5] found that the Autistic children they observed were outpaced by both the typically developing children and children with Down syndrome in the sample group when it came to displaying theory of mind. Eventually, the research began to suggest that theory of mind could be significantly impaired in Autistic people, with issues relating to language and socialisation.

Another widely accepted cognitive theory proposed by Frith in 1989, 'weak central coherence', suggests that Autistic people may struggle or fail to use context – such as someone's tone of voice or facial expression – to understand their environment. They quite literally can't see the forest for the trees. Intriguingly, WCC can be understood as a perceptual bias or difference [6], whereas theory of mind presents a more deficit-based understanding of Autistic experience.

But even as the notion of an Autism spectrum emerged, the misunderstanding of said spectrum as a straight line – from 'low functioning' to 'high functioning', or worse, from 'low functioning' to 'not Autistic' – persists to this day. The reality, as most Autistic people will tell you, is that function (whether perceived or actual) is rarely static. By the time the *DSM-5* collapsed all Autistic and Autistic-adjacent conditions into the one condition, Autism Spectrum Disorder, 'function' was still reflected in the 'levels' – ASD 1, 2 or 3 – that would be assigned to an individual's diagnosis.

The notion that Autism may present differently according to the individual's gender did not emerge until around the 2010s. The misunderstanding of Autism as a 'boys'' condition was built in from the ground up, clinically speaking. Wing, in her 1981 paper presenting the work of Hans Asperger to a new audience, wrote that 'Asperger noted that the syndrome was very much more common in boys than in girls'; indeed, Asperger initially considered whether the condition might be confined to males. Most of both Asperger's and Kanner's charges were young boys and men, so it follows that most of the evidence that became diagnostic fact was skewed towards these male presentations.

As it turns out, Autism can present very differently in girls. Professor Tony Attwood, one of the leading researchers into the gendered differences in Autism presentations, considers it to be less about the specific symptoms (for want of a better word) than the way Autistic females adapt to conceal those symptoms. In other words, their difference isn't so much to do with the nature of their Autism, but the fact that they respond differently to being 'different'. They cope by camouflaging or masking their true selves, sometimes imitating others to do so; when that doesn't work, they may just disappear into their interests and daydreams. It was Attwood's work that sent me off on my first vortex of pre-diagnosis realisation: holy shit, this is me!

Autistic girls may, by comparison to their male equivalents (who may end up as 'loners' among their peers), seem very outgoing, even confident; they may 'perform' confidence, the persona carefully constructed by watching other, more popular girls, or fictional characters. At the same time, an Autistic girl who is shy or a bit withdrawn might not raise any concern in parents or teachers; she might just be seen as well-behaved or thoughtful. But whether she is outgoing or reserved, the Autistic girl is often hiding in plain sight. Eventually, the cost – emotional and psychological – of masking must be paid. As adolescence unfolds, Autistic girls may suffer from identity crises, emotional exhaustion, and low-self esteem; their habit of adopting a different persona in various contexts may lead them to question who they actually are.

Of course, not all women fit the 'feminine' presentation – and, indeed, some men do; gender diverse people also trouble this diagnostic binary – but the emerging understanding of the fact that they *might* present this way and still be Autistic was groundbreaking.

The diversity of Autistic presentation can be difficult for the non-Autistic person to grasp, despite the fact that every non-Autistic person is different, too. There's a phrase that most Autistic people are familiar with: 'If you've met one Autistic person, you've met one Autistic person.' The idea of a monolithic 'Autism', with neatly defined traits and behaviours and a discrete diagnostic presentation, is far easier to comprehend than the notion that there is another multifaceted world of people whose existence is completely unlike that of non-Autistic people, living alongside them *at this very moment*. Acknowledging the diversity of experience and presentation within the Autism spectrum is, to some neurotypical people, I think, akin to scenes in science fiction where a character learns of the existence of a parallel universe. In recognising the humanity and diversity of Autistic people, and in misunderstanding the development of an Autism spectrum, the danger is that a [mis]understanding of Autism forms that is, well, that we're all 'a little bit Autistic'.

In short, no, we're not all a little bit Autistic. I like to think of it like Pokémon, which is itself a very Autistic metaphor. If we think about individual Autistic traits as Pokémon, your average person might have a few of them, like social anxiety, or sensitivity to light or sound. But in order to officially get 'on the spectrum', you have to, as it were, 'catch 'em all'. And then, depending on where you sit on the spectrum, some of your Pokémon might be more 'evolved' than others.

The phrase 'Aren't we all a little bit Autistic?' is, I choose to believe, ultimately well-meaning: it springs from that place of empathy. Told about, for example, the pain of sensory overload, the neurotypical person might recall a time they went to a too-loud concert, or forgot their sunglasses while driving towards the sinking sun; ahh, yes, I understand this. It would be more helpful to extend that thought to consider how challenging it might be to experience those feelings *all the time*. You are, to return to my earlier metaphor, not just playing individually with Pikachu or Squirtle, but with at least a dozen Pokémon, all at once, and they're all vying for your attention.

This 'everyone's a bit Autistic' idea is rooted in the misconception that the spectrum is a straight line that stretches from 'really, really Autistic' at one end to 'normal' at the other. In reality, the spectrum encompasses a variety of Autistic experiences, and is more of an infinity symbol (appropriately, the chosen symbol of the Autism Rights movement) than a straight line. For example: quiet sounds are my nightmare; I revel in the eardrum-obliterating chaos of sideshow alley at the Royal Melbourne Show, or abrasive and experimental sound art. My Autistic friend, on the other hand, likes soft and quiet noises like ASMR playlists, and has to wear earmuffs in loud public places. We are both Autistic, and experience a similar level of both challenges and skills. And yet, the demand for a universal presentation of the Autistic experience prevails.

My own experience is unique to me, but it's also unique in that I am an Autistic person who didn't know I was Autistic until later in life. How many of my earlier challenges can be understood through the lens of diagnosis, and how many were just ordinary, run of the mill challenges that anyone might face? It's difficult to say. My journey to diagnosis began in that office, discussing my screenplay, but my journey to this current moment really began on 21 June 1982. With the relief of diagnosis comes a prism through which to view, and better understand, every experience that has led to that point.

AN AMAZING SECRET

To understand how or why I wasn't 'picked up' as a child, I introduce to you my first primary school.

St Joseph's Primary School was a small and ramshackle school tucked away on Stokes Street, a few blocks away from the Swallow and Ariell factory. There was an upstairs section, where the library and the big kids' (Grades 4 to 6) classrooms were, and a stretch of ground-level classrooms for prep to Grade 3. The only other 'facilities' were a separate modular classroom where everything from lice inspections to class photos to somersault practice occurred, and a small hall that I don't recall being used for anything other than the mysterious annual Mother's Day gift sale of rose-shaped soaps in cellophane bags.

Port Melbourne was small enough in those days that my class was almost entirely comprised of the kids I had spent two years alongside at kindergarten, so the transition to school was reasonably un-traumatic, aided in no small part by our angelic Prep teacher. Mum and Dad did wonder if perhaps I should stay on in kinder for another year, since, having been born smack in the middle of the year, I was six months younger than everyone else, but as I would later discover, my social difficulties would have been apparent in any peer group: it was my Autism, not my age, that was the issue. In the early days – Prep, Grade 1 – I had little trouble making friends; none of my schoolmates seemed especially perturbed by the fact I preferred to be referred to as 'The Horse' (complete with a 'tail' of a plastic shopping bag tucked into my tracksuit pants), or by my habit of imitating my favourite cartoon characters as a sort of parlour trick. It was also, in those pre-anaphylaxis days, the sort of school where birthday cakes could be delivered 'on ground' by willing parents. Mum once delivered a truly spectacular cream-puff caterpillar for me, which we demolished with glee while sitting on the bench seats against the downball wall.

Eventually, when my peers started expressing interest in things like soap operas and romance, I opted out of socialising. Instead, I would spend lunchtime seeking solace in the cool, smooth concrete of the playground 'tubes', and jamming cotoneaster berries into the hole at the top of a treated pine stump and grinding them with a stick until they turned to mush.

The student body was a ragtag bunch drawn from the local housing commission blocks, dock workers' kids, and other rusted-on Port Melbourne residents. There was a long-running blood feud between the students of St Joseph's and 'Snot Street' (Nott Street), which all students were expected to engage in, and the school was run by nuns who enthusiastically embraced corporal punishment. 'The strap' might have been banned in Victorian government schools in 1985, but it hung around at St Joseph's until at least the new decade. Of course, it didn't serve as much of a deterrent; I vividly remember one particularly stern Sister appearing in the doorway of our Grade 2 classroom, bearing the strap and the warning 'I just wanted to remind you …' as we ricocheted around the room in a frenzy.

Lunchtime entertainment often came in the form of someone yell-ing 'QUICK! SISTER'S WASHING SOMEONE'S MOUTH OUT WITH SOAP!', and we'd all crowd around the classroom windows and peer in as some kid who'd said 'fuck' or 'shit' got a mouthful of Sard. Depending on where, and how, you grew up, you sang one of two alternate lyrics to the famed 'my dad picks the fruit …'

Cottee's Cordial jingle of the 1980s. If your childhood wanted for nothing, your footpaths were free of pockmarks and your school well-appointed, chances are you sang the more polite 'my dad picks his nose'. St Joseph's, on the other hand, was definitely a 'my dad picks his bum' kinda town.

Being a Catholic school, we occasionally made the dusty walk across the tanbark to the eponymous church. At the tender age of six I was ushered in for my first (and last) confession, sitting dumbstruck in the booth until I had something of a religious experience. Realising that Jesus didn't really care what I did so long as I didn't murder anyone, I blurted out 'I said "bum" last week!' and dashed out, never to return. I enjoyed going to church, with all the incense and candles, but was never able to commit any prayers to memory, and always forgot what to do with my hands during the various stages of Mass.

my religious education workbook was mostly full of 'prayers' I had written myself

'Dear God, the world changes every day, help us not to destroy it, Amen'

'Dear Jesus, what is it like up in heaven? There might be thunder and lightning brand headphones. Bye, from Clemmy'

To say that the St Joseph's curriculum was light on what might now be termed 'enrichment' would be an understatement: we had no art program (aside from occasionally gluing glitter and macaroni to photocopied pictures of the Virgin Mary), and any formal sport was limited to rounders, a Jump Rope For Heart skip-a-thon and occasional whole-school calisthenics to The Bangles' 'Walk Like An Egyptian' piped through the school PA system. Excursions were few and far between: when Coles New World opened on Bay Street, we went there. And yet, the nuns knew the value of a star pupil, and made a great fuss of Jessica Brady – an aspiring *Young Talent Time* type – and used to regularly have her sing 'You Are My Sunshine' for the class. When Jessica left St Joseph's, presumably to seek stardom, someone found her old jumper in the tanbark and the nuns pinned it to the wall alongside the lyrics of 'You Are My Sunshine'. (This gave me a very skewed idea about how the world regards 'theatre kids'.) Some mornings, in lieu of course content, we'd watch ABC on a portable television; I had no idea about grammar, but I sure knew the 'What? Why? Where? and When?' of *Hunter*!

In a way, St Joseph's was the perfect place to be a stealth Autistic kid: it was total chaos. Objectively, it was a Bad School, and so under-funded as to be almost comical, but we were all equals: naughty kids, disabled kids, show-offs and weirdos alike.

The diversity of St Joseph's student cohort was striking. The kids there were largely working class, with a high number hailing from local commission flats and culturally and linguistically diverse communities. Neurodevelopmental conditions and learning disabilities – although the school was hopelessly underequipped to deal with them in any way other than by the use of shame and scolding – were also well represented.

Even then, I gradually became aware of the haves and have nots when it came to educational development. 'Readers' were introduced in Grade 2, along with a classroom tally sheet to which stickers would be affixed when a book was marked 'read'. That tally sheet became my nemesis, largely because my 'section', like my classmate Matthew's, was empty of stickers. Now, I knew (in a childlike way) that Matthew quite literally couldn't read: the letters and words looked all jumbled up to him. It wasn't like that with me, so what was my problem? My Grade 2 teacher expressed concern to my parents that I might have what we would now term a learning disability, because I 'couldn't' read the readers; the tally sheet was proof I was falling desperately behind.

Problems lurked when it came to maths, too. I was so baffled by the times tables – everything about them, from the way they were organised to the sing-song way they were expected to be recited – that I flat-out refused to learn them.

In retrospect, it's impressive that my teacher even had the wherewithal to observe learning difficulties; the school wasn't exactly firing on all educational cylinders. But there she was, telling my parents that something was wrong, because I hadn't ticked *Spot* off my list like the other kids. As it turned out, it wasn't that I *couldn't* read the readers, but rather that I *wouldn't*. They were boring and dumb and I didn't understand why I couldn't just skip ahead to, say, heretical paleontological theory.

Eventually, a détente was reached: while I wasn't given leave to read whatever I wanted, I was allowed to move ahead to the 'advanced' readers, and so my tally sheet became overstuffed with stickers. I read so many books that I won the jewel in the MS Readathon crown, a cassette Walkman. And yet despite this moment of triumph, that parent–teacher interview sticks in my mind as one of many missed opportunities, one of those *Sliding Doors* moments where something could have changed. What if my teacher had observed my possible learning disability, and recommended that I see a specialist? Would they have uncovered something else? What would have been made of me in 1987 or 1988?

Lorna Wing noted in her 1981 paper 'Asperger's Syndrome: A Clinical Account' what she perceived to be the difference between Autism proper and the condition she proposed be termed Asperger syndrome:

> *The autistic child develops stereotyped, repetitive routines involving objects or people (for example, arranging toys and household objects in specific abstract patterns, or insisting that everyone in a room should cross the right leg over the left), whereas the person with Asperger syndrome becomes immersed in mathematical abstractions, or amassing facts on his special interests.*

I was certainly capable of monologuing on my chosen passions – for example, natural history – but whether or not I *comprehended* all of, say, the collected printed works of David Attenborough (which ended up in the aforementioned MS Readathon tally) is up for debate; those qualities might have seen me tagged as an Aspergian 'little professor'. But I also displayed behaviours more in line with a traditional Autism diagnosis, such as lining my toys up in pleasing orders (by height, or more commonly by colour spectrum) and not engaging in much imaginative play to speak of outside of 'Rats', the byzantine role-playing game I engaged in with my friends Robbie and Alex, a game whose rules or, indeed, characters I have no memory of other than that we were rats, and I was absolutely the showrunner of this particular 'game', which ran for many years. As Wing said:

> In those who do have pretend play it is confined to one or two themes, enacted without variation, over and over again. These may be quite elaborate, but are pursued repetitively and do not involve other children unless the latter are willing to follow exactly the same pattern.

For as long as I can remember, it has soothed me to line things up – toys, clothes, food, the spines of CDs and books – in the order of the colour spectrum. I never 'played' with my toy dinosaurs, for example, in the manner that might seem appropriate; they were *dinosaurs*, der. Even my doll's house was operated with the eye for detail of an industrious floor manager: all furniture was where it should be, and I would park my Sylvanian Families in their appropriate locations (mother duck in kitchen, baby cats in cot) and leave it at that; it was more of a diorama than a site for play. Similarly, My Little Ponies were 'operated' only according to the (comically detailed) biographical information ascribed by their packaging. If one Pony's bio stated that she was shy, well, she was absolutely never going to go to a party with the others. I even took the note 'Let wet curly hair dry before combing', which was printed on every Pony's box, incredibly seriously. Did *any* other children even notice this instruction? Did they spend their childhoods obsessively maintaining their toys rather than playing with them? I was so protective of my toys – I loved them – that I refused to do anything that might get them dirty or damaged, which included letting other children play with them, for which I was often labelled selfish.

There was, of course, a reason for this that went beyond merely not wanting to share my toys. From a very young age, I felt sympathy for things that couldn't return it: I would cry for the can of soup or box of biscuits that Mum or Dad would take from the shelf, consider, and then put back before picking something else. I was once so devastated by a *New Yorker* cover illustration featuring a teddy bear abandoned on a park swing set that my parents had to magic up both a similar looking bear and a letter 'from the editor' insisting that the bear was just fine. As you can imagine, the 1987 animated film *The Brave Little Toaster*, in which a group of abandoned appliances journey to be reunited with their former owner, ruined my life.

Countless online forums detail Autistic people's special relationships with objects, and in 2018, UK researchers Rebekah C White and Anna Remington surveyed both Autistic and non-Autistic people's first-hand experience of object personification, the attribution of human qualities and emotions to inanimate objects, as a preliminary investigation into this apparently paradoxical quality of Autistic experience. (Their paper,[7] published in the journal *Autism*, was very drolly titled 'Object Personification in Autism: This Paper Will Be Very Sad if You Don't Read It'.) In an Autistic context, object personification often leads to heartache; White and Remington noted the 'distressing tone' of many of the online posts on the subject. One Autistic forum member writes, 'I get anxious when cutting up an apple. I get really upset if someone insults an object or even a place. I worry about objects being left in a burning building.' I can certainly relate, having cried while reading the customer reviews of a low-end robotic vacuum cleaner ('It has a mind of its own sometimes', 'Would only do one room then get confused and stop'; #JeSuis). A lifetime of looking glumly at abandoned buildings exploded out in anime tears when I first heard Tom Waits' 'The House Where Nobody Lives'.

I was forever bringing home half-dead mice and semi-squashed baby birds, saving snails from certain doom on footpaths, and attempting to corral ants away from anything that might cause them harm. But even the simple changes of nature, the shifting seasons, are enough to instil a deep sadness; it's not 'seasonal affective disorder', but rather sadness at the knowledge that my routines are changing. Even after all these years, it's still a surprise when the rain stops for the year, or when daylight savings ends and I can no longer stroll around in the evening without a care.

From a young age, I also recognised that other children were different, and observed – with the amusement of an eighty-year-old anthropologist – that they would make their toys 'walk' by grabbing them and making them hop up and down. It delighted me, even though I would never do it in my own time other than to 'try it' myself. ('Trying' something that other 'normal' kids seemed to think was fun would become a recurring theme for me.)

Routines, however, had quickly become a hallmark of my life. One that was quickly set in stone was our yearly visit to the Royal Melbourne Show. For our family, the Show was a chance to live it up for a day in the sun (or, as was more often the case, in the torrential rain and roaring wind). It wasn't a long drive, from Port Melbourne to Ascot Vale, in 1986 but it might as well have been a trip to outer space. 'It was wonderful,' as Mum put it recently. 'We'd go and take $300 out of the bank and pretend we were rich.' Dad always used to say the tickets should be done away with and, in their stead, an array of workers installed at the gate with an army of vacuum cleaners; submit your wallet to the nozzle and then enjoy your day.

Once upon a time, you entered the Show by walking up through the VRC car park, under the train overpass, via a well-trodden path pockmarked with puddles and last night's fairy floss, and eventually ended up in a bottleneck outside the farrier's stables. Before you got to the eardrum-splitting frenzy of sideshow alley, before the yawning money vortex of the showbag hall, before the constant low hum of carnies growling 'mums and dads and boys and girls' into crackling PA systems, you got to watch a couple of ancient stock horses peacefully farting and snorting while you shuffled into the Showgrounds proper. I never knew if this was intentional or just happenstance, but to me it seemed like someone at the Show was issuing a reminder: hold on, hold on, this is what we're really here for ... just watch old Billy unload a few huge poos in the sawdust ... okay, *now* you can run on towards your sugar coma. If you craned your neck you might even see some of the old sheds where farmers stayed, in lieu of a hotel, in wooden bunk beds the approximate vintage of the Jerilderie Letter.

Later in my life I would jet around America, interviewing famous people, being put up in five- and six-star hotels, but to this day the lure of the old sheds looms larger in my mind than any Egyptian cotton bathrobe. A glimpse inside those sheds was like stepping into another world. If I couldn't become a farmer (unlikely, given our sole non-Coles excursion at St Joseph's was to a hobby farm, where I recoiled from a dairy cow's teat), then the next best thing would be to attend the Show for the rest of my life.

Every year, the scent of freesias and jasmine on the breeze heralds not just the turn of the seasons but the return of the Royal Melbourne Show. Barry Dickins once wrote of the Show that 'The whole thing is a celebration of doing your level best, that's what the Show means, really. It's not just for the few winners, but for the battlers. Failing is not the worst thing; not going in something is. It's not about "who can do the best picture" but who gives to it with heart and soul.' We never took big family holidays, but every year in September our trip to Ascot Vale was like a vacation to another dimension, a world where money flowed like water and true happiness could be found at the bottom of a thin plastic bag full of ephemera that an extremely overconfident carnie would assure you was worth at least seventeen times the sale price.

Despite the smell of freesias on the breeze, 2020 was the first in a decade that I did not go to the Show; nobody did, because it was cancelled for the first time since World War II. And yet, I'd been there before: I have never felt agony and betrayal like I did in 1996, the year our parents decided that we had been to the Show plenty of times, and would instead be spending the school holidays visiting Nanna and Poppa in South Australia. (Looking back, perhaps they reasoned that two Firefly bus tickets to Adelaide were a cheaper bet than inserting the vacuum nozzle into their wallets on Racecourse Road.) In other words, the routine of 'going to the Show' was quickly installed as one that should not, could not, be tampered with.

Now, with the benefit of hindsight, I see so much 'Autisticness' in our yearly trips to the Show: the routine of it, the sensory seeking (Sideshow alley music! Fireworks! Farm smells!), the special interest, the unexpected terror of other people and the rides.

In 2014, Dr Thomas Frazier of the Cleveland Clinic and his colleagues assessed 2418 Autistic children, 304 of them girls, and found that in order to have obtained an Autism diagnosis, the girls' presentation was typically more extreme than their male peers – essentially, they 'appeared' to be obviously Autistic, with more obvious self-stimulatory behaviour or stereotyped speech – but that they were less likely to have been noted as having special interests (at least according to typically male-skewed diagnostic criteria).[8] This is also reflected in the results of a 2012 study that suggests that this tendency to diagnose only girls with more 'obvious' Autistic traits is particularly apparent in the failure to spot girls who are considered 'high functioning'.[9]

To put it in lay terms – which is to say, terms that are relevant to the people who were around me in my youth – for many years, if you didn't seem 'like Rain Man', you surely couldn't be Autistic.

To look to popular media to understand Autism, as many people do in order to understand things that do not personally affect them, you could be forgiven for thinking that Autism is a disorder that uniquely affects straight white men of about twenty-five years of age.

These characters are prickly, socially awkward, maybe even rude, but their brilliance – in mathematics, computing, medicine or other STEM fields – tends to bring those around them into hushed reverence. 'My god,' the onlookers whisper, staring as he scribbles at a whiteboard or taps at a computer full of data, 'he's actually done it.' They immediately forget the moment, seconds ago, when Chad/Brian/Ernest insulted his date with a god-tier neg about her pretty cardigan, because he doesn't understand social interaction. In the trailer, this moment will be soundtracked by one of two songs (Peter Gabriel's 'Solsbury Hill' if it's a heartwarming comedy, or Peter Gabriel's cover of 'Heroes' if it's a tear-jerking drama), and will be accompanied by a breathless voiceover promising that *'This summer, Chad/Brian/Ernest is going to learn the most important equation of his life ...'* as he scribbles 'L = $8 + .5Y - .2P + .9Hm + .3Mf + J - .3G - .5(Sm - Sf)2 + I + 1.5C$'[10] on the back of an envelope, gazes skyward in a moment of realisation, then sprints through an airport.

(And/or, if you prefer an Autism-themed page-turner, as Autistic writer Zack Budryk so beautifully put it: 'NOVELISTS WRITING ABOUT GROWING UP AUTISTIC: He stared at his mother savant-ly, doing a series of complex equations on the chalkboard. Her eyes filled with tears as she realized this was how he talked, and loved. MY ACTUAL CHILDHOOD: It's too hot for my coat that I never take off.')

Characters of popular media, whether explicitly Autistic (*Rain Man, Atypical, The Good Doctor*) or implied to be (Sheldon Cooper and BBC's *Sherlock* are what the Autistic scholar Anna N de Hooge refers to as 'Aspie-coded'), form the basis of many people's understanding of what Autism 'looks like'. Well-meaning documentary series about Autistic people's struggles in the workplace or on the dating scene – which for all their pretensions towards 'factual entertainment' are in every way cast with as much of an eye for 'types' as schlocky reality television – also don't stray far from these well-established tropes.

These docuseries do not seek to expand nor explode the average person's grasp of what it is to be Autistic, absorbed as it has been through the filter of popular media. The story of an Autistic young man with an offbeat special interest who struggles to find a girlfriend in between stints at the bank is going to be much more palatable to the status quo than, say, a queer Autistic person who works in the caring industries and goes on three dates a week but can't seem to get a relationship up and running. 'Ah yes,' the viewer nods, watching the former. 'He can't get a date because he's awkward and cares too much about light switches!'

If this strikes you as an odd hill to die on, then consider this: even I, a person who has worked extensively as a cultural critic, who is an early-career researcher, and who prides themselves on regularly clicking on Wikipedia citations (and sometimes even *reading* them), formed my nascent understanding of Autism this way – and, thus, failed to consider the possibility that I, too, might be Autistic.

This lack of representation can certainly play a part in the belief that Autism is something that only affects boys and men. Perhaps if I had seen something of myself in a popular depiction of an Autistic girl, we might have been spurred to investigate further. (Oddly enough, a lifetime of identifying with fictional aliens, robots and even, at one point, a toaster, did not set off any alarm bells.) Even affectionate family jokes at the expense of my 'unique' place in the world came to the family vernacular through this conduit: more than once I have been called 'Kevin', after the probably-Autistic, 'very sweet, sensitive, *extremely tense* little boy' in Ron Howard's masterful *Parenthood* (you know the one, he cries hysterically when he loses his retainer at the fun factory, which is definitely not a scenario that felt horrifyingly real to me at the age of ten). There was no female equivalent of 'Kevin', yet I did not feel seen or represented by the nominally neurotypical female characters on offer either. Ever complained that there aren't many good female characters in film and TV? Try looking for an Autistic one.

The specialists I have spoken to, all of whom were working in the field of Autism research and treatment in the eighties, noted that although 'infantile autism' was separated from childhood schizophrenia in the *DSM* at the beginning of the decade, it was rare for girls to be diagnosed without an accompanying intellectual disability. I have entered many twisting rollercoasters of historical armchair diagnoses, wondering what my IQ would have been deemed, had a moment been taken to assess it: would my voracious reading have outweighed my hopeless lack of mathematical comprehension? Would my capacity to recognise patterns in shapes (and flocked wallpaper) have pushed me up or down the scale?

For every person who receives a diagnosis later in life, there are dozens (if not hundreds) who – despite *being* Autistic – will never be given that gift of understanding because they were born prior to widespread childhood screening for Autism Spectrum Disorders. Even for those fortunate enough to have been born closer to the twenty-first century, there are considerable barriers to diagnosis: it's still much easier for a young white, cis male to obtain a diagnosis than it is for people of nearly every other identity. In Melbourne, for example, you can count on one hand the number of clinics adept at diagnosing Autism in girls and women; as you might expect, it's nearly impossible to 'get in'. Race and class also contribute to vast disparities in diagnosis (and misdiagnosis) rates, and gender diversity can trouble the rigid and male-skewed diagnostic criteria. The cost of diagnosis grows exponentially as a person ages.

For those in their thirties or older, the trend towards underdiagnosis is especially true for those whose diagnosis might once have been termed Asperger syndrome. They may have been misdiagnosed, either altogether (i.e. diagnosed with a different condition, such as OCD, bipolar or borderline personality disorder), or in part (i.e. they may have been diagnosed correctly, in the case of coexisting mood disorders and other conditions, but their Autism was missed). This group of people has come to be referred to as the Lost Generation. In a paper, 'Very Late Diagnosis of Asperger Syndrome', published in 2007, Professor Simon Baron-Cohen and his colleagues described these people as 'those who today would receive their diagnosis by 6 or 8 years old, if they were a 21st century child. They come to our clinic in young adulthood or even middle age, and they tell us a now-familiar story.'

The 1988 film *Rain Man* has been credited by many as being the moment Autism exploded forth into the popular consciousness in Australia. The 'Rain Man effect' cannot be understated; many people's understanding of Autism was, and remains, drawn from the film's depiction of Raymond Babbitt (Dustin Hoffman), the Autistic savant and card-counting whiz whose odd mannerisms became a sort of shorthand for Autistic presentation. It's true that many people *did* see themselves, or someone they loved, in Raymond; imperfect representation is still representation, after all.

At least one study pinpoints 1988 as a 'changepoint' in terms of the 'cumulative incidence' of Autism, though that changepoint is likely due to an increase in diagnoses following the 1987 release of the revised *DSM-III* and its accompanying widened diagnostic definition of Autism; any perceived increase in prevalence actually reflects more comprehensive and sensitive diagnostic practices.[11] Never inclined to let the truth get in the way of a good story, the press prefer to pin the seeming explosion of post-1988 Autism diagnoses on *Rain Man*.

You could be forgiven for thinking *Rain Man* was the first time Autism had played a major part in a narrative of popular media, at least if you were to take its reception at face value. Apparently none of these historians and cultural critics were paying attention, in the two years preceding *Rain Man*'s release, to the rental log at Video Flash Albert Park, where I was regularly borrowing *The Boy Who Could Fly* – a young adult dramedy about a young girl, Milly (Lucy Deakins), and the nonspeaking Autistic boy next door, Eric (Jay Underwood). I watched that movie so many times I'm surprised the tape ribbon didn't snap.

To say I loved *The Boy Who Could Fly* would be an understatement; it was the first 'real' movie (that is, not a Disney animation) that I chose for myself from the video shop. Released in 1986 and written and directed by Nick Castle (aka Michael 'the shape' Myers from *Halloween*!), it is an exquisite exploration of Autism and grief. And while Eric really *can* fly, the film also has some remarkable things to say about the dangers of trying to alter or remove Autistic people's inherent 'Autisticness'.

In some key ways, *Rain Man* and *The Boy Who Could Fly* share narrative similarities: neither film's eponymous character is the protagonist, and in both, the Autistic central character helps the protagonist on their journey of emotional change. *Rain Man* screenwriter Barry Morrow had only a passing knowledge of Autism while he was writing the early drafts of the script. 'The word "autism" never appeared in my original screenplay,' he told *The Guardian*. 'Looking back, *Rain Man* was never a story about autism. It was a tale of two estranged brothers, their journey and then their fragile redemption.'

Watching *Rain Man* now, this holds true: Ray's Autism and savantism is a plot point on Charlie's journey of emotional development; 'a dramatic gimmick,' as Pauline Kael's excoriating *New Yorker* review put it, 'that gives an offbeat tone to a conventional buddy movie'. Information about Ray's reality – he 'can't even express himself, or probably even understand his own emotions in a traditional way' – is delivered as asides.

Eric's ability to fly is, in a way, a comorbidity: it's not that being Autistic means he can fly, it's that he's Autistic *and* he can fly. In this way, his Autism is not a problem to be solved. Crucially, that's because a key turning point of the film is the uselessness of Milly's initial attempts to get Eric to open up. Encouraged by a well-meaning teacher, Mrs Sherman, their work together focuses on trying to suppress his Autistic behaviours: trying to get him to copy her, reading him books he has no interest in, even trying to physically squish his face to model the oral posture required to say 'Milly'. Eric looks as depressed as Milly does through the course of these drill-like sessions.

And then, on 'Day 21' (Mrs Sherman, helpfully for narrative purposes, has Milly keep a diary of her time with Eric), something magical happens: Milly gives up and starts making a paper aeroplane with her notes, and Eric, unbidden, helps her fold the piece of paper with a smile: he loves planes! 'He smiled because *he wanted to*,' she says, not because he was copying her. Eric's behaviour isn't presented as a turning point of assimilation, but rather as humanising: proof that this apparently 'low-functioning' boy has been communicating all along.

In their compelling 2011 *College English* paper, 'Autism and Rhetoric', Melanie Yergeau and Paul Heilker write that 'an autistic's silence is construed as both a heartbreaking tragedy and the cancellation of personhood'.[12] Milly only truly 'sees' Eric's personhood when she accepts his (silent) *Autistic* personhood. The moment is also a sly rebuttal of the notion of speech as the pinnacle of communication. Milly doesn't so much 'give up' on trying to connect with Eric as she does give up on her initial approach. She encourages his special interests, watching home movies of kites and reading him books about flying – *Peter Pan*, *Dumbo*, *A Bird Can Fly* – and revels in his stims. Even as a kid who didn't know I was Autistic, I found this sequence deeply satisfying: yes, let him be who he is!

'Every day,' Milly writes in her journal, 'he tells me a new secret.' We know from the preceding sequences that Eric isn't 'telling' Milly anything in a traditional (verbal or neurotypical) sense; instead, Milly has come to understand the inherent value of Autistic experience. 'I don't know if he's becoming more like me, or if I'm becoming more like him,' Milly writes. It's clear, from the joy she has found in interacting with Eric on his terms, rather than through some neurotypical notion of making him 'function' in society, that the latter is probably true. When Milly eventually flies with Eric, it's their way of escaping all that society expects of them both. They kiss, but not as an act of assimilation; if anything, Eric ends the film more Autistic than he was to begin with.[13]

It's a marked contrast to the presentation of Ray's personhood in *Rain Man*. The audience can recognise that it's bad that Charlie is, for a time, using his brother for his savant skills, but Ray experiences a meltdown late in the film that seems to reflect *Rain Man*'s position statement: here is a person who can never function in society. Charlie's ultimate act of selflessness, as the film presents it, is to let his ego die and relinquish Ray back to an institution. And though one film is magical realism for teens and the other an amiable road movie, I do think there is something telling in the fact that Eric triumphs over institutionalisation – literally flying away from it – while Ray is returned to it before the credits roll.

What's intriguing, in comparing the contemporaneous reviews, is how the critics react to the Autistic themes of the two films. Of *The Boy Who Could Fly*, Roger Ebert notes that institutionalisation 'could crush [Eric's] spirit'. In *The New York Times*, Janet Maslin observed that the film 'has less to do with Eric's magical powers than with the community in which he and Milly live and the questions of how and whether they will fit in'.

As Raymond, the virtuosity of Dustin Hoffman's performance has the unfortunate (and presumably unintended) effect of lessening the empathy engendered in the audience by the narrative. Pauline Kael, decades ahead of her time, questions the decision to cast Hoffman in the first place: 'Slightly stupefied as I left the theatre, I wondered for a second or two why the movie people didn't just have an autistic person play the part [...] But with an actual autistic there would be no movie: this whole picture is Hoffman's stunt.'

And yet what's fascinating about his approach to playing Ray is that he considers his performance, in a way, a work of echolalia, inspired by the Autistic people he spent time with while preparing for the film. 'There's nothing in my performance that's invented,' he told *Los Angeles Magazine* in 2010. In that sense, his embodiment of Raymond was authentic, even if the broader themes of the film were not, and led to the misunderstanding that all Autistic people are genius-level savants who lose it if they don't get to watch *Jeopardy* while eating their Cheese Puffs with toothpicks. In a sense, that's what's frustrating about *Rain Man*: plenty of it is absolutely truthful.

for many years I ate Cheese & Bacon Balls – Australia's own Cheese Puffs – with a spoon because I couldn't bear the sensation of the orange cheez goo on my fingers

I can still draw the patterns of the red flocked gold wallpaper at the Wong Shing Kee restaurant on Russell Street; in fact, I can draw the entire restaurant's layout from memory

of course we get Fanta, short soup, Jasmine tea, steamed rice, combination chow mein

The tone of the conversation regarding Autism at the time of *Rain Man*'s release can be summed up by the opening lines of Roger Ebert's review of the film: 'Is it possible to have a relationship with an autistic person? Is it possible to have a relationship with a cat?' Even in that *Washington Post* piece, the general mood is fairly desolate. 'The film lets people know that in most cases it is hopeless and that an autistic person stays autistic in the end – there is no cure.' *The Boy Who*

Could Fly, on the other hand, doesn't shy away from the turmoil of Eric's meltdowns or the sadness of his isolation from his peers, but it also presents the spectre of institutionalisation and the attempts to extinguish Eric's Autism as low points of the narrative. Milly doesn't love him *in spite of* his Autism: it's part of who he is as a whole person.

Watching both films again now, and thinking about that 'change-point' of society's understanding of Autism that *Rain Man* may or may not have brought about, I kept wondering: what if *The Boy Who Could Fly* had taken this place in the collective unconscious instead? What if this sensitive, funny film that argued for Autistic people (and Autistic people with complex needs, at that) to be celebrated – not used – for who they are, had made as big an impact on popular culture as *Rain Man*?

What's striking about *The Boy Who Could Fly* is that for all my repeat viewings during those formative years, it had buried itself deep in my memory to the point that all I could remember was the tagline from the poster – 'Between the wind and the clouds, between a silent boy and a beautiful girl, lies an amazing secret!' – and flashes of sensation: the dewdrops on the rose that tempts Milly to stand up on the bridge handrail; the agony of Max the dog being hit by a passing car; what I imagined it felt like when Eric and Milly flew down from the high school's roof during the fair, because I too would often dream of running and then diving down towards the ground before swooping up in the air. Did I dream that before I saw *The Boy Who Could Fly*, or did that moment winnow its way into my deepest wishes? Watching the film for the first time since my childhood, as both a cinema and screenwriting scholar *and* an Autistic person, made me feel a little like Wile E Coyote being whacked over the head with an ACME 10-tonne anvil labelled 'HEAVY SUBTEXT'.

Was there a part of me that loved this movie *so much* because I saw something of myself reflected back at me?

SENSORY OVERLOAD

Most of my earliest memories are pure sensation.

Spinning on the spot until the world disappears into a streak of colour and movement and I can feel the pull of gravity against the side of my head, and swinging so high at the playground that the sky shoves me back down towards the hot tanbark. The warmth of Mum's soft body as I'm squeezed into a hug. Picking up chunks of sun-baked sand, the size of biscuits, feeling the tough crust give way to the soft millennia of erosion underneath, and watching them slowly disintegrate in the wind. Or the unparalleled ecstasy of gazing as a flurry of glitter dances around inside a plastic magic baton, a clear tube filled with water and just enough air to form a round bubble that shoves its way through the glitter in a big hurry.

I can stare at sparkles for hours. I will stand in a craft store and regard the little oblong boxes of glitter like I'm trying to pick what to eat for lunch. (The discovery of edible glitter in my twenties was ... huge.) A beam of sunlight hitting a rhinestone and spraying the walls with shards of rainbow light? Better than the entire *Godfather* trilogy. These days, highway robbers who are hip to the Autistic experience flog entire boxes of magic batons as 'sensory toys' in their overstuffed online stores, but in Port Melbourne in the early 1980s you got a magic baton at Scrooges, or perhaps the Royal Melbourne Show along with a Cyndi Lauper-esque tinsel wig, and treasured it as though your life depended on it. Eventually it would spring a leak, or you'd leave it on a hot windowsill and the water would gradually evaporate, and you would have to begin the search for a new one.

One of my most treasured possessions was a museum postcard printed with silver 'laser holographic' paper, which at that young point in my life was quite honestly the most incredible thing I had ever seen. To me, that rectangle of cardboard was proof of a higher power; a future where the entire world is sparkly. At the age of six, I decided that I would attain true success in life if I were to grow up and fill my house full of chandeliers. A single ice blue cut-glass bead, exhumed from Mumple's heaving hall cupboard, was guarded as though it were the Koh-i-Noor. Easter egg foil was to be carefully prized from around its chocolate innards, which I could take or leave, and often did, one morning waking up to a family of mice rolling my discarded eggs out of the basket where I had left them on the floor. Once unwrapped, I would do my best to flatten the pieces of foil into perfect rectangles and watch the sun dance across them. A torn edge was a disaster, much like torn wrapping paper was a catastrophic event. (Who are these monsters who rip their presents open like chimpanzees tearing open an enemy?)

But perhaps the most earth-shattering moment of sparkle in my formative years was my encounter with Barbie's 'Rockers Fashions' wedding dress (#2688) from 1985, a fantasy of white tulle with tiny slubs of pink, green and blue lurex and its fringe of iridescent laminated net. What business did such a full fashion fantasy even *have* gracing the halls of my kindergarten? It must have been brought to kinder by Sarah, who had, or so the rumours ran, an entire washing basket full of Barbie dolls, conciliatory gifts from her father, who regularly travelled for work. I had a hand-me-down Jem, whose big feet and sensible low-heeled pink mules seemed hopelessly frumpy next to Barbie, and also a She-Ra figurine, who I buried in the backyard beneath the fig tree after I discovered she didn't fit inside the Voltron lion.

I knew immediately that Rockers Fashions #2688 was the absolute zenith of doll clothing. Hell, it was the zenith of *clothing*, unmatched until a year or so later, when I danced to 'Twinkle, Twinkle, Little Star' at the 'Port Melbourne community Christmas pageant. My costume was a navy-blue cotton skivvy and tights with a little net tutu, to both of which Mum had lovingly hand-sewn a handful of star-shaped gold and silver sequins, the whole thing topped off by my beloved deely bopper headband (you know the ones: chunky polystyrene stars covered in even chunkier silver glitter, atop 'bopping' springs). To me, that ensemble was every bit as glamorous and mysterious as Rockers Fashions #2688. Finally, I had arrived; finally, I had become glitter. I loved and wore that costume until it disintegrated and all that remained was a single star sequin, with only two points remaining, clinging to that skivvy for dear life.

A certain type of person would think it funny, maybe even poignant, how so many of my most vivid memories of early childhood involve glitter, given that the Port Melbourne of my youth was a tangle of corrugated iron, desiccated weatherboard, busted-open asphalt and brick blasted by the wind whipping off Port Phillip Bay. If you've been to Port Melbourne any time this century, this will be news to you: the suburb is now all silvery mirrored glass and soaring lifestyle apartments and gated mansions, where former AFL players recover from 'exhaustion' and influencers roam freely in high-end activewear. So it stands to reason, surely, that my love of all things sparkling was an act of transportative fantasy. Well, sorry to ruin the writers' festival, but this wasn't some desperate craving for the sweet release of glamour in a sackcloth existence: I fell in love with glitter because I'm Autistic.

Observation of issues relating to sensory input have been a constant throughout the years of Autism's shifting diagnostic sands. Hyper- or hypo-reactivity to sensory input, or unusual interest in sensory aspects of environment, is one of the central tenets of a contemporary Autism diagnosis. Sensory processing, in the simplest sense (ho ho), is how a person perceives, processes and organises sensory information (the stuff of sight, sound, smell, taste and touch). 'Atypical sensory processing', then, is a catch-all term that refers to this core aspect of the Autistic experience. Research suggests that between 69 and 95 per cent of Autistic people experience some degree of sensory processing that can be considered atypical.

This can take various forms. Sensory-seeking behaviour involves unusual curiosity about or desire to engage with certain sensory information; repeatedly touching something of a particular texture, staring at certain moving objects, or listening to loud sounds. An Autistic person's response to sensory input may vary from day to day, and is inextricably linked to their emotional state (and vice versa). Staring at glitter moving in water is a perfect example of sensory-seeking behaviour. When I pick up my magic baton and swirl its contents around, it's a way to focus my attention: by zeroing in on the sparkles, I can tune out the rest of the 'noise'.

Sensory under-responsivity is when a person might be slower to react to sensory input that would ordinarily elicit a response; this might be a muted pain response, or not noticing that the bath water is too hot. Sensory over-responsivity, then, is the opposite: a person's being more attuned to sensory input than others (like hearing tiny sounds, or the specific feeling of certain blends of fabric fibres), with a resulting negative emotional response (such as feeling anger or disgust) that can be described as sensory-avoidant. 'My hearing is like having a sound amplifier set on maximum loudness,' Autistic scientist and activist Temple Grandin has written. 'My ears are like a microphone that picks up and amplifies sound.' It is in the context of sensory over-responsivity that the notion of sensory overload emerges; my anxiousness, if not outright anxiety, has always been linked to the threat of sensory overload.

Sensory overload is one of the aspects of Autistic experience that most non-Autistic people are familiar with, at least in an abstract sense. While all Autistic people react to sensory input differently, there is perhaps a misunderstanding that 'sensory overload' must necessarily relate to, well, an overload of sensory input – too loud, too bright, too hard. But with the exception of fireworks (which I now love), I was not troubled by loud noises or crowded spaces as a child; indeed, I loved *huge* noises, like motorsports and monster trucks and sirens. (I still love sirens, which is a little awkward; nothing marks you as 'unusual' like your eyes lighting up as though you've spotted a celebrity when the specialist stroke ambulance roars past.)

Surprise huge noises, on the other hand, were terrifying. I don't remember much fine detail about my first showbag – Inspector Gadget, 1986 – other than the all-consuming existential fear of the two translucent, glitter-filled pop balls that came with it. For those who did not spend the second half of the 20th century racked with terror, pop balls (those tough rubber domes that you turn inside out, then wait until they turn themselves back with an enthusiastic 'pop'; they are occasionally and more accurately known as 'eye poppers') might be a vague, happy childhood memory. For me they were an exercise in abject dread, as there was no telling when the loud noise would happen, and I would usually start screaming well before the jolly 'pop!'

These days, they are sold online by purveyors of 'therapeutic' toys: 'Excellent for isolating thumbs and building finger strength, while also helping with hand eye coordination when catching them on the way back down.' Sure, I guess that's true, in the same way that one might build finger strength by flipping the pin out of a grenade, throwing it in the air, and then improving one's hand–eye coordination by catching it on the way back down.

Even the term – 'therapeutic toys' – instils in me a vague sense of nausea, like so many hideous euphemisms of neoliberalism. Therapeutic toys are a million-dollar industry, designed to convince beleaguered parents that instead of chewing on jigsaw puzzle pieces and Starbucks straws, their Autistic children could, instead, chew on a $50 hypoallergenic food-grade silicone 'chewy'. I do detect in the entire industry a distinct whiff of bullshit, especially since Autistic people are very good at making their own 'sensory toys'. Spread out in front of me on my desk as I write is my current brace of 'therapeutic' objects: the hang label from an op-shop purchase, folded multiple times into a little cigar of cardboard; three Hi-Chew wrappers in various states of folding and rolling; a kombucha bottle cap squashed in half, a smooth dent on top for resting a finger on, a jagged rim underneath for running a thumb back and forth over; a pile of leathery old mandarin skins that are nice to crumble between my fingers. I do all of those things in order to help me tune out the threat of sensory overload.

Autistic writer and researcher Therese Jolliffe has described the 'unbearably chaotic life' that Autistic people exist within, thanks in no small part to their difficulties in processing sensory information. 'Reality to an autistic person is a confusing, interacting mass of events, people, places, sounds and sights.'

My tormentors were always insidious: the itch of a woollen spencer against my skin, a clothing tag, the grip of sock elastic around my ankles. The hum of electricity in the walls or the jingle of light bulbs and fluoro tubes would put me on edge, and still does. Having my hair brushed was a campaign of emotional terror that had to be approached with military precision. The sensation of someone lightly brushing a hand across my skin feels like I'm being attacked with a vegetable peeler. The sound of people chewing their food (even worse if mouths hang open) makes social dining an act in high-wire terror. To this day, I cannot bear the sensation of the condensation that forms on the outside of a drinking glass or takeaway cup, and will wrap them in paper napkins.

Sensory overload – whether courtesy of a clothing tag, scary noises, or a weird smell – is also often a one-way ticket to a meltdown.

Meltdowns are perhaps the least understood aspect of Autistic behaviour, especially as they manifest in children. To the casual observer, an Autistic kid experiencing a meltdown just looks like, well, a kid chucking a tantrum. There is an essential difference, however. Tantrums are, essentially, wilful: a behaviour a child will engage in consciously, usually to achieve a desired effect. They are goal-oriented performances, and most kids grow out of them, particularly when good behaviour is appropriately rewarded (surely we have all heard a variation on the phrase 'When you calm down, *then* you can have another Bertie Beetle'), or if they realise they're not going to get their way.

Meltdowns, on the other hand, will happen even without an 'audience', and are an innate reaction to feeling overwhelmed. They may involve crying, yelling, thrashing about or striking out; the overwhelming sensation may also lead to the person completely shutting down, going silent and withdrawing (some Autistic people refer to these as 'shutdowns' to differentiate from the more externally explosive meltdown). In Autistic people who are minimally verbal or nonspeaking, a meltdown can also be a reaction to the frustration of not being able to accurately communicate their feelings or needs. As Temple Grandin has recalled of her childhood, 'When I did not know how to talk, screaming was one of the only ways to tell people I did not want to do something.'

Meltdowns and similar 'episodes' of stress and anger (which, let's face it, are really just a meltdown of a different colour) can be thought of as having three stages: the build-up, the explosion and the recovery. The build-up can be triggered by sensory overload, or sensory overload can be exacerbated *by* the build-up. (You know in Looney Tunes cartoons, where everything – clocks ticking, taps dripping – gets REALLY LOUD right before a character runs straight through the wall?) There may be obvious signs of increased stress levels, like pacing, fretting, or tense posture or expression, too. The explosion occurs when the person's ability to regulate their emotions ceases: there may be crying, screaming, thrashing about, self-harm or biting, or fleeing. (In the previous Looney Tunes analogy, the explosion is when the character shoots through the roof like a rocket.) Finally, during the recovery, language processing may slow down and the person will feel drained, and may experience a sense of confusion or shame. (There's no Looney Tunes analogy for this bit, because Looney Tunes characters are rarely contemplative.) It can take a long time to recover from a meltdown.

Unlike tantrums, meltdowns continue to occur throughout an Autistic person's life; they may lessen in intensity, stay about the same, get worse, or a combination of all of the above depending on the person's circumstances at the time. One thing remains a constant: when a meltdown hits you, there's not much you can do about it. I don't know what it's like to be possessed, but I imagine it feels something like a meltdown: a sudden seismic shift that you cannot control.

The first meltdown I can fully remember is still as clear as day – well, perhaps more correctly, the aftermath is. I can't remember what set me off in the first place, but when I emerged from the maelstrom of emotion that had gripped me senseless, it appeared I was lying on the floor of Dimmey's in Richmond, somewhere near the haberdashery section. The bolts of discount fabric towered above me, an old growth forest of cheap jacquard and sateen. My knees were dusty from having dropped to the ancient lino floor in a writhing rage, and my face was red and streaked with tears. My parents were somewhere else in the store, having presumably walked away while I disgraced myself with what must have appeared to be an uncontrollable display of id-fuelled naughtiness.

Time moves differently in a meltdown. It felt like I was on the floor in Dimmey's for a year, but it was probably only a few minutes; a bit like how on Earth, a solar day is twenty-four hours; on Venus, it's 5832 hours. Venus is often referred to as 'Earth's sister', due to its relatively similar size, mass and distance from the Sun, but its atmospheric pressure is ninety-two times that of sea level pressure on Earth, and the mean surface temperature is 464°C; meltdowns, in the eyes of those who don't recognise them, look a lot like tantrums.

Even at a young age, although I didn't have the words to say it, I new that a tantrum was something that a child might choose to do (inasmuch as a child has free will and consciousness), whereas those meltdowns were something else entirely. I'd seen kids crack the shits at the supermarket because their parents wouldn't get them two packets Arnott's Assorted Creams; watched the thought process, the glance from the shelf to the parent, to the onlookers, back to the parent, the thirty seconds of deep thought before the scream came on like a cassette player (and switched off just as suddenly). This wasn't that.

There's a fleeting moment right before a meltdown, like a migraine aura, when I can see it coming, only it's too late to get out of the way; I'm tied to the train tracks. I have seen these referred to as 'rumblings'. It feels like an explosion in my mind; something snaps, sparks into life, synapses fire and electricity scrambles through my brain until it blows out every which way. My throat tightens, like someone is drawing a belt tighter and tighter around my neck. A wellspring of pure rage, or sadness, or injustice, comes shooting up from my core; not being able to understand which emotion it is (all of them at once?) doubles down the nightmare. Hot tears shoot out of my eyes. And then ... BANG!

Have you ever watched those videos where someone drops a Mentos into a bottle of Diet Coke, and the drink explodes up out of the bottle's neck like Mount Vesuvius blowing its top? A meltdown is Eddie Van Halen tearing his guitar apart for one hour and forty-two minutes in 'Eruption' while the screaming-only edit of 'Runnin' with the Devil' plays on repeat. It's the ConSec scanner's head exploding. It's every Donald Duck spin-out playing at once on fifty televisions in a locked room. It's Arnold Schwarzenegger screaming as his eyes pop out of their sockets on the surface of Mars.

Sometimes, the feeling seems sadder; there are more tears, and a sense of hopelessness and despair that bubbles up and explodes out of me before I can register the emotion. In the midst of a period of burnout in January 2008, I had a meltdown after taking an upsetting phone call in a busy train station. The sensory overload was too much to bear, and I fell down on Flinders Street and cried on the ground while people stepped around me as though I were a mud puddle; a dear friend who was with me sent Mum a concerned email, explaining that 'Clem has fallen over and her face is dirty'. Other times, a meltdown is a pure, white-hot rage that explodes out of my throat so quickly that I don't realise what's happening until it's too late. On a summer holiday in 2007, I was mucking around with friends in a river; one 'dunked' me beneath the water (a common human water amusement), and in that moment of sudden terror it was like something broke inside me – I surged up out of the water like a polystyrene bullet, screaming as I whacked him in the face and vacated the river like I was attached to a bungee cord.

Of course, I have learned to control this, up to a point; I feel that synapse starting to fire and I flee. I will literally turn and walk away, or vacate a room, or alight from the tram, anything to stop myself being crushed beneath that wave of rage, my face dragged across the sandbar by the undertow as I claw desperately for air. Some people refer to this Autistic behaviour as 'bolting'. If I remove myself from the stimulus, I can avoid the response. Most of the time.

Suddenly 'losing it' in play situations has been an enduring theme of my life, and – prior to the understanding that came with diagnosis – seemed proof of my ultimate alien nature: who likes a kid who can't play a game without screaming or crying? Worse, my response to bullies was never calm and collected (if *only* I could bolt from them): when made fun of, my reaction was typically to scream at them in my defence, which is of course a sure-fire way to ensure you remain the target of bullies for your entire life.

My emotional responses have never been 'appropriate'; it is the great burden of my life. I laugh too much at violent scenes in action movies; I react coolly in moments of tragedy; I cry when telling funny stories; I explode with fury at gentle joshing at my expense. Even when my response is what might be expected – say, laughing at a funny scene in a comedy, rather than at a character's head exploding – I am too loud, too much, spoiling everyone else's enjoyment of the jokes by laughing over the top of them. When I cry at something sad, it's too much; burst capillaries snake across my eyelids and I am dehydrated by an excess of tears. What is a meltdown but, at its core, an explosion of indiscriminate emotion?

Misunderstanding meltdowns as tantrums – or, worse, 'threatening behaviour' – can have deadly consequences. It's imperative to note that there are countless examples of Autistic people who have been injured or killed by police or security staff while experiencing a meltdown. Courtney Topic was shot dead by police in Western Sydney in 2015; though the 2018 coroner's report found that she was likely experiencing an episode linked to undiagnosed schizophrenia, her mother told SBS that Courtney was also experiencing a meltdown due to her Autism Spectrum Disorder. 'If the police officer on that day had [training in recognising ASD behaviours], I think we probably would not be having this conversation and Courtney would be here.' Locally, there is a slow crawl towards progress. Autism Spectrum Australia provide a 'Tips for Police' sheet, and smaller Autism organisations have offered sensitivity training to police and security staff.

In America, the reality for Autistic people interacting with law enforcement is bleak. In September 2020, a Salt Lake City police officer shot thirteen-year-old Autistic boy Linden Cameron multiple times, severely injuring him; Linden's mother had called 911 to request crisis support. In January 2020, Eric Parsa, a nonspeaking Autistic teen, died after sheriff's deputies are alleged to have handcuffed him, shackled him, and sat on him for more than nine minutes. Troy Canales, who is

Black and Autistic, was seventeen when three NYPD officers punched him in the face and body-slammed him when they spotted him leaning against a car.

Those who have come to recognise a meltdown as intrinsically different from a tantrum generally want to know how they can help when one occurs. And, to be sure, a meltdown (particularly in a teenager or adult) can look really scary!

Many Autistic people and those who care for them recommend the Low Arousal Approach. Devised by Professor Andrew McDonnell in the 1980s, it comprises a variety of behaviour management strategies that aim to reduce fear, stress and frustration in distressed individuals by identifying triggers and avoiding punitive measures, with the goal of preventing escalating aggression. The Low Arousal Approach features an emphasis on humanism (mutual respect, and avoiding dehumanising measures such as physical restraint) and on self-reflection for the (in this context) non-Autistic person (considering how their behaviour – posture, tone, etc. – might have contributed to the situation). Unlike some therapeutic and behavioural approaches to Autism, it is not about 'fixing' the person, or even changing their behaviour long-term, but rather about having empathy for the circumstances that may bring on a meltdown or other challenging behaviours. As McDonnell has written, 'It is important to understand that some people are simply different, and that their ways of being are not wrong or problematic – just different.'

Beyond implementing a formal Low Arousal Approach, there are aspects that can be applied in any situation. In order to prevent stress leading to build-up, this could include helping to provide a sense of routine, or a predictable home, school or office environment: things like schedules and visual timetables (pictures of the things that will happen throughout the day). In the build-up phase, this might include offering a safe and quiet place for the Autistic person to chill out, or recognising things that might be exacerbating sensory input (turning down radios and TVs, not using noisy appliances, offering a weighted blanket or favourite soft toy). During the explosion, a supportive but hands-off approach can work wonders; if you know the person's interests, you could talk to them about these, or see if they want to sing a favourite theme song. The question of what to do if someone has a meltdown in a public space is also concerning to many; acting as 'crowd control' is one option – keeping onlookers away, or asking the shop manager (for example) if there's somewhere quiet the person could go for a while.

Looking back, I don't blame Mum and Dad for walking away from me in that moment in Dimmey's; they didn't know it was a meltdown. To them, it would have looked like a tantrum, and the early-eighties approach to tantrums was to refuse to entertain them. So it's no surprise I ended up crawling, blinking, out of the haberdashery aisle.

Were I given the choice, I would probably walk away from myself in the midst of a meltdown, too, because on some deep level, I am always aware of the shame that will follow it. Sometimes that shame is immediate and intense, and other times it just lurks at the back of your mind as you piece together the memory of what just happened. Once, taking a bus trip to visit a friend on a dark winter's evening, a man dropped to the floor of the bus, in the midst of a seizure. Us fellow passengers sprang into action as the driver pulled into the service lane. When the man came to, he seemed almost disappointed in himself; 'Ah, did I have a fit?' he asked, as though he'd fallen prey to something he'd been trying to keep at arm's length.

There is nothing more embarrassing than coming out the other side of a meltdown, for you have torn off your human costume and revealed your raw and writhing nerves to the world.

WALK THE DINOSAUR

You have to understand: no five-year-old knows more about dinosaurs than I did.

It's also possible that no five-year-old on earth has marched confidently into Brashs (tailed by a willing adult) to purchase the 12" single of Was (Not Was)'s 'Walk the Dinosaur', my first ever record. Did I know – or care – that it was a Reagan-era meditation on a certain nuclear apocalypse? No: it had 'Dinosaur' in the title, in the lyrics and on the cover, and that was enough for me.

I listened to 'Walk the Dinosaur' on repeat while arranging my Invicta British Museum of Natural History plastic dinosaur replicas in various orders: first by height, then by colour, then by order of their extinction.

To this day, in a synaesthetic joy, the name of each dinosaur is linked in my memory with the colour of its plastic: Diplodocus (grey), Tyrannosaurus (rust red), Scelidosaurus (brown), Stegosaurus (peach), Plesiosaurus (grey-blue), Brachiosaurus (teal). They were only available at the Melbourne Museum shop, so the collection evolved over the course of a few years, and there was no gift, not even a new My Little Pony, as thrilling as a new Invicta dinosaur. In 1987, 'Father Christmas' managed to disguise the Brachiosaurus by wrapping it inside a mind-bending contraption of recycled cardboard; I challenge any YouTube 'unboxing' influencer to attain the level of transcendent joy that I experienced when the Brachiosaurus popped out of the wrapping paper that December.

From the archetypal Autistic child who can't stop talking about Thomas the Tank Engine to the 'Aspie' who monologues about obscure systems analytics, circumscribed or 'special' interests are a cornerstone of Autism. In fact, I'd go so far as to say they are perhaps its most well-known manifestation: your layperson's understanding of Autism may very well include the idea that an Autistic person is usually overly interested in something a bit offbeat, be it trains, obscure *Star Trek* languages, or collecting bread bag tags. The clinical literature often refers to the types of domains that special interests can fall in as 'non-social', which seems like a polite way of saying 'you don't make friends with steam train engine facts'.

Sometimes these interests are fixed throughout life, sometimes they may be set aside for even *more* special interests, but the focus and intensity of the fascination remains constant, no matter the topic.[14] Autistic individuals will sometimes deeply investigate their chosen interests,[15] committing vast tracts of information to rote memory (all the better to dazzle you with!), while others may simply enjoy the object of their focus and seek it out for comfort and routine.

Special interests have been noted at nearly every significant moment in the clinical history of Autism, from Hans Asperger observing his 'little professors' chatting animatedly about their chosen interests, to Lorna Wing acknowledging that special interests may be channelled into later employment for Autistic adults. Despite this, it is one of the behaviours of Autism that has received relatively little published research (particularly, like so many aspects of Autism, as it relates specifically to Autistic adults), at least compared to other Autistic behaviours, such as patterns of speech or self-stimulatory behaviour ('stimming').

Where research into special interests does go into detail, it is often presented from the position of what many disability advocates term a 'deficit model': an approach that considers a particular behaviour or symptom through a critical lens, focusing only on the challenges or problems that may arise from the behaviour, rather than any possible benefits to the person. In this sense, special interests are examined as the spanner in the works of 'function', for their ability to distract the Autistic subject from more important things (like schoolwork, or sleep). The special or circumscribed interest is reframed as an 'obsession'. Discussing said obsession will be referred to as a 'monologue' or 'info-dump', the Autistic person talking at, rather than with, a person, and unable to read the other person's lack of interest in the topic.

I prefer to think of 'monologuing' in the same manner as the Autistic author Anthony Easton, who sees it as an act of generosity. They write of visiting museums or galleries with fellow Autistic people, 'where exchanging facts, exchanging the taxonomic list, becomes an act of solidarity and intimacy'. This is what I refer to as 'getting on the wavelengths': getting together with Autistic friends and family and talking for *hours*, at great speed and length, about whatever it is we're interested in.

Special interests are another aspect of Autistic behaviour that have until recently been viewed according to male-skewed diagnostic criteria. There is an emerging school of thought that suggests this is another contributing factor to Autism so often being missed in girls, particularly as their special interests – in horses, celebrities or even ~boys~ (omg) – may be dismissed as ordinary 'girl stuff', at least compared to young Autistic boys' interests in things like public trans-portation systems or garbage trucks (ah yes, the two genders: ponies and garbage trucks), which are more likely to be deemed unusual. The young Autistic girl may appear to be similar to her peers in her chosen interest; only upon closer examination (which is unlikely to occur if the 'it's just typical girl stuff' assumption has already taken hold) will it become apparent that *their* interest will be deeper and more focused than others around them. A neurotypical girl child's shoebox of assorted horse toys will pale in comparison with the Autistic girl child's having read every book about horses at the library, and her notebooks full of sketches of equine physiology.

Take, for example, five-year-old Clem. It's true that a lot of kids go through a 'dinosaur phase', but mine was a love that was deep and pedantic. Like most kids, I can't remember what set off my love of dinosaurs, but *unlike* most kids, the fervour of my love for the extinct beasts was unrelenting: dinosaurs were my first 'special interest'.

It was a good time to be 'getting into' dinosaurs. In the mid-eighties, the so-called Dinosaur Renaissance that had been building since the sixties was hitting its peak: paleontological books were no longer dusty library books that smelled like egg-farts, but bestselling paper-backs with embossed covers and witty illustrations. Perhaps you saw *Jurassic Park* in 1993 and were delighted at the sight of little Tim clutching his hefty dinosaur book and going off about having read 'this book by a guy named Bakker'. Well, back in 1987 I was trying to convince the teacher checking my MS Readathon tally sheet that I – the kid who refused to read the *Spot* books we were assigned – had, in fact, read Dr Robert T Bakker's *The Dinosaur Heresies* ... all 481 pages of it. (Are you kidding? I'd already read it three times by then.)

Bakker's book was *wild*; it was like taking a sledgehammer to the sleepy lizard-like statues of 'dinosaurs' that surrounded Crystal Palace in London, which I had of course seen on my oft-rented VHS copies of literally anything related to dinosaurs. Here was a book that dared to suggest that dinosaurs were, in fact, warm-blooded; the T-Rex suddenly became much scarier when considering Bakker's speculation about the apex predator being able to gallop at speed. (Objects In Mirror Are Closer Than They Appear.) But you will be amazed to discover that most children in Grade 2 at St Joseph's didn't especially want to expound upon what made *The Dinosaur Heresies* such a revolutionary work.

In 1988, Mum went on a trip to Europe with her younger sister, Catie. She returned with what remains the greatest gift I have ever received: a stuffed Pteranodon made of bright purple velvet, which she had bought in the famed toy department of Galeries Lafayette. There was also the news of an impending new sibling, but I was too taken by Pterry to absorb any additional information: dinosaurs, dinosaurs, dinosaurs!

Pterry and I became inseparable; I carried him everywhere by his neck, and the front of his nose soon became glossy and flat, on account of all the food he was served, and all the goodnight kisses he received. I didn't take him to school, but only because I dreaded the idea of anything bad happening to him. Having listened to Meryl Streep reading *The Velveteen Rabbit* more times than is advisable for a child's developing sense of emotional peril, I became fixated on the idea that I might catch scarlet fever and necessitate Pterry's death via bonfire. Every cold, every fever, was made all the more fraught by the lingering dread of the idea that my best friend would be incinerated as soon as I began to recover from my illness. (Happily, he wasn't, and is looking at me as I write this.)

The bicentennial year was to be an auspicious one for our family, with the new baby due in December, but it was also a big one for dinosaur-mad little Clem. Reading the weekend newspaper (yes, I did this) with my parents, it was discovered that 'real' dinosaurs would be coming to Canberra, opening Questacon, by way of the *Dinosaurs Alive!* exhibition of animatronic models. Unlike Pterry, it appeared that *these* dinosaurs were, in fact, alive – as the title of the exhibition suggested, *obviously*. I became fixated on this impending dinosaur invasion. I asked my teacher what the dinosaurs would be fed; I talked to my bemused classmates about the fact that dinosaurs had, in fact, been brought back from extinction and would, of course, be travelling to Canberra (well, it *was* Australia's capital, after all).

Soon enough, the Bastow family piled into the car and made the trip to Canberra. Looking back, perhaps it was designed as a last hurrah for my only-child status, soon to be a thing of the past. I don't think the reality of having to share my parents with a sibling had really dawned on me; birth, like death, was too abstract a concept to really spend much time thinking about. Preparing to meet 'alive' dinosaurs, on the other hand, was enough to occupy my every waking moment! When we finally reached the doors of Questacon, however, the vastness of the experience ahead came crashing down upon me: I was actually *terrified* of meeting these real dinosaurs. There's a photo of me, in my best outfit, clutching Pterry and looking shyly over the railing at a Parasaurolophus as though, despite the fact that they largely ate by grinding low-growing vegetation, the creature was about to eat me. Ever heard the saying never meet your idols? Never tell an Autistic kid with a special interest in dinosaurs that those dinosaurs are 'alive'! Eventually I conquered my fear of certain death and we managed to walk through the whole exhibition at least seventeen more times.

Less than a month later, on 21 December 1988, Atticus arrived. I stood in the corner of Mum's room at the Mercy with my face buried in Pterry as a parade of family and friends came to see the new baby. I vividly remember one grown-up – the late, great Kate Gollings – stooping down from the rarefied adult atmosphere a few feet above me to see how I was faring with all the hustle and bustle of the new arrival. I was, it's safe to say, not a 'baby type'; not for me a chubby-cheeked doll in a miniature stroller nor a tiny kitchen within which to practice making food for my future children, plastic or otherwise. Indeed, my lack of interest in babies bordered on fear; I never wanted to hold them, wasn't especially interested when news of a baby was delivered at Show & Tell, and found them puzzling and difficult to engage with (you can't talk to a baby about *The Dinosaur Heresies*, that's for sure).

> I *was* very interested in those toy baby bottles where the 'milk' or 'orange juice' disappeared, but I spent so much time upending them to watch the liquid vanish that my plastic child would have long ago died of starvation
>> someone gave me a baby doll at some stage and I was so uninterested in it that I left it in the backyard one winter until rust leaked from its blinking eyes
>>> which was, in retrospect, probably a good way to induce a fear of babies

Atti was a very cheerful baby, with a relaxed attitude to life that later extended to carrying Puss, our cat, around the house by the shoulders with her limbs dangling like a pyjama bag toy. I was … not relaxed in the slightest. Photos taken of us two Bastow children in the first year of Atticus's life have the hilarious stiffness of a daguerreotype: Atti, a miniature blonde Alfred Hitchcock with not a care in the world, and me, holding him at arm's length as though I've just dug him out of a space capsule and I'm scared he's going to explode.

A deficit model of Autism frames special interest as something unsettling and obsessive. Why, countless parenting blogs ask, does my son sit for hours reading about The Tube? Why is my daughter constantly telling me about the mating habits of the green sea turtle? It is considered odd to engage with one's (Autistic) passion for hours, rejecting food, socialisation and sleep. And yet, on the other hand, we can observe neurotypical neoliberal fantasies of mastery that essentially present the same behaviours (stripped of Autistic context) as aspirational, such as Malcolm Gladwell championing the 10,000 hours one is supposed to sink into a topic in order to become an 'outlier', or a prodigious talent, as described in his 2008 book *Outliers*.

All sorts of 'disruptors' and 'thought leaders' invoke Mihaly Csikszentmihalyi's notion of flow state – the complete absorption in an active task at hand, with no attention paid to anything else – as a way to achieve greatness. The Hungarian–American psychologist began his research into flow in the mid-seventies, and in a 1996 interview he described the state as 'Being completely involved in an activity for its own sake. The ego falls away. Time flies. Every action, movement, and thought follows inevitably from the previous one, like playing jazz. Your whole being is involved, and you're using your skills to the utmost.'

(Like so many nightmares of late capitalism, I think it's safe to say that Csikszentmihalyi's research has been somewhat repurposed by corporations and brands as another way to increase productivity and 'engagement'; he considered flow state integral to happiness, as opposed to triumph within neoliberal employment structures.)

Spending all day and night consumed in an activity or interest at the expense of time/sustenance/sleep suddenly sounds familiar, does it not? The issue is that when we Autists are tuning into our own personal jazz odysseys – putting in our 10,000 hours on Klingon geopolitics – our attention and involvement is presented as a problem to be solved.

I am not the first Autistic person to make the connection between flow and special interests, and clinicians have also noted the similarities. Just as Csikszentmihalyi's theories have been purloined by capitalism – flow state as a way to improve productivity – so too have some suggested that Autistic people's special interests could be channelled into employment possibilities. Consider the ancient neurotypical proverb, 'Find a job you enjoy doing and you will never work a day in your life'. It is true that many Autistic people *do* find work that aligns with their special interests, but the danger in 'employifying' special interests lies in presenting that as the ultimate way for Autistic people to have value for society.

Anyway, I could never have become a palaeontologist, because I hate the feeling of dirt on my hands.

There would be other dinosaur-related highlights to come in my life, such as the 1993 release of Steven Spielberg's *Jurassic Park*. I attended an advance screening with Mum, only to experience velociraptor nightmares for the next fifteen years. Cool! In 1989, however, a dream came true: ABC screened David Attenborough's *Lost Worlds, Vanished Lives*. Like any Incredibly Cool Kid, I was already a huge fan of Sir David, so this collision of heroes and special interests was big news. We had learned of this world-shattering event early enough to be at the ready with blank VHS tapes. Though his stock in trade was the contemporaneous(ish) natural world, Attenborough, like so many, had fostered a boyhood passion for the secrets that could be held by rocks. In *Lost Worlds*, he's giddy with enthusiasm; watching him looking for fossilised dinosaurs in the Sahara is like getting a glimpse of the ten-year-old Sir David. To me, the notion that one could simply stumble upon a dinosaur in the middle of a desert was absolutely wild; suddenly every salt pan, dried creek bed or jumble of rocks could, potentially, be hiding a dinosaur treasure. I don't believe any fossils of note were ever found in the mud around the various derelict blocks of Port Melbourne, but that didn't stop me from looking.

In the documentary, Sir David wears a khaki jacket; I immediately took to wearing an army disposals jacket in a similar colourway. It was as though by wearing the jacket, I could also be closer to dinosaurs. That jacket was referred to as my 'David Attenborough', and is an almost comical feature of nearly every family photo between the years of 1989 and 1994 (and, no, I did not allow anyone to ever wash it).

In 1991, when *The Trials of Life* was released, Sir David appeared at the Galleria ABC Shop (RIP) to sign copies. The entire family decamped to Bourke Street one cold morning, me in my David Attenborough, where we queued for a good four hours, awaiting our audience with the man himself. I talked the ears off the young couple in front of us about all things Attenborough, in particular my well-worn dubbed copy of *Lost Worlds*. But by the time we reached the trestle table where he was set up with a Sharpie, of course, I was so star struck that I could not say a single word. 'Hello,' he said in *that* voice as I handed him my copy of the book, awestruck. I watched as he scribbled his signature on the endpaper, then handed it back to me with a grin and asked 'How's that?' An officious ABC Shop employee ushered us out of the way so that the signings could continue, and that was that. The entirety of our interaction lasted, at best, seventeen seconds, but I would remember it for the rest of my life.

FEAR RESPONSE

Aside from a fear of heights (reasonable, I think almost anyone would argue), nearly every intense fear I have experienced in my lifetime has been both highly specific and characterised by a fear response that might best be described as 'off the charts'.

Take, for example, the fear instilled in me by the synthesised saxophone theme to the jolly BBC show *The Amazing Adventures of Morph*. It was a terror so powerful that the mere thought of it would bring on a cold sweat; *hearing* it on the TV would induce a meltdown of screaming tears. I vividly remember Dad, presumably having recognised the magnitude of my Morph-theme-phobia, seeing if the same result could be brought on by merely whistling the theme; results were very conclusive, and found that 100 per cent of Autistic kids with a fear of the theme to *The Amazing Adventures of Morph* could have a panic response induced by mere facsimile of the tune.

I had a similar fear of the saxophone solo from Gerry Rafferty's 'Baker Street', when it would occasionally appear on 3KZ
    in an incredibly brave attempt to conquer the formative demons of my youth, I requested to study saxophone in Year 7, but was turned down and given the cello instead

> while tuning my cello one lunchtime, the string snapped and
> whacked me in the face, replacing my fear of saxophone
> riffs with a fear of tuning any stringed instrument – sunrise,
> sunset

There were other screen media terrors, too, some of which to this day I have no context or further understanding of, many of which were not even 'horror movies', which one can generally assume are designed to elicit fear responses. For years I lived in mortal fear of 'the honey man' – some dude wearing a gooey rubber mask, chasing kids down a hillside, possibly riding on hay bales – based on a particularly spooky midday movie I caught no more than seventeen seconds of while channel surfing when I was home sick from school. It's true that many children get scared by things in screen media that they perhaps weren't quite ready for, but this was no standard stimulus–response. These stolen glances at moments of horror on TV – shocking me right out of my brain – were *catastrophic* in terms of effect, even though the relative exposure to fear–response ratio was weighted almost comically in favour of the latter.

Hyper-specific phobias are a common experience of Autism, and were one of the earliest noted hallmarks of the condition. In his ground-breaking 1943 paper, 'Autistic Disturbances of Affective Contact', Leo Kanner observed unusual fears in the children he studied, such as Herbert B's fear of gas burners, and Barbara K's fear of the wind. It could be argued, of course, that all phobias are by their very nature 'hyper specific', to which I would counter that what makes Autistic fears unique is that they're often, well, very unique indeed.

The role that fears and phobias play in an Autistic person's anxiety – a common comorbidity – has continued to provide fruitful material for research. One study, presented in the journal of *Research in Autism Spectrum Disorders* in 2013, suggested that 41 per cent of Autistic children experienced unusual fears, such as of toilets, weather activity

72

or vacuum cleaners; those who also experienced more common fears, such as of the dark, or bugs, lifted the overall number of Autistic kids with phobias, unusual or otherwise, to almost half.[16] And, ironically enough, findings presented in the journal *Autism Research* in 2020[17] suggested that Autistic children have a muted fear response when confronted by things that are *intended* to be scary, like a mechanical spider or a person in a spooky costume. This may explain some Autistic kids' tendency to wander into situations that other children would understand as perilous. (The study itself, and there are many like it, should also give us pause when we consider the ethics of how often Autistic kids are subjected to existential terrors in the name of 'research'.)

It strikes me that the very specificity of these phobias, and in turn (to the perplexed non-Autistic observer) the apparently ridiculous nature of them, makes the depth of the horror almost impossible to communicate to others. It would be fair to suggest that this also contributes to the impatience and frustration that's a common neurotypical response to Autistic phobias: come on, you idiot, it's just a TV theme song; get over it. This is easy to internalise, particularly for the undiagnosed, who have no frame of reference for the intensity of their response. Take my 'issues' with balloons: what sort of idiot is scared of balloons? They're fun, they're colourful, they turn up at parties!

Well, I'll tell you: in 1987, the 'entertainment' at my friend Jodie's birthday party was to fill the front room with balloons and lock us kids in there, while the adults presumably had a smoke and a West Coast Cooler on the back porch. The point of this endeavour – the 'fun' – was that we could pop them all, and certainly everyone around me committed themselves to this activity with unbridled enthusiasm. Imagine, if you will, fifteen or so five- and six-year-olds sitting with glee on a bunch of balloons while I stayed glued to the wall in terror. Like so many aspects of my experience, the only way I could move through a world in which a bunch of jolly balloons is a distressingly common sight was to turn it into a comedy routine. I would switch straight into 'So, get a load of this ...' open-mic-night storyteller mode and explain the context for my fear of balloons, even as my insides were churning in terror. Maybe, the logic ran, if I can make people laugh about the *fear itself*, they won't laugh *at me*.

It's hard to recall any moments in my life when I wasn't simultaneously existing in the world and internally running this sort of thought experiment. And, of course, there were plenty of occasions where people I had trusted to hold my deepest fear would turn it against me, laughing uproariously as they trapped me in a corner and 'squeaked' a balloon by rubbing their hands over its precariously stretched rubber skin. Ah yes, the classic human bonding ritual: torturing each other with our deepest fears!

That's not to say that my carefully constructed facade of normalcy and bravery can't all come crashing down in an instant, of course. During one screenwriting tutorial, another student brought in pages from their script that featured tangential mentions of skin picking. Panic began to rise. Now, some context: I will disembark a train or tram carriage if I see someone picking or biting at the skin on their fingers. Even typing the letters, 's k i n p i c k i n g', is an exercise in determination. Among my Autistic brethren, many of whom engage in skin picking, this is a point of amusement – DO NOT TOUCH YOUR FINGERS IN VIEW OF CLEM – but alone, in the wild, a stranger gnawing at their cuticles will bring on the telltale build-up to a meltdown. Once I observe that it's happening, my heart rate quickens, my skin becomes clammy and a scream rises in my throat. Even if the carriage is crowded and noisy, I can still hear the picking. Forget the fight or flight response; I am already fifty metres down the road, leaving a me-shaped puff of smoke sitting where I was thirty seconds earlier.

Spend a few hours in the online world of 'Autism parenting' and you'll quickly come to understand how puzzling and frustrating these specific fears can be for the non-Autistic person. The tone of the conversation can often be boiled down to 'why can't Autistic kids just get real and stop being scared of hand dryers?' Autistic people, on the other hand, tend to be perfectly happy accepting each other's phobias as fact.

Exact statistics regarding the comorbidity of clinically significant anxiety and Autism are hard to come by; one study has suggested that between *11 to 84 per cent* of Autistic people are affected.[18] Anecdotally, most Autistic people will report that they experience anxiety in one form or another, from simple social anxiety through to debilitating anxiety disorders. The simple fact of existing as Autistic within a neurotypical world can bring on anxiety – trying to fit in, performance anxiety, the unpredictability of the world at large – and issues relating to emotional interception can complicate matters: it's hard to explain what's wrong if you neither know what emotions you are feeling nor are able to explain them. I once heard someone describe Autistic people as uniquely placed to be plagued by anxiety, because our overactive imaginations mean that we don't merely experience a vague sense of unease, but have vivid nightmare visions.

My own anxiety manifests as a constant *Sliding Doors* in my mind in which I see the worst-case scenario of nearly everything I do play out *as I do it*. Stepping inside the supermarket on a rainy afternoon? Slipping over and cracking my head open on the shelves. Waving goodbye to a loved one after a family lunch? Their car being 'T-boned' at the next intersection. Lights change at the crosswalk? Mown down by a runaway truck. Disaster, catastrophe, strangers murdering my dog, blunt-force trauma, rape, torture; this is the daily texture of my existence. And then, at night, I will dream what I came to refer to as 'my Roland Emmerich dreams', after the director who continues to bring us nightmare visions of the (almost) end of the world: disaster scenarios with a scope so vast – enormous waves, huge spaceships crashing to earth, fluorescent purple lightning boiling the seas, dinosaurs so large that I cannot see where they end and the sky begins – that they are awe-inspiring.

(There are unexpected benefits to this: live every day of your life in a white-knuckle hell ride through the disaster movies of your mind and you may find that when a once-in-a-century pandemic follows a once-in-a-lifetime bushfire season, you appear to be significantly less troubled than those around you.)

As a child, this anxiety manifested in much the same way, although perhaps it was slightly less, uh, inventive: typically, it involved scenarios like 'being bitten in half by a shark'. There were only a handful of shark books at Port Melbourne Library, which was probably fair enough, being by the sea (and I knew enough about *Jaws* to know what happens when seaside towns get panicky about sharks), although the likelihood of being speared by a white pointer somewhere off Station Pier was fairly slim; you were far more likely to encounter the bloated, floating corpse of a sewer rat, which occasionally bubbled up out of the stormwater drain near Lagoon Pier that we'd bomb off as though it were the diving board at Harold Holt. The shark books' dust jackets were made of a smooth and opaque plastic that peeled open slowly, with a hiss, like Tupperware containers, and they smelled of rotten eggs. I would grab them and climb up into the carpeted tall ship in the Port Melbourne Library

> yes, a tall ship, with carpet in it, in the library
>> it was made out of the same sort of laminated chipboard as school desks, with colourful split-level decks covered in rough, scratchy dark blue carpet
>>> … didn't everyone have a carpeted tall ship in their local library??

and read all about Rodney Fox being bitten nearly clean in half by a great white shark back in 1963. There's a photo of a recovered Rodney holding up his left arm to show the impact of the bite: a huge semicircle of puncture marks that starts at his stomach and arcs up over his shoulder and into his armpit. And then there was a photo of Henri Bource, whose leg was bitten off in 1964, sitting on top of a dead shark with his left wetsuit leg folded up beneath his knee; incredibly boss. For many years, well before I knew anything about body modifications, I would daydream about 'getting' a shark bite scar so that I, too, could be cool like Rodney and Henri.

Around the same time, the council had started – in typically half-hearted 1980s Port Melbourne fashion – to 'beautify' the streets with some gum trees; just to the left of our front door, two squares were carved into the asphalt and young trees were summarily shoved into the holes. To give you a sense of what a big deal it was to get a young eucalypt on our doorstep, up until that point I don't believe there had been a single tree of note on the entire half-kilometre stretch between Pickles Street and Bay Street; Port Melbourne in the 1980s was busted asphalt, brown brick, blistered weatherboard and corrugated iron (or a combination of all four); the only local 'green space', as they'd call it now, was Lagoon Reserve, a splash of turf with a few cricket cages and a small playground.

Not long after the gum trees arrived, so too did the 'terrible wedges'. Some sort of case moth or bagworm, they feasted on the young gum leaves and spun themselves little wedge-shaped cocoons. One day, I was playing on the pile of sand at the front of our house, and a terrible wedge dropped from the tree and landed next to me. Some sort of grub then began to emerge from its casing. Immediately beset by the horror of this sight, I commando-rolled off the sand pile and onto the asphalt, where a nearly-healed scab on my knee sheared straight off. My horror – at the wedge, the grub, the accidental DIY debridement – soon turned to glee: now I wouldn't just have a scab, but a *scar*.

Once I had read all the shark attack literature I could get my hands on, I realised that even more hideous gore could be found in the accounts of Hollywood's great special effects make-up artists. I would spend idle afternoons in the 790s of the library, working out how masters like Dick Smith and Rick Baker managed to approximate the look of, say, someone being torn to shreds by werewolves. There was considerable irony in this, as I was terrified of horror movies, disliked violent content, and refused to watch anything whose classification I didn't fall in the appropriate age bracket for. But I quickly became adept at mixing up my own fake blood, and stealing globs of margarine to create disgusting pus-filled wounds.

Looking back, I think my fascination with gore and wounds was, in a way, an attempt to wrestle with the existential terror I felt on a daily basis.

There is an emerging field of inquiry that has begun to consider the intersection of Post Traumatic Stress Disorders (PTSD) and Autism. Autistic people are significantly more likely to experience adverse events, such as schoolyard bullying or childhood maltreatment.[19] An initial study conducted in 2020 suggests that Autistic people are at elevated risk of PTSD.[20] In fact, it may be that Autistic people do not even need to experience what the *DSM-5* would define as a traumatic event in order to develop symptoms of PTSD. They can be destabilised by a build-up of exposures to experiences *they find* scary or stressful;[21] in other words, the ongoing trauma of being alive and Autistic.

As a kid, obsessed with wounds and shark bites and worried that Morph might one day crawl out of the TV set and eat me, I was just starting to reckon with this unending low (and occasionally high) level of fear.

When I was twenty-five, I finally told a specialist about this constant marathon of calamitous images that haunted both my waking and sleeping hours.

'I think you are trying to tell me,' my analyst said with care, 'how much danger you feel you are in.'

WHO YOU GONNA CALL?

Of all the aspects of myself that I now recognise as Autistic, echolalia – the repeating of words, sounds and phrases – is my most treasured.

Echolalia is not exclusively an Autistic behaviour, but it's perhaps most commonly understood in an Autistic context, within which it can take one of two forms. There's immediate echolalia, which is the repetition of words as soon as they are heard: a parent asks their Autistic child 'Do you want some juice?' and the child responds 'Do you want some juice?' Then there's delayed echolalia, where the words or phrase are repeated after the fact, such as quoting from a favourite movie, or repeating a phrase from an advertisement they've seen years ago and that everyone else has forgotten about.

Generally speaking, non-Autistic or 'typical' children learn to speak by first grasping single words – 'mum', 'yes', 'cup' – and then learning to string them together in sentences. Autistic kids often, on the other hand, essentially reverse this process: we begin with chunks of language that may be decontextualised, but won't necessarily understand the individual words or be able to use them in a different context.

The best way I have seen this described is by Lauren Lowry, a speech-language pathologist, who writes: 'A child might say "It's time for your bath" every time he hears his father filling up the bathtub. He knows those words have something to do with bath time, but he doesn't know what "it's", "time", "for", "your", and/or "bath" mean individually, and he can't use these words in other sentences. Because he doesn't understand all of the words, he uses the pronoun incorrectly (using "your bath" instead of "my bath").'

In Autistic kids, echolalia can often be a 'stepping stone' to more flexible or functional language, but it rarely disappears completely.

My own language development progressed essentially as expected, as far as everyone can remember, but was peppered with certain turns of phrase that were surely, from the outside, fairly odd. My vocabulary included jumbles of phrases, invented or borrowed, including 'have a shoe' (good luck) and 'agralagra' (relax). I once farewelled my visiting grandfather by earnestly telling him, 'Good bye, Poppa, and don't vomit'. I have racked my brain trying to think where 'don't vomit' came from, and can only assume I watched something where a character took a plane or boat trip and was overcome by travel sickness. When it comes to echolalia, however, I can pinpoint the precise moment it became a fact of life: the time when, in the summer of 1989, I became a Ghostbuster.

It's true that, being a seven-year-old girl, I had postgraduate qualifications in neither parapsychology, paranormal history nor metallurgy. It's also true that my proton pack was made of Duplo, a Cornflakes box and half an old vacuum cleaner, as opposed to an unlicensed nuclear accelerator that emits a way-fire positronic ionised stream of proton energy in order to polarise negatively charged ectoplasmic entities, holding them in the stream even if they are out of phase with reality. Yet, despite all this, in the summer of 1989 (and beyond) I *was* Dr Peter Venkman.

I was perhaps better primed to take the world of *Ghostbusters* at face value than most, because Port Melbourne in the 1980s was *crawling* with ghosts. The old factories and pubs of Port Melbourne all had their own unsettling tales of spectral visitors and unexplained phenomena, as though the old red brick chimney stack of Sandridge Bay Towers was, well, 'a huge super-conductive antenna that was designed and built expressly for the purpose of pulling in and concentrating spiritual turbulence'. Seemingly every resident had a story about a ghost that occupied their house or workplace, like the one around the corner that would throw open the front door, run down the hallway, and slam the back door shut after itself. We even had one at our house, which had formerly operated as a pub in the late 1800s; it would walk up the stairs every night like clockwork. I was too young to have any memory of this, but apparently one night Dad cracked the shits and demanded that the spirit vacate 55 Rouse Street immediately and stop scaring everybody. ('Dad's home' energies are an underrated paranormal extermination technique.)

My first exposure to *Ghostbusters* was, like so many of the films and TV shows I would eventually come to know (inside out) and love (with obsessive focus), a terrifying accidental glimpse on television. These could take a few forms: waking up a few hours after bedtime, when Mum and Dad were watching something; sneaking in a channel surf during the Adults Only Hours after 9 pm; watching something at a friend's house, where the TV rules were different (or, indeed, non-existent). Take *The Empire Strikes Back*, which I discovered by walking into the living room right when the Wampa was attempting to eat Luke. Cue: gnashing of teeth, pure unbridled terror, recurring nightmares, and so on; a real walk in the psychic park. Similarly, for *Ghostbusters*, it was a snippet of the metaspectral hellhound Vinz Clortho exploding out of Louis Tully's wardrobe; like Louis' party guests, I may or may not have fled the room in fear. (Okay, who brought the dog?)

Fortunately, I guess, my initial fear of Vinz Clortho was – given I was a young child who had seen a pretty scary moment in a movie

81

designed, more or less, for grown-ups – deemed a reasonable fear, and I was warned away from going back for seconds even though the tape cover at Video Flash seemed more goofy than terrifying. Despite this ignominious introduction to the world of paranormal extermination, somehow I managed to conquer my fear of Vinz and watch *Ghostbusters* on VHS, in full, in time for the 1989 release of the sequel.

There had been other cinematic special interests sparked in a movie theatre; in 1986, I learned the entire script of *Milo & Otis* over the course of a handful of cinema trips (you had to work fast in those days, when you'd be a year older by the time it was released on VHS). Even in 1989, that year's September holiday blockbuster, *The Land Before Time*, had worked its way into my DNA to the point that I somehow convinced my parents to allow not one but *two* trips to the Pizza Hut on Dandenong Road – once with them, once with family friends – in order to snare two of the rubber *Land Before Time* hand puppets that were available for purchase along with a couple of dreadful family-sized pizzas.

If there was *Ghostbusters II* merchandise available in 1989, it was mercifully kept hidden from me. In other words, the trip to Brighton Village Twin – like so many movie outings of my youth, accompanying my buddy Elliott and his mum Barbara, while Mum and Dad stayed home with baby Atti – was a straightforward affair; just another day out at the movies. Even the very notion of franchise filmmaking was, to us seven-year-olds, somewhat nebulous; if we were aware of the existence of 'cinematic universes', it was only very loosely. *The Empire Strikes Back* and *Return of the Jedi* were, as far as we were concerned, just movies that happened to star the same characters. So, we were aware that the movie we were about to see was a sequel to *Ghostbusters* inasmuch as it had a '2' in its title. (Well, a 'II'.)

In other words, we brought with us precious little context for the gags and winks at *Ghostbusters* proper in this second film, but we laughed anyway. In fact, I think it's probably fair to say that Elliott and I suddenly realised that what we had formerly considered the high watermark for cinematic humour – that is to say, Dudley Moore's performance as a croaking bullfrog in *Milo & Otis* – had been blown to smithereens. As we exited the cinema and burst out into the sunny street, something had shifted. The world had changed: we, mere children, had been initiated into the world of adult comedy, and had passed the test. By virtue of having laughed at jokes like 'You know, I'm a voter. Aren't you supposed to lie to me and kiss my butt?', we *were* adults now.

As far as *Ghostbusters* was concerned, it was over for me: this was to be a lifelong love affair. In Dr Peter Venkman I had a new hero *and* a new persona. 'The Horse' was retired; now, I was a Ghostbuster, with a double doctorate in psychology and parapsychology. This focus reached its zenith when Dad constructed my own proton pack (it attached with my old set of braces; the rainbow striped elastic was not terribly 'screen accurate', but was definitely in the can-do spirit of the team), which took equal place alongside the *Twinkle, Twinkle* tutu and skivvy combo as the greatest costume of my life. Only, it wasn't really a 'costume', and I never actually 'played' in any imaginative sense 'as' Venkman; I just *was* him. I would just pop the proton pack on and wander around (or sit) and reel off lines.

This identification with Venkman was, in its own way, a flight of fantasy; it was obvious to anyone, particularly myself, that in real life I was more like a combination of Ray Stantz and Egon Spengler: too enthusiastic, like the former, about my weird and intellectual interests, like the latter. I also lacked Winston Zeddemore's pragmatism and calmness under pressure. But Venkman was different; funny enough to seem a little bit embarrassed by everything happening around him, quick with a one-liner, but still a scientist. And, importantly, he had the best dialogue.

Lines from the film immediately entered the family vernacular (naturally I convinced my parents to also see the film, posthaste).

Beyond the family unit, dialogue from *Ghostbusters II* – and later, courtesy of VHS rentals, *Ghostbusters* – very quickly became my way of communicating with the people around me. If I were to sit down and attempt to visualise how much of Dan Aykroyd and Harold Ramis's screenplays had entered my vocabulary, in an echolalic sense, well, it would be 'a Twinkie 35 feet long, weighing approximately 600 pounds'.

What's striking about the *Ghostbusters*-ese in our family, however, is that we're not just pinging quotes back and forth for fun (I mean, that happens plenty, too); phrases that have entered the vernacular are used 'appropriately'. If Dad and I say 'Hairless pets: weird', we're not just riffing on Dr Peter Venkman's beleaguered talk show, *World of the Psychic*, we're inevitably reacting to something strange. 'Cats and dogs, living together: mass hysteria' isn't being used to refer to the literal end of the world as predicted in *Ghostbusters*, but to any particularly chaotic situation.

This speaks to a common misunderstanding of echolalia: its presumed lack of contextual meaning. As the Autistic critical theorist Julia Miele Rodas writes, 'echolalia and verbal stereotypy are referred to as "parroting" (an animal language, unconscious, unknowing, without significance) and the autist and her language are described as rigid, robotic, and mechanical [...] The autist echoes because she is hollow, nothing inside; she has no self, no point of origin.' Yet echolalia, when used in conversation, more often than not *has* meaning and purpose.

Had I reacted to the frustration of the 'Reading the Mind in the Eyes' test (which I flunked, for the record) during my own assessment for Autism Spectrum Disorder by yelling 'I'll tell you what the effect is: it's pissing me off!!', it's likely the context would have been lost on the clinician. That is, unless they, too, were a big *Ghostbusters* fan and could locate the quote in its original context (i.e. Dr Venkman's deeply unethical ESP tests upon students at Columbia University) and know that the 'echo' was, however offbeat, relevant to the situation.

But which clinician could ever hope to have an encyclopedic knowledge of *Ghostbusters*, or *Thomas the Tank Engine*, or *The Avengers*, or the hundreds and thousands of conversations an Autistic person has observed and cherry-picked from in order to form their own vocabulary? It is perfectly reasonable that they likely observe all those quotes and idioms as lacking in context. Mine, as kind and insightful as she was, could never have known that 'exactly right' was nicked from my hairdresser and 'okay, it's not' from my friend Lee, nor that repeating those turns of phrase served the dual purpose of providing contextual conversation while also reminding me how much I loved both people.

Some things are said because they have contextual meaning, others because they are just enjoyable to say. I love mimicking other voices; quoting lines from *Ghostbusters* is enjoyable because I like the knowledge that I have learned, like a pianist conquering Rachmaninoff, the exact intonation and rhythms of the actor's original performance. There is satisfaction in becoming a human tape recorder; it's rewarding, and soothing.

That seems to be one of the deepest mysteries of Autism, from a neurotypical and clinical mindset: *why* are they doing that? The thought that a behaviour might be pleasurable or even necessary never seems to occur to the experts. ('Respected texts on autism,' as Autistic writer and researcher Anna N de Hooge notes, 'are not usually authored by autistic people. Even the word itself does not belong to us.')

Sometimes, it's a combination of the two: contextual meaning and textural pleasure. I suppose it's contextual to respond, while watching the daily Victorian government COVID-19 press briefing and hearing an epidemiologist refer to 'recent data', by saying 'I'm worried, Ray, it's getting crowded in there and all my recent data points to something big on the horizon' – but it's also just fun. Faced with the possibility of death – literal, ego, economic, societal – at the hands of a novel virus, why *not* go into Egon mode? Which brings a third aspect into the picture, beyond contextual meaning and enjoyment: it's also reassuring.

Delayed echolalia is, for me, often a type of stim: a self-stimulatory behaviour that Autistic people use (depending on the situation) to express themselves, calm themselves or regulate their emotional state. Most people think of stims, in an Autistic context, as behaviours like spinning on the spot or flapping one's hands. But echolalia itself can also be a stim.

Faced with a chaotic world, and an even more chaotic emotional core, there is always 'Gozer the Traveler' to regulate the storm within and without. The Autistic blogosphere reveals that I am not alone in this, though you wouldn't know it from reading most clinical texts. In a clinical mindset, echolalia is typically regarded as a problem to be conquered, a behaviour to be addressed. I see, in the echoes (yes, I know …) of echolalia that enter the collective discourse, something of this mistrust of the behaviour. You may remember back in 2018, it emerged that Lady Gaga had been telling the same anecdote to refer to her working relationship with *A Star Is Born* director and co-star Bradley Cooper. Every time a friend shared the 'supercut' of Gaga using the same line, or I saw a headline making fun of her, I shrank into myself: I do that ('that' being recycling verbal material that has tested well in previous conversations) every day of my life.

Of all people to swoop to Gaga's, and by extension my, defence, Jonah Hill stood up for her in a *GQ* Live event: 'I actually thought it was kind of amazing,' he said. 'I was like, "Damn, she *is* a good actress" – 'cause it sounds real every single time.'

goddamn right, Jonah, AND THAT'S WHAT IT'S LIKE USING ECHOLALIA TO EXIST IN THE HUMAN WORLD

Whatever enjoyment or emotional regulation I may find in reeling off a favourite quote or borrowed colloquialism, I am acutely aware of the embarrassment that follows if the listener stares at me with blank eyes, unable to parse what I've just said. Leaning hard into movie quotes has been, in a way, a defence mechanism: I am hiding my stimming, my echolalia-ing, in plain sight. If the person I've just quoted at doesn't understand the context or meaning, I can hurriedly explain that it is a joke from a movie. In the sage words of the Red Hot Chili Peppers on *The Simpsons*, everyone can enjoy that.

Of the many things that diagnosis has given me, it's this *understanding* of my own behaviours that has been the most mind-expanding. That's not to say that diagnosis is where an understanding of self begins and ends. Much of that has been hard-won, and most has come through engagement with other Autistic people and by reading the works of others.

Echolalia has been a constant companion in my life. My own understanding of *Rain Man*, funnily enough, was in essence one of doubled-down echolalia. Though I hadn't seen the film in high school, I was vaguely aware of its cultural impact, so when my friend Mel (six months older and *much* cooler than me) started quoting it in giggling outbursts – 'Kmart sucks! C-H-A-R-L-I-E Babbitt!' – I had no choice but to join in. We'd already bonded over *Strictly Ballroom* and *Idiot Box* quotes.

This was huge for me: it was the first time my rusted-on habit of reeling through film, TV and cartoon quotes had actually succeeded in its intended mission: making a friend. Of course (that's a *Rain Man* joke) the fact that I, the undiagnosed Autistic, was parroting these *Rain Man* quotes in an act of bonding without fully understanding the context or even, indeed, the plot of the movie was, well, waiter, bring me my toothpicks: this ironing is delicious.

If there's a poetry to my lifelong commitment to *Ghostbusters*, it's that its co-creator, Dan Aykroyd, is himself on the Autism spectrum, diagnosed with Asperger's in his thirties at the encouragement of his wife. Aykroyd has credited his neurotype with aiding his comedy career. '[It] has helped me creatively,' he told *The Guardian* in 2014.

'I sometimes hear a voice and think: "That could be a character I could do"' – but seems guarded when discussing the specifics. He seems to have a habit of downplaying it in print interviews (regularly employing the phrase 'very mild Asperger's', or referring to having it 'managed'), but in shaggier talk show appearances, he'll make references to 'barking' or talking to himself. Regardless, we have Aykroyd's special interests to thank for *Ghostbusters*. 'One of my symptoms included my obsession with ghosts and law enforcement – I carry around a police badge with me, for example,' he said in 2013. 'I became obsessed by Hans Holzer, the greatest ghost hunter ever. That's when the idea of my film *Ghostbusters* was born.' (Of the badge, he once told NPR's Terry Gross, 'If I don't have a badge on me I feel naked.')

I'm no clinician, but there is certainly something *very* 'Autistic' about the *Ghostbusters* movies, and it's not just that the young Egon had part of a Slinky, but had straightened it, or that he collects spores, moulds and fungus. No, it's something textural and subtextual, something you only detect if your neurological PKE Meter is set to the right levels. The humour is echolalic (the constant nods to classic cinema, pop music and advertising) and offbeat ('Listen: you smell something?'), and the horror is almost entirely sensory (being 'hosed' with slime, or eaten by the bathtub, or the simple fact of the sexual union of the Gatekeeper and the Keymaster being key to an interdimensional catastrophe after which everyone will be covered in melted marshmallow). There's even an entire gag that hinges on echolalia:

> Janine: *'Louis, do you want some coffee?'*
> Louis: *'Do I?'*
> Egon: *'Yes, have some.'*
> Louis: *'Yes, have some!'*

It's possible that I picked up on this as a kid, but there is also the simple fact of *Ghostbusters* being one of the greatest comedy films of all time. It wasn't hard to fall in love with it (once you got over the terror of Vinz Clortho, of course), and if you're going to choose a script upon which to build the bulk of your vocabulary and personality, you might as well go with something that's already tested well with audiences.

It may come as a surprise to hear I was not on board for the 2016 *Ghostbusters* remake/reboot, starring Kristen Wiig, Melissa McCarthy, Leslie Jones and Kate McKinnon. It wasn't because I didn't 'believe' that women could be Ghostbusters, but because from the outset this seemed like a waste of both great comic talent and the possibility of original screenwriting, just the latest in a long line of 'existing IP' franchise filmmaking. My chief problem, however, as someone who enjoys scanning new films for dialogue to add to my mental Rolodex, was that it was just hopelessly unfunny. Take the characters' reactions to the arrival of the team's car, a hearse soon to be converted into ECTO-1: we go from the wry ('You can't park that here!') in 1984 to the spoon-feeding ('You didn't disclose that the vehicle was going to be a *hearse*') in 2016. Throughout the remake, the stars seem slightly pained by the jargon they're required to spout. But it was *specifically* the hyper-specific, Autistic (I did it again; whoops!) quality of *Ghostbusters*' dialogue that gave the 1984 film its gritty sense of, if not reality, then believability: 'Sir, what you had there was what we refer to as a Focused, Non-Terminal, Repeating Phantasm, or a Class 5 Full-Roaming Vapour … a real nasty one too!' In 2016, there's no time for Autistic texture: 'That's a class-four apparition.'[22]

Feig's film also, in positioning Jones' Patty Tolan as the 'oh hell no!' everywoman ('You guys are really smart about this science stuff, but I know New York and I can borrow a car from my uncle'), missed the opportunity to make things right for Black Ghostbusters after the original films' treatment of Winston Zeddemore and, by extension, Ernie Hudson, for whom the role could have been a star-making vehicle. In the earliest drafts of Aykroyd's script, Winston was a

Ghostbuster from the get-go, a former US Air Force major and demo-litions expert. 'The night before filming begins, however, I get this new script and it was shocking,' Hudson told *Entertainment Weekly* in 2014. 'Instead of coming in at the very beginning of the movie, like page 8, the character came in on page 68 after the Ghostbusters were established. His elaborate background was all gone, replaced by me walking in and saying, "If there's a steady paycheck in it, I'll believe anything you say." So that was pretty devastating.'

That the 2016 film's makers saw an opportunity to right the per-ceived wrongs of the original film's gender politics, but *not* to address the devastation experienced by one of its most beloved stars by not repeating the racist mistakes of the past, gives pause. Couldn't Patty Tolan have been a wisecracking doctor of parapsychology? It also makes you wonder if anyone involved in the writing of the 2016 *Ghostbusters* has been involved in higher degree research, a realm where I have met a far greater number of ebullient personalities like Patty than I have people who seem terminally embarrassed by their own research, like Wiig and McCarthy's Erin and Abby.

But truly loving the original films means, as an adult, recognising director Ivan Reitman's determined celebration of Reagan-era con-servatism. The villain of the film isn't so much Gozer or Zuul as it is Walter Peck of the Environmental Protection Agency and his attempts to bring down our small business-owner heroes (and lest we forget how the private sector will 'expect results', unlike the cushy, well-funded world of our university research), but the behind-the-scenes demotion of Winston from high-ranking demolitions expert to Some Guy Off The Streets is the starkest example of the film's positionality.

What can you do? Enjoying *Starship Troopers* doesn't make me a totalitarian fascist (at least I don't think it does; is there an online screener I can take to find out??), and neither does a lifelong love of *Ghostbusters* necessarily make me a centre-right free market capitalist who thinks women 'ruined' the franchise. The facts are simple: without

Ghostbusters, a comedy masterpiece written by an Autistic man, I would not have felt like the universe had given me, an Autistic kid, permission to be as weird as I wanted to be.

In 2012, I attended New York Comic Con dressed as Gozer, a fitting costume choice for a convention in the Big Apple. When in Rome and all that. Having spent my recent recuperation from wisdom teeth extraction examining high-res photographs of the original costumes from *Ghostbusters*, I had constructed a pretty good replica of Gozer's ectoplasmic glamour: a shimmer spandex bodysuit covered in ripped lace, fibre art and iridescent pustules (it's amazing what you can do with some glitter glue and a bunch of chocolate moulds), complete with the 'aim for the flat-top' wig constructed by my go-to wizardess on Hollywood Boulevard, the recently retired Ellen of Hollywood Wigs. After a day wandering around the Javits Center posing with various Ghostbusters and even a few other Gozers, I decided to head back to my hotel; those interdimensional ancient Sumerian heels weren't made for the convention floor, and I was ready to put my feet up on the radiator.

A combination of rush hour traffic and subway works had other plans, however, so I found myself walking through the Garment District to get to a connecting train in Midtown. Despite what my habit of dressing up as fictional characters might suggest, I'm often a little shy about wearing my costumes 'in public', which is to say, beyond the boundaries of the convention's safe space. I was in a hurry that evening, acutely aware of my flat-top bobbing up and down and flakes of glitter sloughing off my Gozerian bodysuit, and concerned that somebody might *really* show this prehistoric bitch how they do things downtown. I needn't have worried: as I wove in and out of traffic, a symphony of car horn honks, claps and cheers started to follow me as

Manhattanites clocked the presence of The Traveler among them; one cab driver leaned out his window and yelled 'Hey, Gozer!'

The lights changed, and as I skipped up onto the sidewalk out of the path of oncoming traffic, I turned my face skyward and yelled the one thing I had been waiting my whole life to say, the true meaning of *Ghostbusters*' love-letter to New York City, the law that Dr Winston Zeddemore taught me as a kid: 'I love this town!'

HAPPY MEALS

Quick! Think of an example of an Autistic character you've seen in a movie or TV, or read about in a novel. Now think about how food was depicted in that media. You're now thinking of chicken nuggets, aren't you?

In 1991 I discovered McCain's Looney Tunes Frozen Meals, a range of nominally healthy microwave TV dinners targeted squarely at kids. When I found an ad for those bloody TV dinners in one of my *Betty and Veronica* comics, the emotions I experienced were akin to what I imagine a committed gourmand feels when they hear that Heston Blumenthal is hosting a pop-up restaurant nearby. Somehow, despite the fact that we did not own a microwave and would have to resort to the dreaded 'Conventional Oven' heating instructions, I talked Mum and Dad into a trip to Coles New World to pick up a Bugs Bunny Chicken Nuggets box. (I'm not sure why Bugs was assigned to flog the nuggets and not Foghorn Leghorn, though I suppose getting Foghorn to shill the reconstituted body parts of his brethren was probably a bit dark, even by Looney Tunes standards.)

The 20–25 minutes required to bring Bugs Bunny Chicken Nuggets to serving temperature were possibly the longest of my life to date. I remember that TV dinner like it was yesterday: the distinct flavour of the cuboid bread crumbs, the rubbery, watery crinkle-cut carrots daubed in 'butter sauce' (don't ask), the Deb-like mashed potato swirled into fanciful clouds by machines of loving grace. Apparently the market for cartoon-themed microwave TV dinners was not booming in the era of cool teen dramas and Hypercolor T-shirts, however; I only managed to finagle another two or three Bugs meals before they disappeared from the freezer cabinet forever. True to my parents' heartfelt and accommodating form, they kept the white plastic tray and would gamely reconstruct the Bugs meal from actual food (as opposed to 'food products'): nuggets made from chicken breast, carrots 'crinkle cut' with a fluted scone cutter, mashed potato squeezed out of a cake icing tube.

I think now about how much time and effort it would have taken Mum and Dad to approximate, with laser focus, the presentation of these TV dinners; I'm sure they would have preferred to just shove some schnitzels on plates and collapse onto the couch in front of *Brides of Christ*. Those fake Looney Tunes Frozen Meals were an act of love, just one of many small gestures that made home the safest place to be as a 'weird' kid.

Issues with eating, with almost everything about it – food habits, food sensitivities, eating disorders, food obsessions, swallowing problems – are a hallmark of Autism, in the discourse as much as the clinical literature. But if we boil this down to its essence, we end up with assertions like 'Autistic people are weird about food' or 'Autistic people want to eat the same thing all the time'. Well … they're not wrong.

The focus, discursively, is often on *what* Autistic people are eating, with less attention paid to *how* they eat it, or indeed *why*. The latter may include any number of feeding issues, either individually or in combination, as this unbroken single sentence from an *Autism Parenting Magazine* article indicates: 'tongue thrust, rumination, texture obsession or aversion, dry membranes, mouth breathing, eating with an open mouth, speed of eating, large bolus (too big a bite), minimal mastication (chewing), rapid oral and pharyngeal transit, pocketing (food accumulating in cheeks), forced hard swallow vs. a spontaneous soft swallow, using large gulps of liquid to initiate a swallow, choking/coughing, nasal regurgitation, and no sense of fullness'. Phew! When we consider that many Autistic people are dealing with at least one if not more (or all) of these issues – and may also suffer from gastroenterological problems, which has become a chicken-or-egg-esque source of much Autism-adjacent research into gut microbiome – then the desire for predictability and textural sameness in food is surely understandable.

Take the 2020 tale of little Tyler Page of Brisbane, whose mum took to Facebook, distraught, when she couldn't find her Autistic son's favourite mini dagwood dogs at her local supermarkets: they were the only thing he liked to eat, and it appeared that they had vanished from the shelves. Word eventually reached Keith's Foods, who made the dagwood dogs in question, and a representative drove an hour and a half to Brisbane to deliver a box of Tyler's faves, and promised to continue to supply the family for as long as Tyler wanted to eat them. Good marketing, sure, but I would rather read 'company supplies Autistic kid with a lifetime supply of [xyz]' than the comments from Concerned Readers on a piece titled 'I Was Very Publicly Food-Shamed For Feeding my Son Chicken Nuggets' (I read them so you won't have to).

Of all Autistic behaviours, food habits seem to be one of the most troubling to the casual, non-Autistic onlooker. Browse any content aimed at families of Autistic kids and inevitably there'll be a question posed by Concerned Mom of Duluth, MN. 'Help!' the letter will read. 'My son with high-functioning autism only eats chicken nuggets and crinkle-cut chips and refuses to try variegated kale!' This obsession with eating a wide range of foods seems to be twofold: there is the perfectly reasonable attempt to comply with government nutritional guidelines, but there is also a particularly Eurocentric notion of broad grazing, of 'trying something new!', of a complete diet being a very literal understanding of the notion of completeness. Complete just means a reasonable balance of protein, carbohydrate and fats with vitamins, minerals and fibre, not trying every food on earth. There are plenty of countries in which a comparatively 'limited' variety of food (comparative to, say, the entire innards of WholeFoods) is eaten and children thrive.

It's natural to worry about your child's eating habits, which is perhaps why 'I'm worried about my Autistic kid's love of chicken nuggets' is the gateway through which far more sinister snake oil salesmanship enters the picture: obscure diets (Casein free! Keto! Gluten-free raw nutrient-dense no sugar!) and bunkum like 'leaky gut syndrome', brought to us by the disgraced former doctor and anti-vaccination figure Andrew Wakefield, whose 1998 paper about the alleged connections between the MMR vaccine and Autism (in short: there are none) was retracted by *The Lancet* in 2010. The tendrils of 'wellness' are starting to infect the 'Autism Warrior Parent' blogosphere, where influencer parents in expensive organic knitwear swear by certain recipes, diets and supplements as cornerstones of their Autistic children's comprehensive care plans.

To be clear, there's nothing wrong with feeding your children a healthy diet, but there's also nothing wrong with an Autistic child who finds comfort and familiarity in certain foods. There is a wonderful nutritionist, Jenny Friedmann, who uses 'food chains' – moving from point A (for example, pea crisps) to point B (say, raw carrots) using stepping stones of similar, but gradually changing, textures and colours – to help introduce Autistic kids and other picky eaters to new shapes, textures and flavours.

The secret is in understanding *why* Autistic kids eat the way they do, and having empathy for their experience of the world. If they want to spend six months drawing pictures with their organic pasta sauce before they try tasting it, who cares? Take it from me: my parents made wonderful food from magnificent ingredients, and I certainly ate it, but you'll never convince me there's anything better than a Macca's cheeseburger. It has long been a running joke in our family that despite growing up with plenty of beautiful, homemade, organic meals around me, I will always crave processed food.

Junk, processed, fake, space, plane; whatever you choose to call it – any food that has the textural qualities of medium-density fibreboard after a heavy rain shower, a healthy dose of sodium, and preferably some sort of marketing boast about having used the same recipe since before the industrial revolution. The sorts of things that sometimes can't even be officially referred to as food, but rather 'food products'. White bread, American cheese, chicken nuggets, battered flake, Cup-A-Soup, TV dinners, potato cakes marinated in the cheapest white vinegar, supermarket sandwiches, microwave hamburgers, convenience store sausage rolls; these foods sing to me of deep comfort and perhaps a slight dehydration headache (a price I am always willing to pay for admission to the kingdom of food heaven).

There have even been food products that I've only dreamed of; things that exist only in the annals of history, or that the Australian food standards dictate might be better used to seal fissures in space shuttle cladding. When I finally tried the legendary Disneyland pineapple soft serve, Dole-Whip, in January 2020, I was disappointed to discover that it tasted like *actual* fresh pineapple rather than the Pineapple™ I had long assumed it would. I went back to my friend's house and drowned my sorrows in Cool Whip, eaten straight from the freezer (it's the 22 per cent hydrogenated coconut and palm kernel oil, sodium caseinate and polysorbate 60 that is the hero of the dish). There is nothing quite like a dinner of 'round food' (chicken pops, 'Pommes', frozen peas), or maybe a lunch of 'beige and yellow' (grilled

American cheese on white bread, served with sauerkraut) to restore balance to the universe and calm to my soul. The things about plane food that make most people's skin crawl are the reasons I spent my teen years poring over the photographs in books about in-flight dining, dreaming of the days when I could pull the foil from my own tray of nuked chicken or beef.

My delight at all things overprocessed and low-nutrient was stoked by the tuckshop at St Joseph's. The strangely dark, cavernous area just near the dunnies (ahh, those innocent pre-WorkSafe days ...) was famous for its snack selection. French Fries chips, Clinkers, Mates, Sherbet Bombs: if it had numbers in its ingredients list, you could probably buy it at the tuckshop for thirty cents. I presume there was actual food available, too, but that was of no interest to me or my peers, particularly in hot weather. The students of St Joseph's were split into two camps: you were either a Sunnyboy fanatic, or a Zooper Dooper acolyte. For me, the choice was simple: Sunnyboys until I die. The solid wedges of tasty ice were superior in every way, in part because unlike Zooper Doopers, whose plastic edges ripped at the corners of your mouth, Sunnyboys' cardboard containers were mouth-friendly, but also because it usually took an entire play-lunch to consume one. As for the best flavour, there was only Glug.

Like Tyler and his mum, I am acutely aware of the devastation of one's favourite food products being cancelled: it's a pain that has followed me my entire life. As the nation's notions of what constitutes good eating (in both a literal and a moral sense) have matured, so too do the surviving 'empty calories' of the eighties and nineties go first to the Reject Shop, and then to snack heaven. I was hysterical when I read, in 2016, that Sunnyboys had been discontinued. The Daily Juice Co announced the news in typically bleak capitalist terms: 'Unfortunately, Sunnyboy has experienced a sustained reduction in consumer demand over a long period of time, making it necessary to delete the product from our range of water ice treats.'

In an era of protein ice-cream, 100 per cent fruit soft serve and green juice icy-poles, perhaps it shouldn't be surprising that the humble 'ambient ice water' wedge had been sent to the big tuckshop in the sky. Who needs a solid block of ice, its syrup gradually pooling in the corner of a tetrahedral sheath of foil-lined paper, when you can have a quenelle of cacao and goji berry semifreddo? As the *MasterChef*-isation of Australian eating habits has continued apace, so, too, has the twilight of uniquely Australian snacks descended. Arnott's Shapes became 'new and improved'; beloved Big M flavours have disappeared; ice-creams have shrunk; Red Rooster has been handballed from owner to owner. Sunnyboys are just the latest victim of our national palate's maturation. Did I contribute to this 'sustained reduction in customer demand' by allowing myself to be dazzled by fancier ice treats? Should I not have been in such a rush to grow up? If I could only seize the means of ambient ice water production, I could live out my days in a bubble of suspended nostalgia, a 3KZ sticker on every car, a Bicentennial Memento for every child, and a Sunnyboy in every hand. Alas, as the legendary Australian band who took their name from the tetrahedral treat once put it, 'Close the doors to the past forever'.

At home, my parents had a repertoire of recipes that were set in stone – schnitzels, homemade hamburgers, meatballs, roast chicken, Madhur Jaffrey's herb pilaf – and so these family classics became their own source of predictable joy. Sleepovers with other families were fraught affairs, and I would often encounter nightmare menu items (Fish! Eggs! Fish with eggs!) that would leave me desperate to return home to the safe confines of a homemade schnitzel breaded with Corn Flakes Crumbs.

My diet *looked* normal enough, but scratch the surface and there were plenty of rules: chicken was to be white meat only; minced beef was always welcome in almost any context; no sauces; no intermingling of vegetables; gravy ONLY on meat and potatoes, never on peas (only mint sauce on peas); toast was only white bread (*occasionally* a 'football' rye, for special occasions) and was barely toasted, covered with butter. We called the latter 'talking toast', inspired by Kenneth Grahame's *The Wind in the Willows*, and an Autistic neologism if ever I saw one. Grahame's book did not actually feature any toast that could literally talk, but rather, 'The smell of that buttered toast simply spoke to Toad, and with no uncertain voice; talked of warm kitchens, of breakfasts on bright frosty mornings, of cozy parlour firesides on winter evenings, when one's ramble was over and slippered feet were propped on the fender; of the purring of contented cats, and the twitter of sleepy canaries.'

Common to my youth was also the sudden and summary rejection of certain foods from my diet. After (apparently) eating a small country's GDP worth of grated zucchini for the first few years of my life, in around 1987 zucchini suddenly became enemy number one and didn't return until 2016. Pasta – any type – went on a watch list in 1991 and remained in exile until the new century. Pea and ham soup was my ultimate culinary nemesis, but that was only because I had vomited shortly after a traditional 'eat it or I'll take it out to the children starving in the street!' dinner time in 1989, thus cementing in my mind a deathly allergy to pea and ham soup. Henceforth, any school excursion or camp parental permission forms featured 'PEA AND HAM SOUP' in the space allotted for 'allergies'.

As for the *way* I ate (and still do), there was no hiding my alien qualities. I would scrape any food from my spoon or fork with my teeth, like some sort of reptilian; the sensation of literally any food, sauce, oil or crumbs touching my lips was what I imagine some people feel when they hear nails down a chalkboard (a noise I can, of course, listen to endlessly). Actually, dryness is a recurring theme; just ask anyone I've ever lived with, who's likely stumbled upon me rolling up dill pickles in paper towel and wringing them free of their brine. Poor Mum now laughs when she makes a beautiful pasta sauce and I gamely eat the 'bits', declaring it 'delicious', and leave the sugo – the prize – in a sad puddle at the bottom of the plate. (Mopping up sauce with bread? Another nightmare.)

When I worked at Il Carretto pizza restaurant as a twenty-year-old, my sauce aversion became a running joke. Billy, the French–Egyptian chef with a booming laugh, eventually became so familiar with my chosen meal order that I couldn't get a word in edgeways: 'Yes, yes,' he'd hoot as he got to work at the mere sight of me rounding the kitchen doorway, 'rigatoni bolognese, with extra capsicum and olives, "not too saucy"!' Once, staying with a friend at a fancy lakeside resort (the type of place where all the desserts were served 'encapsulated' in 'spheres'), just as my order of 'well done' scrambled eggs was delivered, the owner chased the waiter to our table, about to upbraid him for serving such 'revolting' overcooked eggs in such elevated surrounds. I had to explain, sheepishly, that I had specifically requested they be well and truly nuked.

It's easy to laugh about 'not too saucy', or the *Rain Man*-esque quality of needing to use 'the' fork for dinner; there are more abject behaviours that are a feature of my eating habits, the things I have taken great care to keep low-key when in polite company. Let's start with pocketing – chewing food then holding it in your mouth; ye olde 'chipmunk cheeks'. To this day I cannot resist the urge to do this with anything cracker-like: Saladas, Premiums, Saltines, Pizza Shapes. There is something so intoxicating about the shift from cracker to salty sludge that I want to extend the sensation for as long as possible.

The problem is that the longer I hoard a glob of food in my mouth, the easier it is to forget what to do with it, or at least so says my poor brain; the 'executive stage' of my oral phase is more like the lowly casual employee stage. Everything slows to a crawl, like a computer with a processor on the fritz, and suddenly it's as though the next step – swallowing – has been deleted from the code. When I'm stressed or anxious, I will choke on pretty much anything thicker than water (and even drinking is sometimes fraught). It's also hard for me to detect what is an appropriate mouthful, particularly of the aforementioned crackers (three Premiums in one go? Sign me up!), which also results in trying to force too much food down my throat, known as 'cramming'. You know in cartoons, how a character will eat an entire fish and then develop a fish-shaped lump in their throat? If I were Bugs Bunny I would constantly have a protrusion in my neck the shape of a loaf of plain white bread.

Then there's my other love, the other extreme: slimy. Chia pudding, cooked okra, tapioca pudding, slippery vegan jellies, aloe vera chunks, gooey nopales, a smear of frozen yoghurt from the serve-yourself buffet to justify an entire cup of 'popping boba' from the toppings, half-set Aeroplane Jelly eaten greedily from the bowl with the fridge door open, awful overprocessed yoghurts with horrible fruit sludge 'toppers': fantastic. The texture should be like something you'd see in a petri dish; I need to be able to pick up a spoonful and let it gloop back down into the bowl while saying 'Are you enjoying your kep-mok blood ticks, Doctor Lazarus?'

Dry and slimy: the two food genders.

That's just the food itself; now let's talk about the crockery and cutlery! There's a certain teaspoon for gold kiwi fruit ('original' kiwis are banned), and a certain teaspoon for yoghurt. Chia pudding must only be eaten with the dessert spoon with the black plastic handle. The white plastic-handled fork is the only fork, unless steak is on the menu, then I switch to the 1960s fork that looks like a little tree trunk. Butter should only be spread using my late grandmother's rapidly disintegrating spatula knife. Coffee goes in the Penny's Diner mug, tea in the mug with a 'C' on it (tea in actual tea cups makes me deeply anxious; they can't hold enough liquid!), Cup-A-Soup can only go in the vintage Cup-A-Soup mug (der). The dessert spoon that was once used to scoop out Puss' Savings Brand pilchards is cursed forever and cannot be used for human food consumption; ditto The Vomit Bowl, the sturdy white china basin occasionally used in moments of family gastroenterological emergency, which must never be used to, say, serve salad at large gatherings (reader, alas …). Ice-cream can only be removed from the container with a soup spoon, but must be eaten with a dessert spoon.

It seems pedantic to see it written down, because it *is* pedantic, but these rules and routines give me great comfort; they are proof of 'function'.

Like so much clinical literature and popular discourse surrounding Autism, eating is almost always discussed in the context of Autistic children, rather than adults. This could give the impression that 'eating habits' are something that Autistic people simply grow out of. And, to some extent, many of us do manage to improve our relationship with food as we get older. I have plenty of eating habits that don't wash with my love of the over-salted; my 'a punnet of blueberries a day' habit is both expensive and inconvenient in the context of this chapter. Although my palate has expanded somewhat, I still have fairly rigid routines around eating – including obsessions and trends, like the three months of vegan chilli, or a fortnight of 'whole bowls' – and have come to appreciate the beauty of a meal plan.

Reading the results of 'Eating As An Autistic Adult: An Exploratory Qualitative Study',[23] published in *PLoS One* in 2019, is a little like reading my own diary (if I were capable of keeping one). The respondents, twelve Autistic adults, all reported that Autism had some sort of impact on their eating, even if it wasn't as noticeable as it might have been in their youth.

Participant 5: 'I don't like the smell sometimes that forks and knives have on them […] And in fact sometimes mugs out of the dishwasher have that smell in them as well.'

I know that smell, and have been driven to distraction yelling 'Can't anyone else *smell* that??' in the kitchen. I often describe it as bloody, or like bones (neither of which I can admit to having smelled directly, but I *imagine* they smell like That Smell).

It's also true that as I've grown I have come to appreciate the broader possibilities of food; I love to read cookbooks, and watch culinary TV shows, even if I don't generally have the wherewithal to make the recipes myself. Whenever I try something new, I feel a flush of pride – there, I did it! – as if I have clocked another day without being detected as a visiting alien. When I finally, at the age of thirty-two, tried sashimi with a friend, I could hear the Throne Room march from *Star Wars* playing in my ears: look! I'm eating grown-up food! But in times of stress, the food I cook becomes less exciting (at least by others' standards): spag bol, stews, mashed potato. 'CWA cookbook' food in tones of beige and brown.

And then, there is the Happy Meal.

Some people get the molecular structure of caffeine or serotonin tattooed on their body. My version would be 1C+1P+RO+1K+1Mu, which is not a molecule nor a mathematical equation, but rather a code, a prayer, an incantation: begin with regular bun crown, then add one cheese, one pickle (or two smaller ones), 3.5 grams of reconstituted ('recon' or 'rehyd') onions, one shot of ketchup, one of mustard; add one 10:1 meat patty, close with regular bun heel, wrap in yellow paper. And this, my friends, is exactly why you will never eat finer cuisine than a McDonald's cheeseburger. When I sit down to eat a Cheeseburger Happy Meal, I know exactly what I am about to experience, and 99 per cent of the time (provided that Jaden on assembly hasn't honked the mustard gun too hard) that's exactly what I get. That combination of the expectation *and* the confirmation of predictability is extremely soothing.

In 2011, researchers at University of California San Diego's psychology department conducted an experimental study: do spoilers, well, spoil the enjoyment of a story? Nicholas Christenfeld, professor of social psychology, and Jonathan Leavitt, then a doctoral student in experimental psychology, found evidence to the contrary: knowing the ending in advance, even in ironic-twist tales, overwhelmingly enhanced the reader's enjoyment of the story. 'It could be,' said Leavitt at the time, 'that once you know how it turns out, it's cognitively easier – you're more comfortable processing the information.'

Predictability is, culturally speaking, a scourge. Critics complain about movie plots that unfold like clockwork; we roll our eyes when the next line in a politician's 'heartfelt' speech is exactly what we think it's going to be; paperbacks with played-out narratives are sniffed about as *formula fiction*. The dramatist Martin Esslin was unequivocal: 'Predictability is the death of suspense and therefore of drama.' So it follows that the Autistic person's desire for predictability in life is considered restrictive, and where that predictability intersects with food, things get really charged, as though there's something especially weird and unsettling about wanting (nay, needing) to eat the same things all the time, particularly at a time when *MasterChef* is ratings gold and there's a mandoline and a spiraliser in every household. Food has become entwined with virtue and with aspiration. To eat the same thing every day is to, apparently, be suffering from a profound lack: of joy, of interest, of nutrition; a failure to thrive in every sense of the term.

Autistic people may prefer to eat the same things day in day out for any number of reasons: it might be sensory related (only crunchy foods, say, or a preference for nothing with bright colours), or it might be a routine that provides a comforting sense of sameness. My own love of processed foods is a combination of both: it's knowing exactly what I'm going to get, and then getting it. In a world where things often change at the last minute, or turn out differently to my expectations, I can always seek solace in processed food. There is no tension, no stress, no 'what if this is awful??': I already know how the story turns out.

People who complain that, for example, Macca's burgers are always exactly the same are missing the point. That's precisely what makes them a dream to eat: *they're always exactly the same*. They have always been exactly the same, ever since the sainted day in 1987 when we rolled up to the St Kilda drive-thru for a Spaceship Meal. I had seen the ads on TV, and despite my intense fear of anything alien-related, I could not deny the appeal of a cheeseburger that arrived inside a UFO. (And not just one UFO but 'A DIFFERENT SPACESHIP EACH WEEK'! My parents, with the steadfastness of hunger strikers, somehow managed to instigate a one spaceship per household rule.)

There's a beautiful essay by Jeremy Michael Wilson, 'My Autistic Son is Having Chicken Nuggets for Thanksgiving – and That's OK'[24], in which Wilson demonstrates such empathy for the Autistic experience that I think it should be assigned as a key text for any parent of a recently-diagnosed Autistic child. '[I'm] not going to force him to go along with something that causes him horrendous discomfort and anxiety just to go along with "tradition". That's not what I want him to associate with this time of year,' Wilson writes. 'So bring on the nuggets. Bring on the Jell-O. Let him focus on the aspects of the holidays he truly loves, like Rudolph and Frosty and carols sung with butchered lyrics but unmatched heart.' Could it all be so simple? Could it be that there is a world, somewhere out there, where Autistic behaviours aren't a problem to be solved?

Every Autistic person has their 'nuggets and Jell-O', even if those beloved foods aren't, in fact, 'junk' foods. True to its name, the Happy Meal became a culinary comfort blanket, purchased when moving house, when Dad was in hospital, when being driven home in tears after therapy. Every time, the eternally reliable textures and flavours of the cheeseburger provided an anchor in the storm. When stress becomes unbearable, I run into the open arms of space food; it is the alpha and the omega. A chicken nugget is always going to taste the same. I can always go home again.

THE FALL OF THE
APPLE WORM BANK

When I look back over my life, I don't really think of St Joseph's as 'school' in any real or abstract sense. This is possibly a testament to the quality of education received there, but it's more likely because, having only attended from Prep to Grade 3, it was something of a dry run for the real thing. My time there was the last time I remember feeling like I wasn't all that different from the kids around me. Whatever our various neurotypes, cultural or linguistic diversities, we were all in the same boat at St Joseph's (and occasionally, at the library, literally in the same boat). Until, that was, we weren't.

It was December 1989, and this year, our teacher had organised for the class to engage in Kris Kringle: each student was given a fellow student's name and instructed to buy them a Christmas present. Being seven-year-olds who lived in a suburb where the opening of a new supermarket was cause for a school excursion, naturally the thrill of the possibility of even one extra Christmas present was intoxicating. None of us were especially good at keeping secrets, so we all quickly worked out who had who, and busied ourselves dreaming about what we might get on the final day of term. I got one of the Andrews and Ralph got me, which was appropriate given we were best friends.

On a sunny afternoon, at the end of the school year, we gathered around in a circle on the classroom floor, sitting with our legs crossed on the itchy sisal carpet, the discomfort a small price to pay for the impending thrill of Kris Kringle. One by one, gifts were given and enthusiastically unwrapped: top-shelf Scrooges offerings, toys from the outer aisles of Coles New World, bulk lollies from the Lagoon factory. After a few presents had been passed around, I realised that Ralph was absent. Oh well, I thought, maybe he's sick; maybe he dropped off his Kris Kringle early. But as time passed, it became clear that there was no present for me under our classroom's malnourished plastic Christmas tree. Eventually, all the gifts had been handed over, the wrapping paper had been gathered up, and the bell rang to alert us all that it was lunchtime. Our teacher took me over to her desk, pulled open the drawer and retrieved a small wooden jumping jack toy: a concession for not having received a Kris Kringle present. I hated its ugly face on sight.

The rest of the class had already whooshed outside to lunch with their Kris Kringle bounty when a breathless Ralph appeared at the door. He was clutching the best thing I had ever seen: a wind-up money box shaped like a giant red apple. The box art explained that placing a twenty-cent coin on the little red button on the Apple Worm Bank (catchy name) would summon a hungry worm, who would appear and 'eat' your generous offering. Ralph explained that his family hadn't been able to afford to buy the money box until that morning (hence the lack of wrapping paper), but added with pride that he'd been planning to get it for me the whole month because 'I knew Clemmy would love it'. I was thrilled – are you kidding? As far as I was aware, nobody in Port Melbourne had a money box, let alone a clockwork one! I think, in a rare display of affection, I may have even hugged him. But our reverie was shattered when our teacher snatched the money box out of my hands.

Ralph and I looked at each other and then at her, shaking with nervous laughter, unable to parse what had just happened: she's taken ... my Kris Kringle present away? With barely veiled contempt, she told Ralph he was too late for Kris Kringle, then turned to me and insisted that I couldn't accept the gift. I felt what I would come to understand as the putrid nausea of injustice: a hard lump in my throat, my skin prickling as though someone was sticking me with dress pins, hot tears stinging around my eyes. It was a crash course in class power dynamics. I longed to say something – scream, cry, rail at the teacher – but what hope does an Autistic seven-year-old have in standing up to her pearl-wearing teacher, a representative of a school that still regularly beats naughty children with 'the strap', on behalf of her second-generation friend who lives in the housing commission flats? Our teacher probably had enough money to buy ten Apple Worm Banks, and now she was taking mine too. She pointed again to the awful wooden jumping jack I had by that point discarded on a nearby desk: that was to be my Kris Kringle gift, and Ralph would have to go away and think about what he'd done.

There's no neat ending to this story. I don't know if I cried the whole way home, or if my parents marched into the school and yelled at our teacher, or even what happened immediately after that moment, because Kris Kringle 1989 was such a neutron bomb of trauma that my memory only picks up again about two weeks later, on Christmas Eve. But I never got that Apple Worm Bank, and within a year I was moved to a different primary school and never saw Ralph again.

In that moment, the illusion of school as a safe space was shattered. Within a few years, whatever pieces of that illusion that remained were scattered to the wind as school, as it does in the psyches of so many Autistic people, slowly assumed its position as hell.

It is a rare Autistic person who manages to make it through their schooling with any affection for the experience. School presents a variety of challenges for the Autistic child, from changes to routine (including the literal change of routine that happens at the end of each year in the transition between grades) to sensory issues (fluorescent lighting, weird smells, uniform textures, unpredictable temperatures), to issues socialising with peers (different senses of humour, different social 'codes' in the classroom and the playground).

Following the event we will now refer to as The Apple Worm Bank Disaster, Mum and Dad had put plans afoot to get me out of St Joseph's. Middle Park Primary, the state school a few suburbs over, seemed like a better fit; it had an art program and put on school musicals, both things that would surely appeal to my emerging creative sensibilities. I had a year to prepare myself for the reality that, at the end of Grade 3, I wouldn't just be changing grades, but changing schools. I drifted apart from my pals, perhaps aware that soon Pickles Street would form an invisible barrier between us; even though I still lived in Port Melbourne, I'd soon be a Middle Park kid. At lunchtimes, I would gaze up at the upstairs classrooms, with the bittersweet knowledge that I would never unlock the mysteries they held.

Moving schools in Grade 4 was the first time I had experienced significant change, and the effect was profound. As soon as I thought I had conquered some aspect of my day-to-day existence – not just surviving but thriving! – some miniscule change of routine would send me plunging back into confusion. Case in point: I had no idea that my new school's 'recess' was the same thing as my old school's 'play lunch'.

The turmoil of this time wasn't limited to my own playground. The 1989 Christmas ad for Coles New World closes as a working-class family tears open their gifts – one each – and a soothing female voice tells us, as seasonal orchestral music swells, 'There's never been a better time to fight inflation. There's never been a Christmas like this!' There certainly hadn't been: purchasing power (about the only 'power' poor people have) plunged by 7.43 per cent in 1989, meaning that buying the same item would cost 7.43 per cent more than it did during the Celebration of a Nation the year before. Standard variable home loan interest rates had hit an all-time record of 17 per cent per annum in June 1989, a high that continued until April 1990. September quarter accounts indicated a contraction of 1.6 per cent, and in November 1990, Paul Keating addressed the National Press Club: 'The first thing to say is, the accounts do show that Australia is in a recession. The most important thing about that is that this is a recession that Australia had to have.'

Being poor is different to Living In Poverty, I guess, depending on the latest calculations made by pen-pushers who went to university for free and probably thought the diamond-studded gold money clip from Germani Jewellers on *Sale of the Century* was hopelessly déclassé. Then again, maybe it isn't different; maybe poverty is the concept, and poor is the material reality.

Defining 'poverty' in the luckiest country is an exercise in such eye-watering economic semantics that it is, if you've lived it, difficult to read. The 'dollar a day' poverty line introduced in 1990 measured poverty by the standards of the world's poorest countries. The issue is, what do we mean when we talk about 'poverty'? Extreme? Abject? Relative? Relative to what, or whom? And are we talking about a deprivation model of poverty, or one of social exclusion? Here's what I know: even though as an eight-year-old I was capable of recognising Keating's words as a general bad omen for the country, I didn't have any reason to think we might be *poor* until I switched schools in 1991.

On 20 November 1992, my second year at Middle Park, the Kennett government announced that it would close fifty-six state schools, cut 4000 teaching positions, and sack 3760 school cleaners and 830 administrative staff.

Those 'reforms' were, and continue to be, presented as some sort of humanitarian measure: these were schools with shoddy buildings (except when they weren't shoddy) and poor enrolment numbers (except where enrolment numbers, such as at Northland Secondary College, were actually very good), and doing away with them would clear the path for new schools. But the true villainy of the school closures was that so many were wiped from the map in order to make way for private land sales to developers. It was against this backdrop of economic rationalism that St Joseph's pocket of land must suddenly have looked very valuable to the church, and so the fate of the small school was sealed. Catholic schools in the area were rationalised, and 1993 was St Joseph's final year. (The site would sit vacant for decades, the school facilities still perfectly usable, until it was razed to make way for lifestyle apartments.)

On the surface of things, the impending closure of St Joseph's didn't really affect me; I had made the jump to Middle Park and was wise enough to the way of the world to know that, despite the statewide fear of further school closures, Kennett would never swing the axe at a school where so many parents owned swimming pools. Intellectually, even, I knew St Joseph's wasn't a particularly good school, but despite all this, it was *my* not particularly good school. (Well, it had been, but if there's one thing I can tell you about my Autism it's that, for better or worse, I am *extremely* loyal.) For one thing, it had a tuckshop; Middle Park only did 'lunch orders'. But it occupied an increasingly large place in my mind as a school where I had not been 'different'. Middle Park, perhaps due to its enviable programs of enrichment having attracted the attention of local well- (or at least weller-than-Port Melbourne) to-do parents, was not like this.

Middle Park was a state school, officially speaking, but the simple fact of its being located closer to the stately terrace houses of Albert Park meant it might as well have been an entire universe away from Port Melbourne. This was a school where students' parents were often divorced (two houses!), or if they weren't, probably owned a swimming pool. It was the type of school where 'I hear you buy your tampons at BI-LO' was the going insult tossed by popular girls with glossy ponytails. And it was, devastatingly, a school without a uniform. Before January 1991 I didn't have a clue what Nikes were, but boy did I learn in a hurry.

St Joseph's uniform had been typical of an underfunded school in the 1980s: generic navy-blue polyester separates, a raglan T-shirt for summer and a goldenrod skivvy for winter. If there had been any rich kids at St Joseph's, you wouldn't have been able to pick them out by looking at them (you would've had to look inside their lunchbox, probably). St Joseph's was a school where birthday parties involved bowls of Twisties and sitting on balloons in the front room of a housing commission unit; Middle Park birthday parties rented out The Fun Factory for rollerskating parties with ice-cream cakes.

The school did have an official windcheater, but that's where the similarities ended, and I very quickly realised that for all my crammed-in viewings of *Troop Beverly Hills*, courtesy of Video Flash, I had been hopelessly out of the fashion loop my entire life. I was doomed from the outset of my schooling career at Middle Park. Imagine, if you will, the utter tragedy of a nine-year-old in an extra-large *The King and I* T-shirt, maroon cotton stirrup pants, pushed down socks and Jelly sandals striding towards her certain social death in a quadrangle full of children who probably learned to pronounce the words 'L.A. Gear' and 'Billabong surf wear' shortly after birth.

It was only upon shifting to Middle Park that I suddenly realised I was unlike most of the other students. In the winter of 1991, I started repeating everything I had just said, under my breath. Sometimes I said it *before* I spoke, too, instead of repeating it. If the whisper happened first, it was like a dress rehearsal for something I was about to say; if it came after, it was like a post-match review.

Palilalia, the involuntary repetition of syllables, words or phrases, is different from other aphasias because it is typically 'contextually correct'; it is typically expressed in spontaneous speech. Anecdotal evidence – that is, hordes of Autistic people exclaiming 'I do that, too!' in online groups and message boards – suggests that it's relatively common in Autistic people, though it seems to be more commonly associated with neurodegenerative disorders such as Parkinson's. Where the study of palilalia does intersect with Autism, it has been suggested that it can function as self-stimulatory, or as a form of vocal stim. One such study, of course, decried this stereotypy as occurring 'in place of appropriate, more functional verbal behavior', apparently unable to consider the possibility that so-called appropriate verbal behaviour might actually *include* stereotypy.

You can probably imagine how exhausting this was; not so much in the *doing* of it but, like so many Autistic experiences, in the simultaneous suspicion that what you are doing is so completely alien to those around you that you'd be better off dropping to the floor and barking like a dog. It was the shame of it all that made this verbalisation exhausting; the weight of a thousand stares and frustrated exclamations and amused observations. Yes, person who has just pointed out that I'm repeating everything I'm saying, I am aware that I am repeating everything I'm saying; this is one of the realities of Autism. As the Autistic scholar Melanie Yergeau writes, our 'issues' with speaking are framed as a 'propensity to answer "How are you?" with train trivia or decontextualized lines from *Die Hard*'. No fuckin' shit, lady, do I sound like I'm orderin' a pizza?

One of the things that has most occupied my mind post-diagnosis has been the 'what ifs?' about my childhood. What if someone had gone a little further than merely noticing my emerging differences? What if I'd had this prism of understanding *before* encountering so many of my life's challenges?

Looking back, though I can recognise how many of my behaviours were Autistic, most of them occurred within the safety of our home. It didn't really matter if I was lining up my dinosaurs and My Little Ponies, displaying 'interesting' food and sensory tendencies, or reciting lines from *Ghostbusters* and *Milo & Otis* ad nauseum, or even repeating everything I'd just said immediately after I'd said it, because at home I was supported and loved.

I managed, for the most part, to avoid revealing these behaviours, particularly my palilalia, at school. It was becoming increasingly clear that I was behind the eight ball, socially speaking, and the last thing I needed – with my classmates already steaming ahead into the world of dating and gossiping (to say nothing of underwire bras and *periods*) – was another reason to mark myself for social murder.

But let's think, for a moment, about what might have happened had one of my teachers noticed my challenges and stepped in. It's possible I would have been subjected to Applied Behaviour Analysis (ABA), variations of which are, to this day, considered the 'gold standard' of Autism early intervention. ABA involves a number of strategies and approaches, many of them drill-like in nature, that aim to help Autistic children engage in society; this might involve things like toilet training, meal times or interacting with other people (conversation, or recognising others' questions and emotions).

An ABA program may also focus on eliminating so-called 'challenging behaviours', such as stimming, stereotypy and echolalia; this is referred to by many providers as 'extinction'. One Australian provider describes it as 'an evidence-based approach that assesses behaviours and works to both increase positive learning and decrease those behaviours which may be socially isolating, physically harmful or which present a significant speedbump to learning'.

Autistic children who are minimally verbal, or nonspeaking, or whose stims and other behaviours are very obvious, are likely to be recommended for a form of intensive early intervention, typically involving some form of ABA.

It is often reported that the first study into the use of ABA in the therapeutic care of young Autistic children was published by Dr Ole Ivar Lovaas in 1987, but Lovaas had been conducting research into the techniques since the 1960s. In that 1987 paper, Lovaas noted that the children whose results were most encouraging had undergone forty or more hours of ABA each week, for many years. Lovaas worked to eliminate Autistic behaviours such as stimming; therapists employed in his program were called upon to yell at, hit and even administer electric shocks to children displaying these behaviours. Children were tempted with food in order to complete tasks. The approach was drill-like in its application: hours upon hours of repeated exercises.

If we go back yet another decade, in Lovaas' 1973 paper 'Some Generalization And Follow-Up Measures On Autistic Children In Behavior Therapy',[25] published in the *Journal of Applied Behaviour Analysis*, he writes of procedures designed to 'extinguish and suppress' what he observed as 'pathological behaviour':

> *(1) contingent reinforcement withdrawal, that is, the adult simply looked away from the child when he was engaged in undesirable behavior, left the child in his room, or placed the child in an isolation room (separate from the treatment room); (2) contingent aversive stimulation, for example, a slap or painful electric shock; or (3) reinforcement of incompatible behavior, such as sitting quietly on a chair. The rationale for the suppression of self-stimulatory behavior lies in the observations we have made indicating an apparent attenuation of the child's responsivity while he is engaged in self-stimulation (Lovaas, Litrownik, and Mann, 1971). Simply stated, when the child is engaged in self-stimulation, it is difficult to teach him something else.*

(If this reminds you of so-called 'conversion therapy', that's because both approaches have their roots in the same research. George A Rekers used Lovaas' techniques to address so-called sissy boys – children we would now consider either gay, gender variant, or both – and, most disturbingly, a trans child in the 1974 study, 'Behavioural Treatment of Deviant Sex-Role Behaviours in a Male Child'.)

The notion that stimming is a distraction is one of the core tenets of ABA – many practitioners of which aim for 'quiet hands' in their 'table ready' charges. The irony of this is striking; when Autistic people stim, it is often precisely *so* that they can learn 'something else'. If I am struggling to focus on a conversation or a reading, I will jiggle my leg, snap my fingers, or twirl my magic baton beneath the desk. Doing so is a way of releasing excess energy and focusing my attention on the task at hand.

To be clear, most ABA practitioners do not hit or electrocute their young charges anymore (though hold-outs do exist, mostly in the US). ABA is now couched in feel-good language that emphasises things like 'thriving', with a focus on positive reinforcement, even if there is also often a conspicuous lack of the word 'Autism' in their site copy.

Obviously, I have no lived experience of ABA. I can absolutely understand the challenges that parents of Autistic kids with complex support needs face, and how desperate they must be for anything that might help their child, who to their eyes and ears is often obviously distressed. I have read many impassioned, compelling accounts, written by parents, of their children's development after ABA, and I'm willing to believe them.

But my impression of ABA is that it is surely an industry, like any, where there are genuinely caring specialists as well as some who seek to take advantage of these parents' concern; additionally, ABA providers don't need formal qualifications in order to practice. Couple this with the fact that the Australian Government's 'Guidelines for Good Practice' for Autistic children state that ABA is the only early intervention therapy based on established research evidence, and it's easy to see how many parents might think of it as the only way.

Though its proponents may describe it in therapeutic terms, ABA's drill-based approach is designed with one goal in mind: making an Autistic kid seem less Autistic. That may seem like an oversimplification, but it is difficult for me to grasp how training a child out of their self-stimulatory or stereotypic behaviours is anything other than an attempt to hide or remove 'Autisticness' – to work towards 'extinction'. I can only think back to myself as a child, or indeed to any of the Autistic people I know, and to how I feel when I think about them being subjected to hours of 'therapy' designed to extinguish their uniquely Autistic nature – their Autistic *selfhood*.

It is common shorthand for people to describe ABA as like dog training, but as Autistic dog trainer Carol Millman wrote in 2019, 'It focuses on training children by holding their sources of happiness hostage and using them as blackmail to get the children to meet goals which are not necessarily in the best interest of their emotional health [...] I wouldn't treat a dog that way.'

The average working week in Australia, for adults, is 37.5 hours. It is often recommended that an Autistic child undergo up to forty hours of ABA a week as part of 'early intervention'; Australian ABA providers suggest at least twenty (and up to forty) hours as an appropriate intervention for children aged two to seven years. Regardless of whether the program is *effective*, what does it say that society, government and charities consider it appropriate to subject a kindergarten or primary school-aged Autistic child to a drill-based program that runs for the equivalent of a *full-time working week, every week*? Whatever the price of ABA programs (and make no mistake, they are expensive; the fee can stretch into the tens or hundreds of thousands), what is the cost of perceived neurotypicality?

Increasing numbers of Autistic adults who were put in ABA programs as children are speaking out about the impact of the treatment, not all of it pleasant. One preliminary study,[26] published in *Advances In Autism* in 2018, found that there was increased evidence of post-traumatic stress symptoms in children and adults who had undergone ABA; 46 per cent of the respondents exposed to ABA met the diagnostic threshold for PTSD, and of those respondents, 47 per cent reported extreme levels of PTSD severity. The research's quality and methodology were quickly critiqued in a response[27] tabled in the July edition of the journal, by a group of clinicians 'funded by the Autism Special Interest Group [of the Association for Behavior Analysis International] [...] and an anonymous donor who supports ABA-based interventions for individuals diagnosed with autism'. It seemed clear that it was unwise to suggest that ABA wasn't necessarily the miracle 'cure' that uncritical commentary (such as *The New York Times* essay, 'The Kids Who Beat Autism', and numerous 'Autism parent' books and blogs) would have you believe it was.

There are aspects of early intervention that I think – *know* – would have helped me navigate the world, particularly therapies focused on emotional regulation and speech-language pathology therapies, and help with navigating social situations. In any case, by 1991 there was every chance that a teacher or guardian would have had to look very closely indeed to notice any divergence in my behaviour, because this was when I began putting nearly all my energy into appearing 'normal': masking. This campaign had, shall we say, mixed results.

Between 9 am and 3.30 pm, all my energy went into appearing as normal as possible. The tragedy of this is that, of course, I did an absolutely hopeless job of it; no matter how casually I introduced the topic of conversation, my special interests would always reveal me as a complete outsider. I'm prepared to believe that there is a generation of young kids, raised on *Glee* and *High School Musical*, for whom the act of loving musical theatre is *not* social suicide, but this was not the case in the early 1990s. And though I had long been interested in musicals, when my sister Blazey gifted me the original Broadway cast recording of Stephen Sondheim's *Into the Woods*, dinosaurs were summarily shown the door. Everything I understood about the world was shattered. Sondheim's verbose lyrics and his knack for syncopated rhythms were intoxicating to me; singing along with his shows was its own form of stimming.

Aware of both my immense interest in musical theatre *and* my burgeoning social issues, my parents enrolled me in the National Theatre Drama School's Saturday morning youth program. Mum had studied at the National years ago, completing its 'grown-up' course, and most of her classmates were close family friends. The Saturday program, by then well established, was mixed-peer – students were aged anywhere between eight and seventeen – and despite occurring under the auspices of the Drama School proper, it wasn't really about 'acting' as such; as the playwright Michael Gurr (one of those family friends) wrote in his memoir *Days Like These*, 'It [seemed] more connected to learning how to live.'

Each class was commanded by a small group of teachers, whose expertise was drawn from all sorts of backgrounds: one term you might have a mime artist, then a Russian theatre nut, then a former cast member from *STOMP!* (which was, as you can imagine, *very* thrilling for true 1990s kids). No improvisational exercise was too weird ('Okay, she's chained to the train tracks, but all you have to save her is a fire extinguisher!'), no character too strange ('She's a deaf Russian drunkard, I'm a koala').

At drama school I was still, more or less, a complete outsider, but the crucial difference was twofold: in some way, we were all outsiders (the *real* 'theatre kids'; the ones who wanted to end up on *Neighbours* went to St Martins), and at drama school I was an outsider under the watchful eye of the legendary Joan Harris, the school's director. Every Saturday she held court from within her office, which was so jammed with memorabilia and stationery that it seemed improbably small for such a huge personality. Every now and again she'd wander out and around the hallways, but she never set foot in our workshops; that was a sacred space. Her motto, and by extension the motto of everyone who set foot in the National, was 'TRUST. RISK. ALLOW.', and we were all expected to abide by it. As Gurr noted in a memorial of Harris' life written for *The Age*, 'If Joan Harris cast her beady eye on you and picked you as someone worth encouraging, it was no easy ride. Not for her the easy compliment, nor the lazy endorsement.'

I quickly became used to the sound of Harris yelling 'CLEMMY ...' from inside her office, summoning me for another dose of extreme tough love. One Saturday morning during my first year of classes, I sat glumly in her office, having escaped whichever theatre sports exercise was currently being undertaken in our group. I tearfully explained that I felt I was being shunned by my fellow drama students, and could I please change into one of the other groups? After listening with great care and compassion, it became clear that Joan was having none of it; she issued one of her many malapropisms-turned-edicts (something to do with rotten apples in a barrel) and marched me back to class. I'm glad she did; the days I spent at the National were some of the happiest of my entire life.

If there was one silver lining to my shift from St Joseph's to Middle Park, it was in fact a platinum one: it was where I met my best friend, Tash. Well, we had *met* plenty of times before – our dads were old friends – but when she enrolled at Middle Park not long after I did, we suddenly spent nearly every day together. In Tash I had found both a kindred spirit and a protector; she was six months older than me, and had both a flair for the theatrical *and* a video camera (well, her parents did). For once I was not the only one trying to stage manage the production of (checks notes) 'Cooking with Monica Seles'.

Tash and her family lived in a terrace house in Albert Park that was as chaotically homely as ours – full of her dad's artworks, Balinese icons, musical instruments and overflowing costume baskets – and I quickly learned to feel as at home there as I did at our house. We were as thick as thieves, devising plans for backyard theatre productions and cooking up April Fool's Day 'treats' for the teachers (which in Grade 5 included cupcakes full of castor oil and black pepper). Tash didn't care that I wore my David Attenborough on nearly every outing, and unlike our peers, she wasn't interested in the vagaries of fashion or soap operas, preferring instead to rewind *The Making of Michael Jackson's Thriller* for the forty-seventh time so we could get special effects make-up tips from Rick Baker. We would put on performances, starring a cast of Barbies in various stages of undress, lit by candlelight, and once screamed with laughter for a good four hours when we found a wind-up comedy plastic penis. We took our inspiration to the Barbie movie studio (Tash's bedroom) to shoot an incandescently rude film, no doubt 'rated "x" for sex!!!'.

When I had finally begun my investigations into assessment for Autism, I read Tony Attwood's foreword to Liane Holliday Willey's *Safety Skills for Asperger Women*; he spoke of how Autistic girls may forge a single, intense friendship with another girl who becomes a sort of protector and mentor. It was like I was staring at my favourite photograph of me and Tash, with our Barbies shoved through a spare-sheet backdrop, her giving an Oscar-winning smile and me with my gaze ever so slightly on her, learning how better to be a confident person in the world.

For years, I had no context nor understanding for this experience I had lived through; the act of readying or repeating my speech was just another example of how 'weird' I was. I say that my palilalia 'started' in the winter of 1991, but in truth I don't really know when it started, only that this was the year it seemed most noticeable, because it was the year nearly everybody pointed it out. Some clinicians consider palilalia to be a sign of high anxiety. Which came first, the crushing realisation that I was unlike everybody else, or the anxiety? Post-diagnosis, I was browsing a Reddit thread titled 'Autistic people of Reddit, what is something you do/did that you thought was completely normal until you learned it was a symptom of Autism?' I saw a comment, and recognition hit me like a bolt of lightning:

As a child, I whispered what I was going to say before I would say it, and would sometimes whisper back what another person had just said to me. I wanted to make sure it was the right thing to say, so I would 'test it out' before saying it, and I'd repeat things because it helped me to process what was being said.[28]

The only respite from my own echo was, somewhat ironically, echolalia; I could quote my favourite movies and repeat jokes from TV without so much as a verbal stumble. The process of creating original and 'normal' speech patterns out of thin air, on the other hand, was such a high-wire act it required preparation and review. The esteemed British neurologist Macdonald Critchley, in his 1927 paper *On Palilalia*, wrote, 'A point of great interest and importance lies in the fact that the palilalia (as with stammering) disappears during pre-formed speech automatisms, as for instance, when the patient reads aloud, sings or recites. Thus if the patient is ordered to repeat from memory some well-known speech pattern, such as the Lord's Prayer, the alphabet or a nursery rhyme, there is no trace of repetition.' (He also, rather poetically, notes it as a disorder of *speaking* rather than speech.)

Happily for me, right around the same time that I was battling with my own echo, I had the opportunity to make echolalia earn its keep: I was cast in the lead role in our school musical, *It's a Fine Life!*, which is what our production of *Oliver!* was called in order to confuse any visiting copyright lawyers.

Despite what my assiduous study of Broadway culture had suggested, getting the lead in the school musical does *not* garner you much social capital. To be more specific, getting the *straight* lead doesn't; getting the role with laughs is what you want. What you don't want, as a lanky eleven-year-old girl, is to get the very dull, soprano-singing role as a goody two-shoes orphan boy. Well, I mean, you *do* want it, because all you want is to be in musicals, but it turns out there's a large chasm between the Broadway fan fiction you insist on writing in your class journal and the not-so-bright lights of the Phoenix Theatre at Elwood College. Now I wasn't just an outsider, I was an outsider who – by virtue of being the lead in the musical, as though it had been my decision – reckoned she was a bit good.

Students who had previously not given a shit about musical theatre were suddenly looking askance at me for nabbing the lead; what's she got that we don't have? Like so many of the subtleties of human interaction, I didn't get it: wait a minute, I'm in the school play, aren't they meant to be happy for me? ('I'm a voter: aren't you supposed to lie to me and kiss my butt?')

Making matters worse, when the props department put the call out for handkerchiefs to decorate Fagin's quarters, I offered up, at my parents' suggestion, some of my late grandfather Stewart's silk ones. I turned up at the dress rehearsal to discover they'd been chopped into smaller squares, and had to deliver the news to my immediately furious father. Had I misunderstood the brief? Was this another example of me taking things at face value, only to discover a reality to the contrary? How was I to know that World War II-era silk hankies were bigger than 1992 hankies, for fuck's sake?! It was the same emotional routine as ever: the naivety, followed by the shame at the naivety, followed by the volcano of rage at the injustice of it all. Rinse, repeat.

It was all worth it, of course. Rehearsals were a blessed *exeunt* from the hell of the playground; sorry, I can't hang out and play *Perfect Match* near the rounders court, I have to go practice my solo! And the musical itself, once it was up and running, was of course everything I'd ever wanted. I know, intellectually and from looking at photos of the event, that the set was just a jumble of scaffolding and second-hand furniture lit by the blue and red gels of the nearby high school's poky theatre, but to my eyes, we were all appearing in a Cameron

Mackintosh blockbuster at the biggest theatre in the land. We only did three performances, but I could have done seven a week plus a matinee on Saturday. Day to day, I was beginning, in earnest, my life's work of hiding my true self away; constructing an engaging persona and vernacular by consuming and repeating dialogue and turns of phrase I'd borrow from screen media and others; whistling and singing to control my emotions. On the stage, I was applauded for pretending to be someone I wasn't, for remembering my lines, for singing. It was like walking into another world.

If the common misconception about actors and performers is that they are all limelight hogs, the considerable concentration of Autistic people in their ranks complicates things. Daryl Hannah has spoken of her realisation as a young Autistic girl that acting was a space within which her vivid internal world could take flight. 'I was about 11 when I understood that movies weren't something that just happened in reality and someone caught it on camera. Once I realised that it was actually a job I could have, I actively pursued it,' she said in a 2015 interview. 'I wanted to go and live in the land of Oz and meet the Tin Woodman and the Cowardly Lion and the Scarecrow. I wanted to go to those places. Literally. It wasn't that I wanted to be an actress as such. I wanted to be physically transported to other realities.'

I didn't especially want to be transported to the slums of midnineteenth century London, but anything was better than reality, and acting took me inches closer to the Technicolour life of my daydreams, in which I wasn't just friends but *family* with the famous people I admired. Autistic children may well lack 'imaginative play'

why would I invent what I'm doing with my toys when every single
My Little Pony comes with a character biography?
so-called 'typically developing' children invent imaginary friends,
and *we're* the ones being given MRIs for 'asynchronous brain
activity'?

but their *imaginations* can be extraordinarily active. I was by this point so comprehensively obsessed with the idea of being in a Broadway show (I had read Alan Jay Lerner's *The Musical Theatre: A Celebration*) that I spent my idle moments thinking about all my (imagined) close personal friends 'in the biz', stars like Jonathan Pryce and Geraldine Turner.

The daydream was so real that taking a chance on reality felt pointless. After all, in my mind, I was already a star, already a 'Broadway Baby'. The fact that that song is delivered not by a precocious preteen but by an exhausted, ageing hoofer, the great joke of 'Broadway Baby', was also immaterial; I never let the deeper subtext of my beloved musicals get in the way of my performance. Perhaps that's Autism: no subtext, only text. I certainly had the pipes, but very little else: as a child whose awkward gait and lack of hand–eye coordination had already been noted, what hope did I have of becoming a triple threat performer of international renown? Besides, dance lessons were expensive.

Once the musical was done and dusted, the glow of the bright lights dimmed, the friendships forged in the wings of the theatre eventually also started to fade. It was my first experience of circumstantial friendship – the bonds you make through shared experience, which aren't always 'for life' – though it wouldn't be the last to confuse me. (To this day, I'm still surprised when someone I've shared a house, a job, or some other experience with disappears into the ether once the circumstances of our relationship dissolve for perfectly normal reasons, such as the end of a shared lease; what is a friendship and how do you keep one?) Within months, I was back to being a plain old weirdo, and I couldn't understand it. I vividly remember writing a note to a clutch of classmates I had considered to be friends

friends??

'friends'

127

in class, in pastel felt-tip marker, that said 'Is this because I had the lead role in the musical?' I can't remember if I sent it. I hope I didn't.

There were a handful of other kids who were on my level, which is to say, in the dungeon of the social order: Jess, who had a learning disability *and* an accent (catnip for bullies); Alexander, given the typically Australian nickname of 'Unco' (as in 'uncoordinated'); and the mysterious brothers Dusty and Sandy, country kids (everyone thought they were weird because of their hippie names). In a sainted irony, the one student who might otherwise have been outcast as a 'wog' or a 'reffo' was given god-tier social status because of his family's incredibly boss escape from occupied Czechoslovakia in the boot of a car. The lord really does work in mysterious ways.

If I had been nominally on the outer in Grade 5, it was Grade 6 where things really started to go off the rails. I even had my own tormentor, Patrick, a hawkish boy with the tan and blonde hair that suggested regular seaside family holidays. Patrick had apparently forgotten the fact of our once-upon-a-time co-starring in *It's a Fine Life!* He started terrorising me, with the crushing wit and great delight common to all great villains, by cornering me and singing the *Four Corners* theme in a menacing fashion. Get it? What has four corners? If you answered 'a square', well done – perhaps you, too, have spent a lot of money on therapy. (Google tells me Patrick is now a commercial law specialist.)

Confused by this apparent echolalic battle of the wits in which the opening numbers of popular current affairs shows were employed as weapons, I would reply by 'ticking' like a clock, à la the *60 Minutes* theme. I thought I was incredibly clever – Two can play at that game, sir! – but of course it only made things worse.

As the Autistic child is also usually identifiably 'weird', this typically marks them as a target for bullying. One meta-analytical study[29]

found that Autistic students are at a significantly higher risk of victimisation and bullying than typically developing students and students
with other disabilities. Issues with interpreting social situations – and
a lack of strong friendships – may also lead to Autistic students
misinterpreting bullying as normal peer interaction.[30] To return
to Lorna Wing's case studies of children with Asperger syndrome,
consider the story of C.B.: 'He is not socially withdrawn, but he prefers
the company of adults to that of children of his own age, finding
it difficult to understand the unwritten rules of social interaction.
He said of himself, "I am afraid I suffer from bad sportsmanship". He
enjoys simple jokes but cannot understand more subtle humour. He is
often teased by his classmates.'

After the musical faded into memory, palilalia came back in a big
way, bringing with it a profound existential agony that could probably
be described as separation anxiety. Grade 6 camp was a rolling disaster
that culminated in a meltdown on the final night. Imagine, if you will,
a small girl in shrieking tears at the bottom of a staircase at The Old
Priory in Beechworth. A kindly teacher suggested I was homesick and
plied me with extra potatoes from the bain-marie; it seemed like a
reasonable enough explanation, even if I wasn't entirely sure it was
true. (I recovered enough to disturb and delight everyone at the 'talent
quest' on the last night of camp by imitating The Chipmunks; like
so many Autistic people throughout history, I had learned to use my
powers for good.)

Over the course of the year it became increasingly difficult to be
away from home. Sleepovers were fraught with danger. I knew that
it would be 'daggy' or 'embarrassing' to bring Pterry to a sleepover,
so I was stranded, without comfort, in other people's houses full of
bewildering textures and smells. More than once I had to be rescued
from someone else's living room at 2 am because I was feeling sick;
my parents would dutifully roll up and usher me into the car, and the
drive from Albert Park to Port Melbourne would be enough for me

to magically recover from what had previously been a deathly serious case of nausea. Maybe this habit of spending gossip-fuelled parties forever teetering on the brink of chundering all over the *Beaches* and *Nightmare on Elm Street* video boxes was what led to the drop in birthday party invitations.

There was even, as I vividly recall, the 'big test' of going away to Lorne for the week with my friend Stella and her family; I lasted a day before, once again, Mum and Dad had to show up, driving two hours each way for their troubles. Eventually, my reluctance to be away from the safety of home extended beyond sleepovers and vacations, and started to affect my attitude to school.

Years later, in therapy, I asked Mum about something relating to Grade 6 that had come up 'on the couch'; she replied that 1993 was the year I started refusing to go to school. Apparently, there were quite a few weeks where I just straight up said I wouldn't go. I was stunned: I had absolutely no memory of this. There was certainly precedent – my refusal to learn the times tables, my refusal to read the 'boring' school readers – but looking back and piecing all the evidence together, it seems fairly clear that this was a desperate attempt to avoid the trauma of bullying.

A 2017 study suggests that Autistic students are at a far higher risk of so-called school refusal,[31] at 42.6 per cent, compared to a 7.1 per cent risk for typically developing kids. The study observed behaviours such as pleading, clinging to parents, crying, and a physical refusal to enter the school grounds. While the outcomes, educationally speaking, of school refusal are fraught, Professor Tony Attwood has noted that discussions of school refusal in Autistic kids tend to focus on the problem to be fixed (i.e. how to get the kid to school), rather than considering the reasons behind the behaviour. Of those reasons, one of the most compelling can be that, to the Autistic child, the school is tantamount to a war zone, where bullies lie in wait to ambush them. There may also be feelings of social exclusion, and the lack of acceptance, if not outright rejection, by their schoolmates can lead to the Autistic child suffering blows to their self-esteem and self-identity.

I am yet to meet a fellow Autistic person who didn't experience some form of bullying at school, and I have also met many who were eventually homeschooled due to the virulent nature of their treatment. I was 'lucky'; aside from Patrick and his *Four Corners* campaign, the bullying I received at the hands of my classmates was more insidious than direct. More than once I sat down at my desk to discover, too late, that it had been sprinkled with thumbtacks. My favourite pens and pencils would go missing, then turn up after lunch, gnarled with bite marks and still glistening with someone else's saliva.

It was, of course, baffling to me; I was doing all I could to keep up with my classmates, feigning interest in *Melrose Place* (which I wasn't allowed to watch, nor did I have any desire to) rather than assailing people with facts about whatever had happened on *Dr. Quinn, Medicine Woman* that week. Why was I still on the outer? How do you do, fellow youths, it is I, Clem, your very normal classmate! But my attempts to pass as 'normal' could only go so far. I thought I was being so cool when I sidled up to a group of classmates to tell them about the new Sondheim musical I'd been listening to; 'It's pretty cool, it has swearing in it,' I said, with what I can only assume I thought was a terrific impression of a nonchalant pre-teen.

Maybe this masking was why my 'out of school hours' speech patterns were so off the charts: the privacy of home, the library or the park were the only safe places to be myself. Some Autistic people feel that they are most Autistic when they are out in the world; that's where the social model of disability dictates that their experience of the world around them is different to those it is designed to accommodate. For me, as I'm sure is the case for many others (particularly those diagnosed later in life), I am most Autistic at home; that's where it is safe to let it all hang out. It's difficult to explain the burden of masking to those who don't need to do it. I have seen clinicians – specialists, apparently, in Autism – dismiss masking and camouflaging, particularly as a marker for diagnosis later in life, as akin to a shorter person deciding to wear shoes with a heel: not much of a big deal, and certainly not necessarily a sign of Autism. For me, masking was a matter of safety, psychic if not physical, because I was well aware of what would happen to anyone who dared to seem 'different'.

There was one girl whose bullying at the hands of literally everyone other than me in our Grade 6 class was a breathtaking example of Wilfred Bion's theories of the psychopathy of group dynamics. Her name was Anne. In a testament to the cruelty of children, I can't recall what Anne's crime was, other than to be withdrawn enough to favour a hoodie, which led to the rest of the girls roaming in a pack, wearing hoodies with the drawstring pulled tight around their faces and yelling 'I'm an Anne-berry!' in a stupid voice as they chased her around the quadrangle. It became obvious to me that the only safe solution was to remove myself completely from the social dynamic of my class, and by the last few weeks of fourth term, I spent my recesses and lunchtimes playing with my Prep 'buddy' and her friends.

I knew this was probably not 'normal', and I admired Atti for his seemingly preternatural ability to make friends. (Indeed, he once entered the kindergarten grounds, grabbed another kid in a hug, and announced 'Love me and be my friend'.) Atti was so relaxed and confident, in fact, that in one of his kindergarten photos he's lying in a billy kart with his legs crossed and his arms behind his head, as if to say, 'Ah, welcome, make yourself at home'.

With the fights against school closures looming large in local media, my low-key war against Jeff Kennett reached its climax at the school talent quest in 1993. My reason for both entering and helping to organise the talent quest was transparent: surely I, with an encyclopedic knowledge of the collected works of Stephen Sondheim and the singing voice to prove it, would win. I'll show them! This will be the moment my career takes off and I never look back! Forget you, rich kids, I'm off to NIDA!

This plan hit a speed bump early when my parents suggested that my choice of 'Being Alive' from *Company* was – as a song sung by a 'confirmed bachelor' at the end of a very grown-up musical about 1970s sexual politics – probably not the best choice for an eleven-year-old girl to sing. Disappointed yet undeterred, I settled on my second choice: 'Getting To Know You' from *The King and I*, the winning power of which would be upped by a gaggle of adorable Grade 1 students cast as the children of the King of Siam. Tash appeared, wearing fisherman's pants, a sequinned waistcoat and the worst-fitting bald cap ever known to humanity, as an award-worthy imitation of Yul Brynner. I even convinced Mum and Dad to hire a ballgown from Rose Chong's, for the princely fee of $50, to better evoke the sumptuousness of Roger Kirk's costumes. Unfortunately, my tendency towards baffling political comedy meant that I also cast my classmate Katie as Jeff Kennett: she was to walk across the stage periodically, dressed in a business suit with a Jeff Kennett mask, and remove the mask to reveal hideous zombie make-up, only to ('He's behind you!') replace the mask whenever I turned to see what all the fuss was about.

The talent quest catastrophe was the final nail in the coffin of my primary school career. What hope did this brave and groundbreaking hybrid theatre performance have against the combined power of all the popular girls of Grade 6 dressed as nuns and performing 'My God' from *Sister Act*? The audience was probably full of Kennett voters.

THE UNDISCOVERED COUNTRY

It's a funny thing, really: one of the best years of my life was also one of the worst years of my life. I only remember snatches of it, good and bad, because the fact of its being the worst has also, bittersweetly, extinguished my memories of some of the best moments.

1994 started off on a good footing: I had escaped primary school! I was to begin my secondary schooling at Elwood College. Elwood was a state school with impressive arts, theatre and music programs, and a diverse student body. Despite the nerves of starting at a new school, I immediately felt at ease on its then slightly scratch-'n'-dent grounds. If you've ever watched *Heartbreak High*, it was like that. In a way, it felt like being back at St Joseph's. There were kids with learning disabilities and recently arrived Russian kids and hippies and weirdos and show-offs. Nobody gave a shit about *Melrose Place*, and people wrote poems about Kurt Cobain in English class. Ahh, I thought, I will fit in here.

I quickly made friends with a few fellow oddbods, including Alexandra, a theatrical type too, and Naomi, who had an undercut and smoked like a chimney, and became a swimming champion thanks to her deathly fear of sharks (the secret: imagine there's a shark waiting to chase you from the starting blocks). It eased the pain of Tash and her family having recently moved to Queensland, though none of them could hope to take her place in the firmament of best friends.

Everywhere I looked, there were kids of all ages who seemed like they wouldn't fit in anywhere other than Elwood. Rebecca, who got sent home from science class for wearing a Cypress Hill 'Cone Flakes' T-shirt. A punk, Seamus, who had dragons tattooed on his temples (he was in a higher year level). Sometimes I'd watch him, awestruck, at the canteen; he'd order 'ten dim sims with tomato sauce, please', then turn and grin at me as he tucked into his revolting lunch.

Elwood was the sort of school where a kid like me could flourish; the type of school where all the teachers were overworked and slightly stressed, but had a real passion for helping their charges thrive. I got a small role in the school musical and relished the camaraderie of the mixed-peer cast, and the proximity to cool, weird students like Amiel (the future 'Totally Addicted to Bass' vocalist) and Ashley, who played saxophone in the school jazz ensemble, the hilariously named Jazz – Off The Rails. This was high school as film and television had told me it would be: it was like my mental Rolodex of popular media had come to life at last. Never had I been more thrilled than when, at musical camp, Ashley flushed Corey's head down the toilet in a truly Shakespearean battle for the affections of Liz, the walleyed opera singer. When we all returned from musical camp and were waiting for parents to come pick us up, my friends started giving me shit for something (take your pick). I have never felt cooler than I did in the moment when Ashley sauntered up behind me and whispered in my ear, 'Why don't you tell them to all go fuck themselves?'

What I didn't realise was that behind the scenes, my family life was about to experience a seismic shift.

We were in the thick of Keating's 'recession we had to have', and Dad was working long, long hours. He had an intern who didn't seem to be helping with the workload an awful lot, and a bunch of clients who weren't too keen to cough up when the invoices went out.

We had a block of land in Gippsland back then, a cheap wedge of nearly vertical farmland pockmarked with puddles and ponds (and, occasionally, the neighbours' cows). Mum and Dad had bought it as a possible site for a holiday home, or a tree change, or maybe just a carrot dangling out in front of the recession. We'd occasionally go down there and camp, and I had fond memories of the time Blazey came down from Sydney to join us. The land overlooked the almost incomprehensibly beautiful landscape, down across the rolling fields with Wilson's Promontory in the distance.

Dad worked from home, but was often out and about, so there wasn't much to be concerned about one night when he seemed to be staying out late. But as the night wore on, it became clear that Dad wasn't just out. This was the pre-mobile-phone era, so when Mum had exhausted all the possible places he could be, starting and ending, really, with Mumple, the mood plummeted. Dad had gone missing.

The rest of that night is hazy in my memory. Apparently I went to Dad's big filing cabinet, pulled out all of my drawings he'd saved, or that we'd done together, spread them out on the floor and sat among them. I think my aunty Catie came over to help with Atticus, who had just begun Prep. And then, very late at night, Mum came up to me, face streaked with tears, sort of half-smiling in a hesitant way, and said, 'They've found Dad.'

Down in Gippsland, the neighbours had spotted our family car, a pea-green Renault TX, parked by the gates of our block.

A family friend leapt into his car and floored it all the way to Gippsland. It was another few hours until we saw Dad. When we did, in the emergency room of the Alfred Hospital (bless them), he seemed distant, if happy to see us.

Through it all, Mum was a pillar of strength. Despite being only thirty-six and having recently returned to university (not to mention having only just begun her own therapeutic journey), she managed to juggle two young kids *and* Dad's architecture clients while reckoning with the earth-shattering realisation that the man she was married to had nearly left her in the most profound way possible. Nobody would have blamed her for packing me and Atticus into a car and driving it onto the *Abel Tasman*, never to return. Even Nanna, her extremely traditional mother, thought something of that nature would be a good idea. Instead, Mum poured her heart and soul into keeping our family together.

The next day was Saturday, and I went to Drama School as usual. I remember Joan taking me aside and saying how proud they all were that I'd come to class that weekend, considering the circumstances. As far as I saw it, there was no time to crumble – I just had to keep going, for my sake and for everybody's sake.

This was my first experience of being calm in a crisis, and perhaps also of not displaying the sort of emotion a person might be expected to. But just because I didn't *show* it didn't mean I wasn't *feeling* it.

My whole life, I have been aware of the disconnect apparent in my behaviour: devastated by an abandoned teddy bear or a lonely can of soup, apparently cool and calm in the face of someone else's emotional distress.

In Term 1 of Year 7, while sick at home with chickenpox, I watched a rented copy of *Star Trek IV: The Voyage Home*. I was struck by the scene where Spock undertakes Vulcan computer training of his mental acuity. Initially I enjoyed the scene because Spock is working on two computer panels simultaneously, and I felt seen by this detail, as I had a habit of reading both pages of a book at once. Moments into his test, however, having aced questions such as 'ADJUST THE SINE WAVE OF THIS MAGNETIC ENVELOPE SO THAT ANTI-NEUTRONS CAN PASS THROUGH IT BUT ANTI-GRAVITONS

CANNOT', Spock is stumped by the question 'HOW DO YOU FEEL?' The question repeats as he stands, stunned, in front of the screen. His human mother, Amanda, observes his confusion, asking what's wrong. 'I do not understand the question, mother,' her son responds. Amanda explains that, although Spock has been retraining his mind 'in the Vulcan way', the computer has recognised that he has human feelings (emotions), and that they will surface.

'How do you feel?' is a question I can rarely answer, at least not with words. It has been suggested that around half of all Autistic people experience alexithymia, a subclinical difficulty in recognising and expressing emotions (literally: *a*: lack, *lexis*: word, *thymos*: mood or emotion). I am aware of my emotional state, which is to say, I know I'm feeling *something* – indeed, I feel emotions deeply – but it can be unclear as to what that emotion is. I also find it incredibly difficult to articulate what I'm feeling, so much so that the very questions 'how are you?' or 'what does it feel like?' can bring on a complete brain shutdown. When prodded to articulate my feelings I might play a song, or find a photo, or a clip from a film or cartoon that will illustrate my answer, but to explain my emotional state with words? I, too, do not understand the question.

A common misconception persists that Autistic people lack empathy; the popular depiction of the curt, thoughtless Autistic hero of screen media (Sheldon, Sherlock) has helped to embed this at an almost cellular level. The reality is more complex. Issues tend to arise in the chasm between cognitive empathy (recognising and understanding the emotional state of others), itself an aspect of the social-cognitive skill known as 'theory of mind', and affective empathy (*feeling* the emotional state of others and responding appropriately). Many Autistic people will tell you that the opposite of the misconception is true: if we 'suffer' from anything, it's *too much* empathy. I am prone, as many Autistic people are, to emotional contagion; one person's bad mood is to my own sense of emotional equilibrium what a bad cold is to someone with a compromised immune system.

My own experience of empathy is something raw and unfocused, as though feeling everything and nothing at once. The various representations, on the page and on screen, of Superman first recognising that he can 'hear' the thoughts, hopes and fears of every human being on earth are a good parallel: almost too much to bear.

The most painful aspect of this disconnect between cognitive and affective empathy is that I will often *feel* a person's distress but be unable to address it in any helpful way beyond attempting to 'fix' the situation through a series of complicated thought experiments and hypotheticals. Here's an example: for many years I simply could not believe that anyone could have a dysfunctional relationship with their mother, because my own mum was proof, somehow, that all mothers were godly. Any criticism of *any* mother (including by Mum of *her* own mother – their relationship was complex) felt like a slight against my own. I would prod for evidence – citation needed – as though, surely, they had got it wrong. Let's look at things from her perspective, maybe she didn't mean that, perhaps it was a bad day, who knows what she's going through. Ironically, in an attempt to perform an empathetic consideration of the mother's role in all of this, I would negate the child's experience, and ruin any attempt at offering sympathy. Highly illogical, captain.

Maybe I *shouldn't* have gone to drama school that Saturday morning, no matter how important it was to my sense of routine; maybe I should have stayed home and cried and hugged Mum and Atti, and called Blazey. With better (or any) social skills training, would I have put my foot in it a few less times? Would I have chosen not to barge in on emotionally charged discussions where I was expected to listen with care, not solve a riddle? Would I be able to tell the computer how I feel? Or are mistakes, no matter how painful, just an unfortunate fact of life? These are questions that can never be answered, though merely considering them in the context of my diagnosis has helped me to sketch out the path that stretches out beyond me.

Or, as the tagline for *Star Trek IV* ran, 'A catastrophe in the future can only be averted by a journey into Earth's past.'

Years later, I spoke to Dad about what he thinks drove him to the brink that night. Aside from the obvious stresses of being self-employed during a recession, the regrets and pressures imparted upon him by his strict, English father seemed to weigh overwhelmingly on his mind. 'I think I carried this with me from then on and spent far too much time and effort trying to make male clients think highly of me, clients who really just needed me to do my job satisfactorily,' he told me. 'I invested far too much in that quest, so that when the rather patrician one of a couple I was designing a house for, who reminded me a bit of Dad, expressed disappointment that the estimated cost for the project was too high, I took it out on myself.'

I asked Dad what he remembers of that night in 1994, and he replied, 'It's funny, Clembo, I have no memory of the time between leaving Mumple's and being found on the block. All I do recall is that I had Jessye Norman on the tape player singing the last song of Richard Strauss's *Four Last Songs*, 'Im Abendrot'. The most lovely and comforting of the four.'

Gradually, through counselling and hyperbaric therapy, Dad started to return to his old self. I remember my birthday that year as a turning point. Mum wrote in my card 'The year Dad got better! xx', and every single one of my presents, though they were clearly from the toy aisle at Coles rather than the more expensive toy shops, was a treasured gift. I wasn't even mad when Naomi and Alexandra gave me a hamper stuffed full of condoms (rude!) and cigarettes (cancerous!).

Mum and Dad made the decision to sell our house not long after, to clear out the mortgage and move to the suburbs for a fresh (and less expensive) start. This was the moment my feelings finally exploded to the surface: after narrowly avoiding the loss of my father, the thought of such massive change – moving away from the only house I'd ever known, and leaving a school at which I felt welcome and supported – was almost too much to bear. Eventually, however, the storm passed, particularly as Mum and Dad dazzled me with the promise of my *own* garden (the house we were moving to, the worst on a decent street, had a little courtyard outside the window of what would be my room).

To celebrate the simple act of *surviving* that year, in September we went on our first real family holiday, flying to Cairns. Everything about it felt absolutely magical, particularly the lagoon pool at the slightly down-at-heel beach resort we stayed at; I spent approximately 75 per cent of my time there swimming in loops around the pool, underwater, with my goggles on. (When I returned home I sent a hand-written letter to the producers of *Ocean Girl*, just letting them know that if misfortune should befall the star, Marzena Godecki, I would be willing to take her place.) Atticus and I, terrified of the Nemo-esque fish on the Great Barrier Reef and their habit of suddenly appearing from within an anemone's fronds, spent the entire snorkelling trip standing on the shore of an atoll like blue-wet-suited aliens. We also went to visit Tash and her family; it's difficult to describe the relief I felt at being able to again make absolutely demented Barbie movies with my best friend while our parents got blasted on cheap red wine to the tunes of Dire Straits and Deep Forest.

When we returned to Melbourne, I – in an unusually upbeat and mature twist – did my best to enjoy the last of my term at Elwood. I signed up for lunchtime gymnastics. I went to birthday parties. I joined the Christmas choir. Towards the end of the year, I was invited to join a mixed-peer writing workshop, with other gifted students from Years 7 through to 12, that would be run by the legendary novelist Arnold Zable.

We moved house on a hot day early that summer; the goldfish didn't survive the journey. Just as we started to pull out of our car spot, the postie arrived, carrying with him a reply to a fan letter I had written to

Steven Spielberg. It was a form letter, and the 'autographed photo' was clearly printed, but I took it as a sign: things were going to be okay. By the time we arrived in Ivanhoe – *very* much the square pegs in that suburb's leafy, middle-class round hole – I felt sanguine about the rest of my schooling career. I was sad to leave Elwood, but hopeful that, perhaps, this year had been the beginning of a new direction.

Of course, we didn't magically pop out the other side; dealing with the aftermath of a loved one's suicide *attempt* is a very different, strange sort of grief; you wonder if it will happen again, you wonder if it's hereditary. It's always there, in the background, in the nooks and crannies of family interactions, in simmering resentments and deep, age-old wounds.

Like many Autistic people, depression and anxiety have been a constant companion in my life, and in my darkest moments I have fixated, panicked, on whether or not I had inherited what the writer Anna Spargo-Ryan once called 'the suicide gene'. After all, suicide is one of the leading causes of death for Autistic people; this risk is increased in those who have coexisting conditions, or who experience psychosis.[32] Some research has pointed to the loneliness and social disconnection experienced by many Autistic people as a possible cause for elevated risk of suicidal thoughts.[33]

The one thing that has kept me from the brink, without fail, is the fear of hurting my family, and particularly, of hurting Mum. To this day I am amazed at the strength and determination she showed in getting the whole family through the catastrophe of 1994. She was the glue that held the family together for another decade, after an event that would have quite reasonably shattered even the strongest bonds, and it is only because of her that we are all still alive.

A ZERO-SUM GAME

'That didn't look very spontaneous or romantic, let's try it again.'

Great. Not only is my first kiss with David Mould, during a closed rehearsal for the school musical, *Guys and Dolls*, but now Mrs Clayton is giving me notes on it.

We try the kiss again, and evidently this time it's even less spontaneous or romantic than before, because now Mrs Nisbett is chiming in as well. I'm surprised Mrs Carroll, the accompanist, doesn't turn around and offer her two cents, too. There's a strip window above the classroom, which is rapidly filling with the faces of students desperate to get front-row seats to this unfolding catastrophe. So much for a 'closed' rehearsal.

'Again! Start at the top, Mrs Carroll.'

I wish I could dance. I wish I didn't have a soprano voice, so I could've played one of the funnier roles, like Miss Adelaide. I wish I hadn't had to move to the eastern suburbs and abandon drama school. I wish it wasn't a big deal that 'Year 9 students don't usually get lead roles in the musical!' I wish they *still* didn't get lead roles in the musical so I could've had a normal first kiss like a normal girl, and auditioned for the next musical in Year 11, a glamorous and sophisticated adult woman who has kissed at least three people.

'Ugh ... Let's move on to the next scene.'

By 1996, things at Balwyn High were, well, *fine*. I had managed to score myself a role in the school musical, giving me a blessed escape from the drudgery of class. The universe, in a rare moment of feeling, had somehow replaced the outright bullying of primary school with its equally distressing yet less immediately noticeable cousin: being mostly ignored.

To be clear, I *did* have friends. There was Max, *Star Trek*–mad and with a penchant for the colour purple; the mysterious Gill, who dressed as Morgan le Fay for Halloween; and Kira, an academic whiz who was such a huge Take That fan she once made us watch an entire bootlegged concert on VHS. (I, a prude, was *not* impressed when Gary Barlow started humping the stage.) When Mumple died, drifting away after experiencing a massive stroke, it was Kira who wept alongside me after Jim Stynes gave our year level a seminar about emotional wellbeing. Thank the merciful heavens, Tash and her family moved back from Queensland towards the end of the year, and she enrolled at Balwyn (shortly before becoming a goth, a time-honoured rite of passage). Being something of a tomboy, I also started hanging out with the *Freaks & Geeks*-esque boys: the *Magic* players and music nerds, including Daniel, who once wore a cork hat with 'I LOVE ALBY MANGELS' scribbled on it to free-dress day, Darren the drum nerd, and Nick (Nick was kinda just there). We were a ragtag bunch of outcasts who became insiders on account of our shared experience of outcastness.

Adolescence is a tricky time for most people, but for Autistic people it's especially chaotic: hormones, social changes, body horror. My body started to produce smells, but my complete lack of interest in social norms and shaky grasp of executive function meant that I didn't realise I needed to do something about it. Mum very kindly took me aside one particularly sweaty afternoon and explained that spraying my supermarket-brand lavender 'cologne spray' in the middle of the room and walking through the mist (as I had seen done in a Hollywood movie) wasn't quite going to cut it.

The onset of puberty is also particularly fraught for Autistic girls, as it's when they may cease hiding in plain sight, through no conscious decision of their own. 'When puberty hits,' Rudy Simone writes in her wonderful Autistic autoethnography *Aspergirls*, 'it flips us on our heads and you can see our autistic underbelly.'[34] Even if Year 9 was in every other way a completely forgettable year, it was memorable for one thing: it was when my vague sense of being different began to grow into an echoing chasm of anxiety.

I'm prepared to believe that high school is reasonably diverting for the people who have nice hairstyles (not just hair*cuts*), those whose privilege manifests in a total inability to recognise their own privilege, and who see themselves reflected in the cast of *Home and Away*. High school for an undiagnosed Autistic girl from a hard-up family, on the other hand, was mostly an unrelenting white-knuckle hell ride peppered with occasional moments of levity. Most of those moments occurred in 1997, the one year in my high-school career that I look back on with any sense of sentimentality. It was the only time I ever truly felt like 'a teenager' in the manner I understood that to feel, based on my careful examination of teen movies and Blink-182 lyrics.

Year 10 was, most notably, when I made friends with Oliver. We'd been in the same art class all year, but it wasn't until free-dress day (pay $1 to express yourself!) that we interacted. 'You look like a lesbian,' he said, referring to what I thought was a very convincing facsimile of one of Miranda Otto's 'looks' from *Doing Time for Patsy Cline*.

I knew it was going to be an above-average year when I discovered that our Year 10 home room teacher was Mr Foster. Mr (Dale) Foster was one of those rare legends of the Australian high-school experience, an art teacher with a beard and a rat's tail who looked a bit like he got lost en route to the siege at Glenrowan, and who probably wouldn't dob you in for making a bong in woodwork class or smoking behind the shelter shed.

> Balwyn thought of itself as such frightfully elevated company I don't
> think it even *had* a shelter shed
>> the closest I came to smoking in high school was dressing as
>> Withnail for a costume party and spending the entire night with
>> a rapidly decaying fag dangling soggily off my bottom lip
>>> when I got home I was convinced I had developed
>>> sudden-onset lip cancer

By that year, we were starting to find that certain teachers preferred to be addressed by their names rather than a droning 'Miiiisssss' or 'Sir', so after Mr Foster took the roll, a student raised a hand. 'Sir, what do we call you?' Mr Foster looked up from his clipboard: 'God.'

Aside from the presence of God in our home room, there were plenty of reasons Year 10 was tracking to be above average, among them the release of Red Earth's Azure perfume, a new season of *Recovery* and the premiere of the school musical. But most of all, there was the thing I had been waiting nearly a decade for: my final year of mandatory maths lessons. There have been a few formative moments in my life, but nothing compares with the momentousness of being able to yell 'SMOKE YOU, TEACH!!!!' at the entire concept of mathematics. Maths: bane of my life, proof of my stupidity, the thing that could ruin days, weeks, terms.

My inability to understand human social interaction might have caused me existential pain, but my inability to grasp even basic maths unsettled me at a cellular level. What does it matter if you can converse like Clive James if you can't even work out how much change you get from a $5 note when buying something that costs 95 cents? I was constantly being caught out by my subpar mathematical skills – baffled by simple calculations, confused by phone numbers, never able to remember if there were 60 cents in the hour or 100 minutes in the dollar – and nowhere was this more apparent than in maths class.

Recall, if you will, the fact that I was so bad at maths that my Year 8 teacher enquired, at parent–teacher interviews, if there had been a recent death in the family. Any day I had a maths class was cause for great dismay. I would lug my apparently twenty-seventh-hand copy of the textbook out of my locker (where it inevitably stayed most of the time, since attempting to do maths out of school hours was a certain recipe for a meltdown) and drag myself to the classroom; never late enough to get in trouble (the horror), but not a second earlier than necessary.

My struggles with maths have put paid to many dream careers, from medicine to air traffic control, but it is also a mundane, daily struggle. Being 'bad at maths' (Autistic) and also 'bad with money' (grew up poor) is a truly catastrophic combination for someone whose neurotype dictates they work as a freelancer. Over the years, I have scratched out a hard-won grasp of the times tables I once flat-out refused to engage with. I don't understand them so much as *know* them; I learned them the same way I learned the 'Gozer the Traveler' speech from *Ghostbusters*. A year shy of forty, I still count on my fingers. The near-meditative state I have to enter in order to finger-count without getting confused is, I imagine, similar to the state that neurotypical people refer to as 'mindfulness', just without the neutral-toned natural fibres and expensive herbal supplements.

Dyscalculia, or 'maths dyslexia', is a common comorbidity with Autism. Its behavioural signs may include finger counting and difficulty retrieving number-based facts from memory. A study conducted in 2018 by researchers at Queen's University Belfast's School of Psychology found that, of children identified as potentially dyscalculic, 81 per cent had another existing diagnosis (such as Autism, ADHD or dyslexia).

What's remarkable about my schooling is that not one teacher or coordinator thought to – or perhaps more accurately, had the information that would lead them to – look a little deeper at my situation. Here was a girl who was in multiple 'gifted' programs (art, writing, science), yet for whom maths class brought on panic attacks; who could express herself eloquently at the debating platform yet who could barely comprehend times tables. She could adopt an uncannily accurate French accent in language class but had no idea what she was saying. She had the lead role in the musical but had low muscle tone and was uncoordinated in physical education class

> to quote one highly supportive phys ed teacher at Balwyn during a
> speed session of step-ups against the wall of the basketball stadium,
> 'My grandmother is more coordinated than you, Clementine!'
>> shortly after that exclamation, I slipped and smashed my knee
>> against the step
>>> in Year 12, the sports captain asked why books were
>>> given for speech night academic prizes and I called him a
>>> 'dickhead philistine footballer'

and so the contradictions continued. I will state for the record that the gifted activities themselves were *absolutely fucking sick*: if you're going to go through high school as an outcast, you might as well do so with the ability to breed butterflies at the zoo or run around the Melbourne Museum as though you had the keys to the place. But for all the perks for gifted students, it fostered a paradox deep in my soul: why am I so good at this stuff, and so bad at other things?

Surely to any observant educator, my chaotic performance in maths must not have computed when considered alongside my constant shipping out to Future Leaders conferences and the like?

The Victorian Department of Education and Training provides a helpful checklist of attributes that gifted children might demonstrate, from 'knows a lot about topics' and 'changes their speech according to who they're talking to', to 'uses a lot of "how" and "why" questions' and 'can be unusually sad and emotional when things do not go to plan'.

The overview is quick to note that 'most gifted children will show several, but not necessarily all of these'. Well, this is awkward, because if that checklist was a test, I scored 100 per cent. I was constantly debating, with both my teachers and my peers; my determination to argue, in media class, that the image of a V8 bursting through a Big M billboard in an advertisement for the flavoured milk in fact represented male phallic primacy was met first with stunned silence, then with '... Well you're just obsessed with sex!' from Troy in the back row. As for 'unusually sad and emotional', that's an understatement.

Every single one of those dot points referred to me as a young person, and yet to look at them now through the prism of understanding, every single one of them could also describe the Autistic presentation that might once have been labelled Asperger syndrome. I sometimes wonder if many of my teachers were simply entertained by this seemingly eccentric mini adult – 'little professor' – who constantly refused to accept the syllabus at face value. How else to explain my Year 8 science teacher agreeing, with an amused chuckle, to my demand that I should be able to do my energy essay on psychokinetic energy instead of choosing between the assigned topics, kinetic or potential energy? It was a great essay, too; Mum borrowed a bunch of absolutely cooked 1970s books from the La Trobe library for me and I somehow managed to work in a deft explanation of parallel dimensions. For my troubles I received an A, so get fucked everybody!

It's hard to tease apart which of these qualities were due to my being (actually or deemed) gifted in some areas, and which were due to my Autism; it's doubly hard to assess which gifts were, in fact, Autistic behaviours. I have seen gifted Autistic children described as 'twice-exceptional'. Giftedness and Autism can often coexist, though the 'Autistic genius' stereotype persists, both in the 'idiot savant' model of the nonspeaking person with complex needs who can also create breathtaking artworks, or the 'high functioning' wizard of STEM fields. The latter is pervasive enough that many Autistic people slip through the cracks because they don't feel they have the spectacular gifts they've been led to believe are a side-effect of Autism; ergo, they must not be Autistic.

An editorial in *The Hollywood Reporter* for 2018 World Autism Awareness Day addressed the portrayal of Autism in *The Good Doctor*, writing that 'the Hollywood production of the "model neuro-minority" elevates some while excluding others on the spectrum [...] Hollywood depictions underscore the false belief that autistic people only have value if they have savant skills that can benefit non-autistic people, and offset their supposed societal burden'. The prevalence of these depictions – white, male, straight, brilliant – can also lead to underdiagnosis and delayed diagnosis in women and people of colour; 'if they can't see it, they can't be it' in its most disruptive form.

I think it's fair to say that most Autistic people are not 'the Good Doctor'.

Towards the end of Year 10 I began to suspect I wasn't truly 'brilliant' because I was shithouse at maths, and I also couldn't read sheet music; at the time I had recently read something about how there are only two forms of innate genius: mathematical and musical. My alleged gifted status felt like a high-level subterfuge that would surely soon be revealed as a terrible lie. Adding insult to injury was the very un-Australian notion of giftedness itself. You have never felt acrimony like the burning glare of fifteen to twenty children who, unlike you, have *not* just been called upon to leave a very boring class in order to attend a gifted program. Any desire I had to share, say, how cool it was to visit Melbourne Zoo's butterfly breeding centre with my schoolmates was snuffed out by a 'You reckon you're good' that echoed through eternity. I began to wonder just who this gifted label was meant to benefit. Did the school dine out on it with stakeholders? Would universities care? Employers?

At one gifted excursion, to the Melbourne Museum (where we learned essential life skills such as 'taking a rubbing from a replica

Rosetta Stone'), I saw a familiar face across the mezzanine of the old Russell Street building: my friend Ivy from Elwood. She was as cool as ever, accessorising her school pinafore – a recent introduction – with combat boots and a beret, and filled me in on everything I was missing at Elwood (a renovated art department! A musical every year!). Once again I felt a pang of recognition, and the bittersweet knowledge that somewhere out there was a school full of cool poor kids and weirdos just like me. At Elwood, being labelled as gifted meant getting to do a mixed-peer life writing workshop with Arnold Zable. At Balwyn, it was a mixed blessing: it brought the relief of out-of-school enrichment, followed by the searing resentment of my peers.

There is a growing movement against the notion of labelling children as gifted, led in tandem by those who suffered under the weight of the label as kids and psychologists who realise the implications of the burden. Giftedness (the concept, not the natural act) instils in a child a sense of supernatural talent that is difficult for them to claim ownership of; they are 'just' good at their dictated area of giftedness. This lack of ownership leads to broken connections between effort and outcome. As Dr Jim Taylor, a specialist in the psychology of sport and parenting, has put it, 'If gifted children attribute their successes to their ability, when they fail – which they inevitably will sooner or later – they must attribute their failures to their lack of ability (they must be stupid or untalented) and, though children can acquire more skills, they cannot gain ability beyond what they were born with.'

So it was, ever thus, for me and maths (and its cousins, chemistry and physics): I was 'just not good at it'. Cruel teachers whose idea of motivation was to chastise me for my idiocy did little to improve this mindset. No matter how hard I concentrated, no matter how many times I read and re-read my battered maths textbook, it was gibberish. (If I could insert an animated GIF in a book, I would add the 'maths lady' GIF here. Look it up, then come back.)

In Year 10, I had a teacher whose approach – perhaps due to his own comical enthusiasm for maths – was to encourage even those of us who were struggling; I was rewarded with my highest ever maths grades (a C+ and a B, rather than Es and Fs). It is bittersweet to think what might have been different had I received this type of guidance earlier in my schooling.

I began to identify profoundly with the malfunctioning robots of popular culture, C-3PO and R2-D2 from *Star Wars* in particular. In 3PO, I saw my frustration and existential agony ('We seem to be made to suffer, it's our lot in life'); the golden droid is never far from a melt-down, constantly baffled by the irrational behaviours of his human companions and their unwillingness to address the odds of success. In R2, I saw my enthusiasm and my loyalty, and my raw nerves of emotion ('[sad beep]').

It would be dangerous to assume that identifying with robots is due to being 'robotic' myself. In truth, I struggle with the numerous studies where robots are used to teach Autistic kids social skills, since such studies live and die on the implicit assumption that Autistic children are, in a way, robots themselves. Art therapies and assistance animals have been proven to be just as, if not more, effective than robot-assisted therapies – even old-fashioned hand puppets are – but in a click-driven age, a story about Autistic kids learning about emotions from a sock puppet is far less racy than 'Autistic kid makes friends with Siri'.

If there's one overwhelming reason I have found myself drawn to robot characters, it's that storylines concerning robots (and cyborgs and androids and replicants) so often concern their attempting, not always successfully, to learn the ways of the human world. I can watch a heart-wrenching family drama and be largely unmoved while those around me weep, but from *Short Circuit*'s Johnny 5 to *A.I.*'s David on his quest to become 'a real boy', any storyline about a robot trying to become a person will leave me collapsed and sobbing in the aisles.

DEAR DOLLY DOCTOR ...

There are three things about Year 10 that I remember vividly: feeling disappointed that the 'cute girl' in Hanson was a boy, and being delighted that the 'cute guy' in Jebediah was a girl. Despite all this, at the time, I hadn't really thought deeply about my sexuality. I don't think I had thought particularly deeply about sexuality in general, for that matter, unless we consider the sole surviving page of my Year 10 media workbook on media tropes, pasted with clippings of noted lesbians, entitled '5. LESBIAN'. There is just a small segment of my notes remaining:

> since k.d. lang and Ellen DeGeneres came out there has been a clamour in the media for stories about how cool it is to be gay. The media is always stressing how great lesbianism is, and unfortunately, they often become quite patronising along the way. On TV & in film,

(We will never know what came next!)

That same year, Prime Minister John Howard cancelled a federal youth suicide campaign initiated by the Keating government, 'Here For Life', which was aimed at teenagers who were 'gay, lesbian, bisexual or simply attracted to people of the same sex'. He would later tell A Current Affair that he'd be 'disappointed' if one of his kids turned out to be gay. It was, in other words, despite the presence of '5. LESBIANS' in the media, a confusing time to have any non-heteronormative thoughts about your own sexuality.

It wasn't that our family home was unwelcoming to the notion of queerness – quite the opposite. I had grown up surrounded by a diverse range of people, including Mum and Dad's old friend Adam, who used to dress in a Sgt. Pepper's costume and paint naked murals of himself and his beautiful trans girlfriend in a utopian garden ('They're nice pictures, Adam,' was apparently my response, aged seven, to one particularly hair-raising slide night of his BDSM-themed artworks). We watched loads of camp British comedy, and were possibly the only family in Ivanhoe East whose vernacular included Polari words, the cant slang used as a secret code by British LGBTQ+ people prior to legalisation. But the twin perils of being surrounded by heteronormativity and aspiring to neurotypicality (even if I didn't intellectually understand it in such terms) dictated to me that, even though I was clearly experiencing thoughts and feelings to the contrary, it was time to start looking for a boyfriend.

One of the many misconceptions about Autism is the idea that all Autistic people are asexual, or perhaps more correctly, desexualised. The limited media representations of Autistic sexuality have been, until quite recently, heteronormative, and it's true that there are many Autistic people who are magnificently, confidently heterosexual; who dream of a white wedding and a nice house with a picket fence and 2.5 children. The broader reality, however, is that, like all people, there is a vast spectrum of sexuality among Autistic people. In fact, various studies have recognised a greater diversity of sexual orientations among Autistic people[35] than their neurotypical peers, and particularly among Autistic females. Anecdotally, nearly every Autistic person I know has some aspect of non-heterosexual sexuality. It would be some time, however, before I truly understood that about myself.

In the winter holidays of 1997, we stayed at the Mt Buffalo Chalet, in the cheap rooms at the end of a long hallway that stretched so far from the Chalet proper that we started referring to it as 'steerage class'. The Chalet had a drawing room, which featured a bookshelf dotted with the usual ragtag bunch of old paperbacks and musty coffee table books that tend to populate B&Bs. Among these was a copy of the second edition of Derek Llewellyn-Jones' *Everywoman: A Gynaecological Guide for Life*, shoved somewhere between the Tom Keneally books and filled-in crossword collections. It had a *very* 'groovy' cover design and had been published in 1978, so as I was both fascinated by the 1970s *and* comically naive as to all matters sexual, I grabbed it from the shelf.

Now, despite taking to my gynaecological and sexual education with the enthusiasm of an anthropologist, I knew enough of human niceties to understand that this was a bit embarrassing, so I didn't dare take the book back to my room where it might be discovered by a family member. Instead, I would read as fast as I could, whipping through the pages at speed, and then shove it back in the bookshelf, behind a stack of outdated cookbooks that were certain never to be removed, ready for me to later resume my studies.

Despite this newfound understanding of Masters and Johnson's four phases of women's sexual response, I was unfortunately also hopelessly awkward. I had gathered (from observing my peers, and the bulk of teen-focused TV programming) that, at fifteen, it was time for me to start Talking To Boys, but I had no idea how.

To say I wasn't particularly good at socialising, either with The Opposite Sex or in general, would be an understatement. My solution to feeling baffled, anxious or confused in social situations was to over-compensate: I became one of *those* people at the party (and later, the dinner party), treating the entire night as a performance. Sometimes, this was literal: I was once dismissed from a Year 10 birthday party for performing the TAC road safety ads – every character, every line – in a symphony of echolalia that was dismissed as 'attention seeking' by the attendant parents. Other times, it was a performance of confidence:

adopting the air of a witty dinner party raconteur, like my parents, was a handy way to disguise my fear. Couple that with a post-'gifted program' reluctance to ever admit I didn't know something, and it was a heady cocktail.

Why, you ask, had I not been given the 411 on human teenage romance by the glossy magazines of my youth? Well, there are certain things – moments, feelings, dilemmas – that are so hyper-specific to the experience of growing up poor they must border on incomprehensible to those whose adolescence was flush with cash. Here's one of mine: as a teen, I would borrow *Dolly* and *Seventeen* magazines from the library, a habit I didn't start until I was well into Year 10 (when most of my female peers had already abandoned *Dolly* for *Cleo* and *Cosmo*).

I'd borrow those teen magazines and occasionally come upon the holy grail of an unopened 'sealed section'. These supplements, of ten or so pages, typically contained racy information about sex – how to put a condom on a banana! – or less racy but potentially embarrassing lessons about vaginas – they all look different! Whether it was sexy or educational, the sealed section presented a unique dilemma to the library card–carrying teen. Not wanting to rob the next borrower of the excitement of ripping open those closed pages, I'd leave it intact, and so would the next considerate borrower, and the next borrower, until months had passed and none of us had any idea what wonders the 'Sex Extra!' held.

Imagine, I would think, having the cash to just tear open any sealed section you damn well wanted. Then, in the same breath, I would chastise myself for engaging in such unbridled capitalist thinking. The same was true for the perfume samples held within the pages of these magazines. Those strips of scented cardboard remained unrubbed by local wrists, lending the library's periodicals the heady scent of Impulse Liberté body spray and So? perfume – olfactory memories I chase to this day, like a boomer trying to remember Woodstock.

These borrowed magazines were a site of intense emotion. Beyond the universal 'teen girl' experience of reading them, and discovering which hunks were deemed most 'babelicious' by the *Dolly* editorial staff circa 1997, they were also laced with a feeling I would later come to acknowledge as shame. I read these magazines in the safety of either the library or my own bedroom because I imagined having a months-old barcoded *Dolly* slip out of my backpack would be akin to the time I wore no-name zebra-print jeans to free-dress day and Liza sneered at me to 'go back to the zoo'. I retaliated in the impotent manner of many powerless people throughout history, by drawing devil horns on her photo in the yearbook.

Young people may lack the vocabulary to discuss class, but they are keenly aware of it – just re-watch *Pretty in Pink*, or return to the skin-crawling relatability of ABC's sorely missed *Heartbreak High*. By the time I owned the 'white babydoll T-shirt and black shoestring strap dress' combo we'd all read about in *Dolly*, it was months after the trend had passed. I was so proud of my outfit – a Christmas gift – but knew I was hopelessly out of date.

What I *did* learn from those borrowed teen magazines was altogether more Socratic: the wisdom that comes from knowing that you know nothing. I would *without fail* pick the multiple-choice answers in *Dolly*'s various quizzes that revealed me as utterly clueless. There is nothing quite like confidently choosing, at the age of seventeen, 'C) It's when a woman blows gently on a man's penis' only to discover that is *not* the definition of a 'blow job' to make you feel the world crumbling around you.

For all of Dolly Doctor's care and kindness, teen magazines were too full of euphemisms and social structures I had no idea about. *Cosmo* and *Cleo* were even worse; they appeared to have been written by a Dadaist who encouraged the willing participant to, say, put a bag of coins in the freezer and then unload them over your vulva, or to scrape a fork along your boyfriend's penis. Surely, I reasoned, this is not actual human sexuality, but instead some sort of satire? *Everywoman*, on the other hand, was just the sort of dry, scientific text for me: no poetry, no social cues, just straight up physiological information about what happens and when. I didn't notice at the time, but perhaps I was also absorbing some of its *very* 'seventies' opinions, among them 'some 25% of lesbians have considerable emotional problems'.

It was around this time that I started focusing intently on having a flat stomach. I don't think, despite what the popular assumption might be, this was *Dolly*'s fault; it just emerged, ephemeral, as a goal in life: if I have a flat tummy, I will be attractive. The fact that I barely knew how to style my own hair and regularly forgot to apply deodorant was, apparently, immaterial in this understanding: a flat tummy would solve all my problems! It was the beginning of a long, disordered approach to exercise and dieting.

Links between Autism and eating disorders, particularly anorexia nervosa, have been recognised since the mid-1980s. The cognitive rigidity of Autism can mean Autistic people are especially at risk of eating disorders and avoidant or restrictive food-intake disorder. One investigation into restrictive eating disorders in Autistic women[36] revealed a wide variety of triggers, from sensory issues to difficulties with emotion, that exacerbated disordered eating and exercise behaviours.

Autistic blogger Carrie Beckwith-Fellows, who was diagnosed at thirty, has discussed the role Autism has played in her relationship to her body, and associated eating disorders. 'For me, it is a way to cope with a world that scares me,' she wrote in an essay for the National Eating Disorders Association. 'Autistic people can become fixated on certain facts, numbers, and patterns. I am fixated on a specific weight and every day begins either happy because I am below it, or miserable and full of anxiety because I am over it. Black-and-white thinking makes food good or bad and dress sizes acceptable or not acceptable.'

Searching for a boyfriend meant constantly worrying if I was cute or sexy, in a way that had never occurred to me before. And this flat-stomach obsession manifested itself as surreptitiously doing lots of sit-ups in my room. Eventually, the flat-stomach goal led to disordered eating, if not an outright (but undiagnosed) eating disorder, though that wouldn't really take hold until my twenties. As a fifteen-year-old, I was just busy doing (not very good) sit-ups and wondering why I didn't suddenly have washboard abs like Cameron Diaz.

During the school musical, I'd made friends with Claire, one of those incredibly cool and carefree 1990s girls who *definitely* had a flat stomach. She wore chokers and dark brown lipstick and her long black hair was never far from a packet of LiveColour. She was one of Miss Adelaide's dancers in the school musical, so we spent more time together than we ever had in class. Words cannot describe how proud I felt that Claire was my friend – Claire, the sexy dancing girl who all the boys were in love with. Even more indescribable was my pride at knowing that Claire also lived just a few blocks away from me; somehow, the idea that someone as cool as Claire was living in the same postcode made all the times local gremlins belted eggs at our house and yelled out 'WITCHES!' and/or 'HIPPIES!' worth the agony.

On 27 November 1997, I switched on Seven to watch Michael Hutchence's funeral. It was a sunny day in Sydney, but – appropriately, to my teenaged mind – it was raining in East Ivanhoe. A few minutes into Garry Wilkinson and Anne Fulwood's coverage, I heard a knock at the door. Claire had wandered over to my house, and we wordlessly watched the funeral together.

Looking back, it's hard not to see my friendship with Claire as being tinged with a crush. I admired her confidence and sass, sure, but was there also a part of me that wanted to be *with* her, not just around her?

It's hard to say, because whatever nascent feelings were starting to bubble up inside me, they were soon muffled by reality: at the end of

Year 10, I 'got' a boyfriend. His name was Geoffrey, and he was the perfect nonthreatening boyfriend for me: he looked a bit like George Harrison, was pretty weird himself, and we communicated – initially, at least – almost entirely in written notes. Like me, he was also a fan of obscure British comedy shows, and both our sets of parents were music-mad eccentrics. Our relationship lasted for all of Year 11 and mostly involved trips to the zoo and occasional late nights of staying up to watch *rage*, punctuated by make-out sessions.

Most striking to me was the facade of normalcy 'having a boyfriend' afforded me. That facade was multifaceted, but the most important part was that it made me look like, perhaps, I wasn't such a weirdo after all; I was, objectively, loveable.

that meant, in the eyes of others, we might even be *having sex*
of course, we weren't; he once got 'a stiffy', in terrible op-shop
cream linen pants, and I nearly died of fright
whatever Dr Derek Llewellyn-Jones had written about
stiffies, I had completely ignored

Having a boyfriend also meant having someone else to socialise alongside; I no longer had to operate as a sort of satellite person, floating from group to group. And, crucially, it meant that I had achieved my life's purpose: I had reached the end of my own romantic comedy. A few years ago, I mentioned some strongly held belief I had about relationships to a friend who is also Autistic. I vividly remember her response: 'But is that something you *know* from experience, or is it something you learned by watching romantic comedy movies in order to become a human being?'

When Geoffrey and I first started Going Out, I was beset by anxiety and nausea. Mum took me to the local GP, who upon conducting a thorough examination, suggested with great kindness that I might be 'love sick'. It's a treasured memory, but looking back now, I wonder if it was the first experience of what I would come to understand as

the panic I would inevitably feel upon the beginning of any relationship with a guy – 'Oh no, not another one' – the alarm that would
bubble up as I prepared to delay my true feelings for another few
weeks or months.

It's hard to know, other than to say that this relationship set me on
a path that I would not stray from for another two decades.

BUCK'S FIZZ

I had my first alcoholic drink in March 2000.

Up until that point, my lack of interest in socialising with those in my peer group had been a growing concern to my parents. In a way, I can see where they were coming from. What sort of teenager *doesn't* want to sit around a pebble-glass table in a freezing backyard in Balwyn and sink a few Two Dogs while debating the merits of Korn's *Follow the Leader*? Like many aspects of teenage behaviour I didn't understand, drinking was a mystery to me: not only was it dangerous (see: TAC ads), but it was also *disgusting*; no amount of artificial sweeteners and day-glo food colouring could disguise the fact that all the beloved alcopops of the 1990s tasted, to me, like actual vomit with a light misting of sugar. And given that by the age of sixteen or so I was so terrified of vomiting that I had, in effect, trained my body not to do it, why would I actively drink something that reminded me of spew?!

There is increasing evidence that many undiagnosed Autistic people engage in harmful alcohol use. They may drink to mask their symptoms, or to self-medicate due to the depression and anxiety that can come with masking and feeling socially isolated.

Matthew Tinsley, the Autistic co-author of the book *Asperger Syndrome and Alcohol*, resorted to 'extremely heavy' use of alcohol to deal with his anxiety. 'I also was socially awkward and discovered alcohol turned me into a much more relaxed person,' he wrote in 2016. 'Of course, I was unaware of my autism at the time and it's only in retrospect that I can understand why it worked so well.' Tinsley's experience is not uncommon. One large population-based Swedish study of Autistic people, the first of its kind, found that they were at a vastly increased risk of addiction to alcohol and other drugs.[37]

My reluctance to socialise had reached enough of a crisis point by VCE that my parents had begun to bargain with me: if I went, for example, to Emma's eighteenth birthday party, I could get a Happy Meal on the way home. Just in case you're preparing to undertake a retrospective child endangerment investigation, my parents weren't on at me to *drink*, but there was an assumption that it would probably be normal, maybe even healthy, if I were to at least socialise with my peers. In doing so, the expectation was that I might have one [1] single cup of the Passion Pop punch that typified the long run of eighteenth birthday celebrations that began in late 1998 and stretched well into the new millennium.

Tales of amusing alcoholic misadventure were part of the family discourse. Mum spoke of a friend whose parents, in a masterstroke of reverse psychology, allowed him to demolish the liquor cabinet on the night of his eighteenth while they went to a dinner party; he woke up feeling crook the next day and swore never to drink again. And we all knew the story of Dad's ill-fated sixteenth birthday party at his family home. In his words: 'I got hopelessly drunk, and one of my last memories before passing out in the front garden, is of a Number 42 tram pulling up at the stop outside and ALL the passengers getting off and coming in through the front gate! My friend St John had casually dropped the fact at, of all places, Tattersalls Hotel in Russell Street, that there was to be a "rage" happening at 272 Cotham Road, Kew. As I lay semiconscious in the front garden, our fine Georgian dining table had been danced on by dozens of revellers, leaving it decidedly V-shaped, and Dad's basement wine cellar had been ransacked, which accounted for pools of red vomit all around the garden. I awoke in horror at dawn. The revellers had by then gone home but for one good friend who was a dab hand at carpentry and thankfully with Tim's help, I managed to repair the table before my parents got home.'

My habit of taking things 100 per cent at face value meant that I had (accidentally) had the fear of god put into me: parties = drinking = complete catastrophe! Of course I had my own observations of that nature, such as one birthday girl being carried out the back door of her family's cream-brick Art Deco manse on a stretcher due to alcohol poisoning while the cover band played the assorted hits of Rage Against the Machine and Grinspoon on the front lawn.

Though I had spent the past five years at Balwyn essentially on the outer, Year 12 was an exercise in disappearing into the background, socially. Geoffrey and I had broken up (poetically, at his end-of-childhood-themed seventeenth birthday party at McDonald's) and our group splintered. Most lunchtimes I worked on my pet project, a screenplay adaptation of Shakespeare's *King Lear*.

With handy access to Dad's Xerox machine, I amused myself by creating Barbara Kruger-esque posters that I'd Blu-Tak around the common room and hallways. At one stage I made posters railing against the fact that the 40 Hour Famine offered motivational trinkets (I believe my slogan was 'KIDS IN REAL FAMINES DON'T GET PRIZES FOR STARVING', which went down about as well as you'd expect). As the posters became increasingly obscure and more likely to be torn down, I moved them to the inside of my locker door. I don't think anybody else ever noticed my one-girl public art installation. Fiona, whose locker was under mine, was always off doing drugs in the toilets, and the only time anyone else came within spitting distance of my locker door was when someone poured fish sauce through the vents and all over my books.

As Year 12 ground on, I found myself more alone. At the time, I thought myself incredibly cool when I spent nearly every lunchtime floating around the art teachers' staff room, occasionally cracking jokes with Mr 'God' Foster, although in retrospect that scenario is exactly as poignant as I'm sure it looks on the page. But as I ate my sandwiches near the big window by the door, gazing out on students socialising in the quadrangle, I thought of myself as frightfully elevated company: not for me the fripperies of a teenaged social whirl, I have *adult* friends, adult friends who are absolutely not being paid to provide me a duty of care! Sometimes I thought about what might have turned out differently had I been able to stay at Elwood, where odd kids flourished.

I still 'officially' had my weirdo mates, but even they were starting to drift away towards the fruits of young adulthood. Geoffrey started dating Kathryn, the mysterious girl from the country whose legs were *always* hairless and whose skin was tanned to a honey colour like a *Dolly* model. Robert dropped out of school to become an apprentice and spend all his money on guitars. Nick ran over a dog the first day he went out on his L plates and was never the same again. I developed a rather Georgian friendship – largely based on scholarship and rhetoric – with Megan, who would sit with me in the Year 12 common room and pore over the Daimaru catalogues. 'I can't wait to be a housewife', she'd tell me conspiratorially, like she wasn't on track to becoming dux of school

> she *did* become dux
> > I don't know if she became a housewife, though
> > > *por que no los dos?*

Through it all, Oliver was the only constant fixture. Most of my memories of our time spent hanging out together involve him marching up the hill to his parents' house, punctuating his chain-smoking with occasional drags on his ventolin inhaler. We'd spend most of our time there playing *Mortal Kombat* or listening to Me First and the Gimme Gimmes while his giant Lagwagon poster stared down at us, dreaming of the day that Blink-182 might tour Australia. (In a poetic twist of fate, we *did* get tickets for their November 2000 show at Rod Laver Arena, which was summarily cancelled. Well, I guess this is growing up.)

Crucially, Oliver, like me, was not interested in drinking; if we'd known what Straight Edge culture was, what with its punk music and political stance against alcohol, drugs and stimulants, we probably would've identified with it (well, except for Oliver's chain-smoking). Both of us were too poor and uncool to attend the 1999 winter trip to Lorne that quickly passed into legend among the student cohort. Nobody really knew *what* happened in Lorne, other than the fact that everyone came back yelling the lyrics from Marcy Playground's 'Sex and Candy' as some sort of uproarious in-joke, so naturally we assumed that it had been an absolute frenzy of sex and maybe even *drugs*.

Towards the end of my final term of school, I was engaged to create the photo montage that would conclude our graduation evening at Ivanhoe Town Hall. This was probably because earlier that year I'd made the only Year 12 Media film (a hyper-violent fantasia on what I imagined share house living to be) that required an R rating at the annual screening; amusing, given at the time I was still staunchly refusing to watch anything rated 18+ because, obviously, I was not yet eighteen myself. Perhaps fellow classmates were impressed enough by my 18+ status that they gave me the gig.

For two weeks' worth of lunchtimes I toiled away in the tiny Media Studies 'studio' (actually a broom closet jammed with ancient VHS gear). Students gave me envelopes full of photographs from parties, afterparties and holidays, and I dutifully scanned them and/or filmed them with the video camera, then assembled them with copious Ken Burns zooms to the accompaniment of Green Day's 'Time Of Your Life'.

I wore my Studio Art assessment project – a gown I'd designed to look like a Pre-Raphaelite painting, or words to that effect – to graduation, with Mum's vintage *Desperately Seeking Susan*–style pink bustier underneath it. Unfortunately, in every photo taken on the night, the bustier's pink scalloping looked, peeking up from the neckline of my dress, like giant, rouged comedy nipples. It was a fitting end to high school.

By the time the Year 12 exams were grinding to a close, I was so exhausted and relieved to have finally escaped from the hell of compulsory schooling that I returned home, threw my backpack in the corner of my room, and didn't touch it until I remembered, three months later, that it had contained a chicken sandwich.

It was a blissful summer, albeit one marked by the spectre of the Y2K bug. We decamped as a family to Lorne (eat it, former classmates, now who's cool?) to spend New Year's with Dad's best mate Chris, his partner Wendy and Chris' cool daughter Sophia, who had flown in from Sweden. On 31 December we went, en masse, to The Falls (me in my hand-painted Beastie Boys T-shirt), then returned to the foreshore for the fireworks. It was a new millennium at last and I was free.

So, that alcoholic drink. On 17 March 2000, Mum had to drop an essay at uni, so I accompanied her to Parkville. Once we'd visited the submissions slot, we walked out into the quad, where a St Patrick's Day event (read: mass irresponsible serving of alcohol) was in full swing. Now, cast your mind back to the Port Melbourne of my youth: I was well aware that St Patrick's Day was when great rivers of green vomit flowed in the gutters, so I was in no hurry to get among it. But Mum spotted a colleague, and thought it would be fun to have a beer together! I had no choice but to acquiesce. As we sat down, her with a Guinness, me with my pot of dyed-green beer (with a straw), I hissed, 'Mum, I'm only seventeen and a half; we're going to get *arrested*.'

Of course, we didn't, and my *second* – and third, fourth and fifth – alcoholic drinks were consumed on one night in August 2000: my first all-nighter. My friend Monica asked me if I wanted to come for a 'night out', which turned out to be a pub crawl of all of North Fitzroy's most infamous spots, culminating, most egregiously, in a visit to the Park View, aka the Park Spew. Though I begged, at 3 am, to borrow her keys and go to her share house to secure some desperately needed sleep before the trains started at 6 am, I had discovered something about alcohol: drink enough of it, and you might convince others, and by extension yourself, that you're just like everybody else.

SINGLED OUT

It's a new year, a new century, a new *millennium*, and there is only one thing standing in the way of my ascent to rock superstardom: my complete inability to publicly play a single note without crumbling into a panic attack.

This is immaterial, of course, as at that point I had already spent most of the summer planning my reinvention from humble school swot to infamous goddess of the stage. Plenty of rock superstars suffer from stage fright. And what's more, if I'd learned anything from spending the past few years listening to the entire history of popular song rather than socialising, it was that a lack of discernible confidence on stage (much less talent) was no barrier to becoming an icon of 'the scene' – and I was willing to put in the hard yards.

Having gradually built up the confidence to venture out into the world by myself, each week I dutifully travelled to Elizabeth Street to pick up my air-freight copies of *Q*, *Mojo* and the *NME* from McGills newsagency, then turned around and went straight home again to pore over every word. I borrowed CDs from the library, racking up reams of fines for overdue Eels or Harry Nilsson or Hole albums, eagerly awaiting the start of the academic year when I could start blowing my Austudy on second-hand CDs from Burke Road Dixons instead. Every weekend I would record *rage*, then hook our cassette player up to the

169

VHS player and dub mixtapes of whatever took my fancy, which I would listen to on my rapidly decomposing Walkman.

MELBOURNE MUSIC STORES CIRCA 2000, RANKED IN DESCENDING ORDER OF HOW LIKELY THEY WERE TO INDUCE A PANIC ATTACK

1. Missing Link (absolutely terrifying, abandon all hope, ye who enter here)
2. Au Go Go (I remember very little about this place, which can only suggest that the experience of entering it was an experience of great stress)
3. Gaslight (I will gladly pay their inflated prices if only to avoid the judgement of the Au Go Go staff)
4. Burke Road JB HiFi (there is one very angry man who works here, but the $2 bargain singles bin is worth the fear)
5. Burke Road Dixons (depending on the day, very friendly staff; I will one day make out with one of them after a show at the Hi-Fi Bar shortly before he falls bum-first into a rubbish bin; two days later I get worms)
6. Polyester Books (okay, not strictly a record store, but who could feel anything *but* comfortable in this wonderland of 'totally fucked up shit'? Where, I should note, my own parents will buy me a VHS bootleg of the Rolling Stones *Cocksucker Blues* for my twentieth birthday)
7. Voyager Home Entertainment (level of comfort self-evident in the business name, surely)

Music was both special interest and stim, the alpha and omega, an all-consuming passion that left precious little brain space for anything else. This quickly proved to be an issue when I began studying a BA in Fashion Design at RMIT, the course that I had been accepted into at the end of Year 12.

With the encouragement of our school careers counsellor, I had applied for fashion design, due to my love of sketching paper fashion dolls and cutting Versace ads out of magazines. Alas, I had not considered the possibility that a fashion degree might include activities other than becoming the next Gianni Versace. There was also the fact of my being hopelessly and utterly unfashionable. Not in the way we might now describe as 'normcore', but just actually terrible at dressing myself. (In the Year 12 yearbook I was dubbed 'Most Outrageous Wardrobe', which seems like a nice way of saying 'she once wore an entire ensemble – bell bottoms, T-shirt, cardigan – of mismatched vintage lurex crochet to free-dress day'.)

Personal hygiene was still something of a mystery to me, as was hairstyling, and while I enjoyed the fantasy of *designing* Bob Mackie-esque haute couture gowns, I had absolutely no idea how to put an outfit together for myself. This was partly due to the fact that most turn-of-the-century fashion – with its handkerchief-hemmed boob tubes and retro-futurist printed spandex – was a nightmare to the Autistic body: sweaty, too-tight, weird fabric textures.

Fashion trends had not yet swung back again to make my wardrobe full of tatty sixties and seventies offerings from the subterranean Ivanhoe church op-shop cool (fashion's loss; I think we can all agree that a disintegrating fluorescent purple Bri-Nylon body shirt with weblike holes under the arms is, in fact, the height of style). My sole engagement with fashion was to buy very cheap Miss Shop tops and hand paint my favourite bands' logos on them, because I couldn't afford actual merch. So, showing up on the first day of a three-year fashion degree in ugly jeans that I hadn't washed since the Big Day Out, topped off with a boat-necked three-quarter-sleeve tee painted with the Nine Inch Nails logo, was a little like doing a giant poo on the floor at a perfume convention. I owned a leopard-print velour bucket hat, for Christ's sake.

It became clear very quickly that the fashion school life I had dreamed of in escaping the grind of Year 12 was just that, a dream. In reality, the Fashion Design BA was not so much non-stop sketching of elegant fripperies as it was ten pages of 'development' just to design a T-shirt. 'Development', as my desire to skip rehearsals, lessons and homework on the path to glory should by now have demonstrated, was not a natural state for me. In even worse news, pattern design was eerily similar to my high school bête noir, maths, and the Computer Assisted Design (CAD) module was so baffling they might as well have asked me to bring QF94 in from Tullamarine air traffic control in high winds. It was the first time since maths that I had felt that sting of assumed stupidity: why could everyone else seemingly take to CAD like they were firing off text messages when the very thought of the class sent me into racking shivers?

Happily, though the course content was alienating (and I had the exponentially decaying grades to match), the cohort was everything I'd thought university life would be: a bunch of older, *much* cooler people who seemed to find the presence of a very awkward seventeen-year-old entertaining. And, even better, they were all really into music, from Geoffrey, the breakdancing streetwear designer, to Andrea, who looked like the lost member of B(if)tek. A captive audience at last!

anybody want to talk about that music video that played on *rage* at 2.37 am on Saturday?

has anyone heard the Damon Albarn remix of Cornelius' 'Star Fruits Surf Rider'?

can anyone explain how to insert an invisible zip? I wasn't listening

I don't think I have ever felt cooler than when all of my older, groovier friends from fashion came to my eighteenth birthday party. The theme was 'fashion through the ages'; ever the stage manager, I assigned eras to each individual invitee, nabbing Regency for myself. In a stroke of thriftiness that Jane Austen herself would have been proud of, I found my (electric magenta; not very Regency, but who can truly say?) gown at Miss Shop, recycled my gloves from the debutante ball, and wore a set of clip-in ringlets from my beloved $2 Shop at

Melbourne Central Station. Was my choice to sing vocals on Reef's 'Place Your Hands' with Geoff's band (i.e. the entertainment) while dressed in Regency fashion incredibly cool, or the complete opposite? You be the judge, but I received a Discman as my 'big present' (RIP the old MS Readathon Walkman, 1989–2000), opening up a whole new world of antisocial music consumption before my eyes.

As the year wore on, my attention drifted from fashion design. Somehow I managed to convince Oliver, whose interest in bass was about as passing as my ability to do my guitar scales, to start a band with me. We called ourselves Rimbaud, after the poet, because I was pretentious, but also liked that it sounded a bit like Rambo; I loved a double entendre. I didn't realise any implied second meaning was expected to be risqué, not to imply action heroism. We had no songs, no instruments, and Oliver thought Shihad sucked where I reckoned they were definitely the most exciting band on earth. Still, we were a band, and that was all that mattered: as though by simply speaking those words aloud we could somehow will it into being.

So certain was I of this reality that during the mid-semester break, I helpfully interviewed myself, in case, perhaps anticipating the eventual death of print, any music publications needed to feature me but were short on staff. Oddly, though my mind replays most of the embarrassing or shameful things that have happened to me on a daily basis, I have no memory of having written this 'interview', and yet here it is in front of me and now, also, in front of you:

Clementine hails from Melbourne, Australia. She attended four different schools, all of which left lasting impressions on her. She began her musical training at age seven, learning piano formally for five years, although she is now self-taught and plays mainly by ear. She learnt guitar for five years from age twelve, continuing to be self-taught after her guitar teacher moved interstate. 'Learning guitar was a turning point for me. I had the honour of being taught by Alain Valodze, who had a great relaxed style and was an exceptional guitarist (I also used to 'forget' my guitar so that I'd be able to use his beautiful old Les Paul) and the lessons were more about the experience of playing than notching up some mysterious grade or technical rating, which I think was very important.'

For about a year in 1997, Clem played bass (again self-taught) with her friends Robert De Groot, Darren Angelo and Geoff Dickens, usually doing a mix of Smashing Pumpkins, Led Zeppelin and Status Quo 'in Darren's living room'. When she got an electric guitar, her duties were 'playing one note, an A I think, in a Blur song. Other than that, I did some impressive vogueing. I found my new guitar a little formidable for a while, and I think everyone else picked up on that.' Eventually, there were fewer rehearsals, and finally none.

In early 2000, Clem went along to a rehearsal with the guys, now joined by Nick Taylor, Robby Haddad and Andrew Mogford, which was in preparation for Robert's eighteenth birthday party. 'When none of the guys could or wanted to sing "Enter Sandman", I stepped up to the mike. Anyway, I did it, and I think the guys felt a mixture of terrified and impressed. So anyway, I did that, and the Romantics' "What I Like About You" with them at the party, which in turn led to more gigs.'

Unfortunately, tensions built during the year, and Clem left in late July, though not entirely of her own will. The rest of the guys are now called Beyond Egg. Clem took a week-long holiday to South Australia just before she left the band, and focused on writing some original material, ending up with about twenty songs, 'of which I chose eight to refine, and also wrote a few more later'. There are now around twenty songs which are presently being refined for recording. They will hopefully be recorded soon, 'even if it's just me and a guitar, or even just me. I'm willing to see where it takes me'.

It's bittersweet (once the embarrassment subsides) to read this 'interview' now. While at the time I thought it was an incredibly sophisticated bit of music journalism, what I now see is a simulacra of confidence, cobbled together from the sort of journalism-isms I'd absorbed from the various magazines I didn't so much read as *consume*. You know that old urban myth about Tom Scholz from Boston having programmed a computer with all the greatest guitar riffs of all time, and the computer spitting out 'More Than A Feeling'? That was me teaching myself how to talk about music: endless rereads of *20 Years of Rolling Stone: What a Long, Strange Trip It's Been*, constantly listening to my tapes of *rage* guest programs, beginning to position myself as worthy of interviewing.

The agony of not quite being able to behave in the way a human being is expected to is a very unique pain. The knowledge that you are constantly on the verge of saying the wrong thing, exposing yourself as frightened and confused about social niceties *you have no access to*, is exhausting. Have you ever had one of those dreams where, say, it's the present day, but you've for some reason been cast in the school play, only due to your busy adult life you have no time to attend rehearsals or even read the script until opening night, and you have to ride a bike (which you can't, in fact, do) down Beaconsfield Parade with your costume stuffed into the basket and hope you can just wing it? It's a bit like that. Gobbling up interviews with musicians – people who are paid to Be Themselves – was an exercise in learning how to move through the world with maximum confidence and verve.

Despite having never written a song, had a rehearsal, nor touched our instruments within shouting distance of each other, the band was going great guns. Though Oliver had no interest in Shihad, my friend Monica and I had 'managed' to 'get tickets' (as in, our parents bought them from Ticketmaster) to see Shihad at the Corner Hotel. This would be my first 18+ gig, and even though my inner monologue regarding this fact was something like the rooftop stake-out from *Can't Hardly Wait*[38] –

William: Okay, we're gonna rendezvous here at 0030 hours, all right?

X-Phile 1: Wait, William. There's gonna be drinking in there.

William: Yeah, so?

X-Phile 2: So what are you gonna do? They're gonna kick you out if you don't drink.

William: Well, I will be drinking.

X-Phile 1: But William, you could get drunk.

X-Phile 2: You could get *addicted*.

– I was determined to embrace the terror. Decked out in spiked bracelets that could very well have been considered deadly weapons, and lots of eyeliner, Mon and I arrived moments after doors opened and endured supports from Weta and Motor Ace (scientific fact: the breakdown at 2:47-minutes of 'Death Defy' still canes, and fuck you if you're too cool to admit it!) before the very sight of Jon Toogood sent us into apoplectic screams. Was the gig any good? Who knows: I was too busy having some sort of religious experience. 'So this is *living*,' I thought, churned about by the maelstrom of moving bodies, my nervous system flooding with endorphins as the sweaty elbow of a very large man made perfect contact with my eye socket. 'You *can* go home again.'

I was a person who couldn't enter a store or restaurant before my companions without crying from fear, who flew into a rage if my sock fell down under my heel while wearing boots, yet here I was: deep in the spray zone, nuking the membranes of my cochlea one by one. I'd like to personally apologise to anyone I injured with my spiked bracelets in that mosh pit, but I hope you understand, Shihad were officially the best band I had ever seen live (they were also, in that moment, the *only* band I'd seen live, aside from the Jimmy Barnes Rock & Soul Revue in 1992, and the satirical disco cover band Stone Cold Boners at the RMIT Brunswick campus cafe in 1998). How could anything that lived inside the pattern design classrooms at Building 8 hope to compare to this newfound reality?

Within a few months, Oliver and I would fall victim to an ever-green music industry euphemism: creative differences. This wasn't so much rooted in our disagreement about Shihad as it was the fact that we'd inevitably end up playing *Mortal Kombat* rather than our instruments, and spent more time writing entries for the Frequently Asked Questions section of our website than writing songs.

I persevered for another year or so, and even, at one point, attempted to start a punk trio with a friend who happened to own a drum kit and some dude called MJ Clash, who answered the 'COLLABORATORS WANTED' flyer that I nearly died of terror pinning to the Missing Link noticeboard. We had one rehearsal in the East Ivanhoe scout hall before MJ disappeared off the face of the earth, returning briefly to send me a very cranky email about a year later. For all my determination to become the next Chrissie Hynde, there were two fatal flaws in my plan: I was absolutely terrified of playing music in public, and didn't especially like to be around strangers. It had become clear that my true calling was not to *perform* music but, rather, to *love it*. And how better to love music than to start writing about it *all the time*? Being in a band was too terrifying, so I decided to try a different approach: music journalism.

Well, 'rock critic' was the term I used, because that's what happens when an Autistic girl watches *Almost Famous*, then reads *Let It Blurt*, then realises there's no better way to make up for being desperately uncool her entire life than by setting her sights on the coolest job on earth. Encouraged by Mum after she'd read a piece I wrote for my 'website' (vale, Geocities), I started sending reviews in to *Beat* magazine; I settled on 'Clem' as my pen name because I liked that it had a sense of the indeterminate, gender-wise. (To this day, I am delighted every time a publication I've written for receives a grumpy email about 'that Clem Bastow guy'.) And, at the tender age of just eighteen, it struck me that I could even lay claim to being the latest in a storied line of rock critics who 'started young'; I cut a sidebar out of *Mojo* magazine, detailing the youthful beginnings of writers like Caitlin Moran and Emma Forrest, and carried it, talismanic, in my wallet. It was fate. Back in the early days of my writing career, I filled out one of those personality quizzes on my MySpace profile

status: 'How's My Writing? Call 1800-EAT-SHIT'

glitter GIFs: enabled

auto-play song: Nikki Webster's 'Strawberry Kisses'

and stated that the person I most wanted to meet was Moran; in another act of talismanic optimism, I added her and put her in my 'Top 9' alongside Andrew W.K. and a few other heroes. Weeks later, I awoke to a comment notification: Queen Caitlin herself had left a note on my wall. 'I flew halfway around the world to write this: Clem has excellent taste in music, and even better taste in journalists.'

I can still remember what I was wearing the day I went for my first 'assignment' (which is to say, the first time I visited the *Beat* office after having had a few live reviews printed): cheap fake Doc Martens Mary Janes, a dark grey knife-pleat skirt, a sheer rose-tattoo-print top with lettuce-hemming at the cuffs and collar, and a red knitted beret I'd had since I was four. It was an outfit that said, in my eighteen-year-old mind, 'music journalist'. Here at last, my Cameron Crowe dreams were becoming reality – never mind the fact that being an eighteen-year-old correspondent who still lives at home with her parents is far less interesting than a fifteen-year-old boy going on the road with Led Zeppelin and the Allman Brothers for *Rolling Stone*.

This was the beginning of the rest of my life – and so soon: I hadn't even finished reading Jim DeRogatis's biography of Lester Bangs yet! As I ascended the staircase to the *Beat* offices I thought, well, if there's any important music critic lore I haven't read yet, I'll just have to be fast on my feet. I also tried hard to pretend that my parents weren't, in fact, waiting outside in the car.

'You're that chick whose reviews we keep getting hate mail about,' one of the editors snapped as I walked into the chaotic open-plan office, her eyes flashing in the shadows under a tangle of bleached blonde hair. This wasn't how I expected things to unfold. My brain scrambled and I tried to think of something nonchalant and music-critic-y to say in response. In my mind, an amalgam of Nora Ephron and Lillian Roxon's finest zingers presented itself. Do I go for Carrie Fisher, or maybe something from the collected works of Ben Elton and Richard Curtis? One of the withering put downs I learned while watching *Yes, Minister* when my schoolmates were glued to *Neighbours*? 'Ha ha, yeah, that's me,' is what came out of my mouth, as I felt tears pooling in my eyes. There was no time to cry, thank god, because the other editor – the one who I was there to see – shot his colleague a look and told her to shut up.

I was given a desultory tour of the office and handed a few free CDs – as I would later come to understand, all music offices are *crawling* with a forest-floor detritus of CDs so thick that the only way to carve out space to move is to give them away – and was told to keep sending in my stuff. I was IN.

My 'training' was almost entirely conducted by reading as much music criticism as I could, and attending the weekly rock trivia night hosted by Helen Razer at Cherry Bar. (To this day, Helen is one of the sole people allowed to utter the words 'Clem, I've known you since you were eighteen ...') There, safe in the company of fellow weirdos – such as the team comprised solely of Polyester Books employees – I put my encyclopedic knowledge of music to the test. In some quarters people still talk in hushed tones about how I could tell the difference between Michael Jackson's 'Billie Jean' and No Doubt's 'Hella Good' within one snare hit (thanks, Weak Central Coherence!).

After two unhappy years, I dropped out of Fashion Design and enrolled in Professional Writing & Editing at TAFE. Halfway through the first semester, a local arts journalist gave a careers talk. Careers talks were usually meant to be inspiring, but this one had the bitter edge of someone who'd been forced at gunpoint to eulogise their enemy. The bulk of the talk seemed to hinge on the notion that none of us who were planning to become freelance journalists – particularly those interested in music or arts criticism – would ever make any money in Australia. Perhaps he was trying to dissuade anyone who might have been angling for the same 30c-per-word assignment as him. As his dour tirade continued, I looked around the lecture theatre and saw my fellow non-fiction students close their notebooks, one by one, with resigned sighs. The aspiring romance novelist stared ahead with glassy eyes, having already astral travelled to the fantastical beaches where their protagonist rubbed her clitoris against the tide's edge and 'called it "sexy sand"'. Some got up and left early. When the talk finally ended, the remaining students shuffled glumly out of the lecture theatre. I, on the other hand, stormed angrily towards Melbourne Central Station. Can't make money from freelance criticism, you say? *Just watch me.*

Back in those days, the major street presses in Melbourne were like the Capulets and Montagues. After I had written a few pieces for *Beat*, I decided to approach *Inpress* instead (because their layout was less busy and thus, easier for me to read). After swearing a blood oath that I would never write for the competition again, I was welcomed into the fold. Soon enough, my determination to write – anything, everything – meant I had scored myself both the role as singles reviewer *and* a part-time job as editorial assistant: I'd come in two days a week to help put the gig guide together and go over proofs for copy errors. My time at *Inpress* was not quite the *Rolling Stone* fantasy I had imagined, but it was at least proof that there was a job I was capable of doing without crumbling into anxiety at interacting with the public or getting confused about how much money was in the till.

(That's not to say there weren't *some* moments of *Rolling Stone* fantasy, such as the time Justin Hawkins from The Darkness tore open my catsuit in a storeroom cupboard at Cherry Bar – later that evening, after a night of dancing to AC/DC's *Powerage* on repeat, he gently refused to take me back to his hotel room by assuring me, 'You're too good for that, and you don't deserve to get your heart broken' – or when Clem Burke from Blondie left a voicemail on our family answering machine.)

Very quickly, I demonstrated an inhuman ability to write *reams* of content; I was like a computer that could spit out album reviews and interviews at a rate of knots. In one weekend alone, I wrote the cover story, three interviews, the singles column, an album review, a live review, and conducted and edited thirty-five small interviews for the wrap-around Fringe Festival program guide. It turns out, if you reveal a skill for turning in masses of content at a quick turnaround, you will be repeatedly asked to do so. I did not, it's safe to say, have any notion of a 'healthy work–life balance'; we lost count of how many interviews I had conducted around the 450 mark. But through it all, my true love was writing about music, and my column, Singled Out, was the playground within which I could try on different voices and personas, experiment with form and structure, and even, at one stage, write an entire review as a sort of grammatical exquisite corpse.

Making music criticism my job also meant that I had the income – albeit modest – to move out of home, living first with a friend, and then by myself, in a variety of Carlton fixer-uppers. The fact that I had no idea how to actually be in the world by myself (I was so excited about the idea of independence that I forgot about things like bills, taxes, even eating three meals a day) was immaterial: I was now a Professional Woman, living in my own apartment, just like Dana from *Ghostbusters*. Eighty per cent of my earnings went on rent, the rest on CDs and beige food.

I was so committed to elevating the art of Australian music criticism that I banded together with my colleagues to take it to the small screen, with big dreams of Molly Meldrum-esque influence. Dance music critic Tim Finney, metal fanatic Mia Timpano and I co-presented two seasons of perhaps the most niche chat program in the history of television, the music criticism panel show *Dancing About Architecture* on Channel 31.

We discussed the vagaries of musical genres so often that one week C31 received an email that read: 'I just love the Dancing about architecture show. It's the best jonra that I have ever seen. We have set up a drinking game every night that the show is on. Everytime someone says jonra we all get to drink. As I'm writing this Macca is passed out on the floor. None of us even know what jonra means. I have set a bet for the next episode that you guys will say jonra at least 15 times. Don't let me down.'

Being the only woman on the *Inpress* editorial team had its ups and downs, of course. One of the writers asked me on dates by leaving apples on my desk each time he would visit the office; we had subpar sex while he was on ecstasy and he broke it off after a few weeks because I was 'too cynical'. Towards the end of my time in the office, my bosses nervously checked if it was 'okay' to print, in the weekly *Pub* comic strip that ran at the back of the magazine, a nude drawing of me as the inaugural 'Panel 3 girl' (yes, it was indeed a very witty spin on the Page 3 girl tradition), because its cartoonist had decided to honour my critical legacy by drawing me in the (imagined) nude. I reacted exactly the way you are supposed to react when you're the only female member of the team and your superiors have implied that they're heading off a potential workplace sexual harassment case by 'running it past you' first: uproarious laughter. (For the record, at the time I *wished* my norgs were as big as Fred's fantasy vision of me.)

Behind the scenes, I was starting to crumble: the mask I had constructed for myself had become such a constant feature of my life that I was starting to wonder who I was, if not for my snippy music reviews. By 2005, the wheels were falling off; it was the beginning of a period of slow and steady burnout that would last the next few years. It was my dear bosses at *Inpress* who that year first noticed the depth of my depression. Mum and Dad had broken up, and though it wasn't as acrimonious as some friends' nightmare tales of divorce, it cast a pall across my happy memories of family holidays that I found hard to shake. I was drifting through the days, buffeted by dodgy dates and perplexed by the realities of living alone. They pulled me into the conference room – to fire me, I was certain – and insisted that I take a week's paid leave, saying they wouldn't let me back into the office without proof that I had engaged a counsellor's or therapist's help. I realised that something had to give, and I wondered if the answer might be pulling back from editorial work to focus on writing: to regain my love of music.

Later that year, I made the switch from my editorial roles to freelancing from home. Making writing my sole gig was also a protective measure: in working remotely, I could avoid the vagaries of the office, which was still a sensory and social nightmare, even when working with friends.

Music criticism eventually led to other forms of writing – bar reviews, opinion pieces, film criticism – and my love of music found its way into other parts of my professional life, too. In 2006 I started presenting shows on Triple R, and have done so on and off ever since. Becoming a professional writer, and particularly a music critic, was a *magnificent* way to continue my subterfuge of convincing people that I was, in fact, very cool and confident, because I would never have to reveal my true self so long as I had the keyboard in front of me. As the famous *New Yorker* cartoon goes, on the internet nobody knows you're a dog; well, on the page, nobody knows you're Autistic. I mean, I say that now, but when I go back and read my early work, it's screamingly obvious that I was a dog: everything is very detail-oriented, with a curious lack of focus on emotion, and enthusiastic overuse of the secret rock criticism thesaurus. (Excoriating! Angular!)

I 'retired' from full-time music journalism in September 2011, which is to say, I told *Inpress* I was hanging up the Singled Out hat. Reflecting the gravity of this momentous changing of the guard, my editor responded by emailing me a photo of a dude with a crepe draped over his face, stamped with the words 'FUCK YOU I'M A PANCAKE'.

A CERTAIN TYPE OF MAN

'Clem has had many boyfriends,' my friend Luke's speech for my twenty-first birthday began. 'Some of whom we've met, some of whom we've only seen drawings of.' To say this was a prescient way to announce my arrival into adulthood would be an understatement.

Working in (or at least adjacent to) the music industry exposed me to a smorgasbord of wildly inappropriate men, the affections of whom I could shrug off as an occupational hazard before enthusiastically following them to hell.

Take the much older bassist (I was almost twenty-one, he was thirty-seven), whose idea of a pick-up line was a philosophical lecture about how bad condoms were. It's difficult to know exactly when I realised that agreeing to date him had been a bad idea, but it might have been when he did a standing backflip in front of my parents on Degraves Street. The sole silver lining of it all was that the relationship meant I got to know his housemate's girlfriend, now a good friend, who, when commiserating with me after the bassist revealed he'd been sleeping with someone else the whole time, described his new girlfriend as 'like a daggy skeleton with the personality of a donut'.

To this day I regret leaving my leopard print coat in his house. He was just the first in a long line of dodgy dudes who'd sidle up to me when I was DJing, or slide into my DMs on the various music-related message boards and blogs I spent too much time posting on. He was also, in retrospect, not the worst man I ever dated.

Numerous studies have pointed to Autistic females being at greater risk of sexual victimisation and coercion than their neurotypical peers,[39] with one study suggesting that Autistic girls are three times more likely to be subjected to sexual abuse during childhood and adolescence than their typically developing peers[40] (females with ADHD are also at an increased risk). At the Yellow Ladybugs mental health symposium I spoke at in 2019, Professor Tony Attwood put it bluntly, warning the assembled crowd that the number-one danger to young Autistic women is neurotypical male predators. In that moment, so much of my life made sense. Autistic people are taught compliance from an early age (particularly undiagnosed girls, whose behaviour may be addressed as 'naughtiness' or 'rudeness'), whether informally or through early intervention therapies, which can make us soft targets for unscrupulous people. Couple this with difficulties in understanding social cues that affect our ability to 'read' situations, and you have a recipe for possible disaster.

In 2002 my friend Leah wondered aloud, as we sat in her car at the intersection of Elgin and Nicholson Streets, 'Clem, are you sure you're not gay? Because I'm starting to feel like you just pick any guy out of a line-up and say "Mmm, he's 'hot', I'd like to 'hump' him!".' At the time, I laughed, even though I knew she had a point: both about the line-up of dud dates, and the fact that deep inside me lurked the feelings I'd had since noticing Vanessa in a Jebediah video clip. Despite Leah's insight, that line-up would continue to stretch forwards, for many years.

The rogues' gallery of men who have successfully pursued me includes a variety of men of such pantomime villainy and/or idiocy that they are referred to by code names coined by my friends – 'Crazy Eyes', 'Crazy Life', 'rappin' Ronnie Reagan' – but the worst was a man whose behaviour was so abhorrent he is no longer referred to, neither by name nor nickname. He asked me to marry him not long after shoving me over mid-argument; we had been dating for only a few months. I believed this act of apology, and that the romance was real.

A report put together by a group of Autistic women advocates, 'Multiple and Intersecting Forms of Discrimination Against Autistic Women', was submitted to the United Nations' Special Rapporteur on Violence Against Women in 2017. In that report, one woman, Morgan, said that prior to developing an understanding of her Autism, 'I thought if people smiled at me, they were nice and that they liked me. I could not and still cannot see the signals that help many women to avoid certain men. I let them get too close. I have been badly physically abused. I believed people who said they only did it because they loved me.'

In Rudy Simone's *Aspergirls*, there is a sentence that absolutely knocked me for six: 'Relationships with other people is where we are most out of our element, so we may not realise it when someone is treating us badly.'

My relationship with my fiancé lasted only a year, and I only really remember fragments of trauma. I remember the day of our engagement party, when Mum rang me in tears to tell me he'd yelled at her for asking if she could bring food to the party, and that she was worried I was making a terrible mistake. I remember agreeing but thinking that the party was set, and I'd already bought my dress at Sportsgirl; I had to go through with it. I remember the way I was slowly isolated from my friends and family, and the times he'd upbraid me for gently asking if he could remember to flush the toilet, accusing me of belittling him. The time he turned to me at a supermarket checkout and hissed 'I'm not paying for your fucking yoghurts' because I had the temerity to add a few Yoplaits to our shopping basket. The hundreds of dollars I spent on placatory gifts for him the same Christmas he gave me an unwrapped, second-hand Matchbox car and a book he wanted to read. The way he'd inspect my receipts, when I'd dared to buy myself something small from the sale rack, and sniff, 'Centrelink's obviously paying you well.' The road trip where he refused to speak to me until

I was nearly hysterical, driven mad by his neglect. The time Mum and Dad, estranged at the time, reunited for an intervention disguised as a 'family dinner', to no avail. He waged such a sustained campaign of emotional and psychological terror upon me that it took me years to pull myself free of the wreckage.

Once I escaped, the thrill of being free soon morphed into three or so years of total emotional chaos. I overcompensated for the pain I felt by adopting a 'Samantha from *Sex and the City*'-esque persona, treating casual sex as a tour of duty, and drinking to numb the pain. Sex was *fine*, sometimes even enjoyable, but there were plenty of aspects that I didn't enjoy (especially from a sensory perspective, shall we say, certain tastes and textures). My masking persona became so abrasive that I lost work at one publication after getting into online arguments with its senior writer on Twitter. The shame at having not only 'allowed' myself to be abused, but also at having tried to convince everyone what a great guy he was – see: engagement party – was all-encompassing. How could I have been so stupid?

In 2010, still poleaxed from the trauma of the abusive relationship, I fell into a friendship with an old colleague from 'the scene'. He was about to leave the country, and I was ricocheting through the mirror maze of what would later be diagnosed as PTSD, after the adrenaline of escaping that abusive relationship had worn off. The friendship that developed involved the two of us, unspokenly, each trying to drink as much as the other.

We would meet at the pub, or wherever someone (sometimes him) was playing a gig, drink until closing, then wander around to other bars and pubs, skipping away as *they* closed, before resorting to the 24-hour bottle-o on Lygon Street and then returning to my house or his mother's terrace to continue drinking. We were both big fans of *Withnail and I*, so each litre of beer and vodka was consumed with a merry 'Chin, chin'. Eventually we'd pass out, wake up at 7 am or so for breakfast at Ti Amo, swim some laps, and then do it all again the next night. Late one afternoon we marched into Borders (RIP), made a beeline for the area where people could browse while having a coffee and croissant, and staged a dramatic reading of the sex scenes from Nick Cave's terrible novel, to the bemusement of nearby readers.

That was the fun stuff; it was clear that in every other way my life was starting to disintegrate around me. During the day, when my anxiety and fear would be at its peak, I'd get into fights on the internet, channelling my rage into meaningless disagreements. To my shame, one night I turned up for a dinner party at a friend's house still drunk, unable to sit up straight at the table. Another night I woke up alone on the living room floor, the DVD menu for *Ghostbusters* looping on my television and a half-drunk bottle of Moët next to me on the floor. The sole comfort was screenwriting, which I had recently taken up again to fill my empty days, working on a fantasy adventure script in an act of transportative optimism.

Eventually, my newfound friend came by to say farewell en route to the airport; I gave him twenty Euros folded inside a picture from *Withnail and I* (to get a round, on me, upon his arrival; chin chin). Despite the departure of my drinking buddy, I maintained my drinking. Without a moscato or Zubrowka I would have to face the full nightmare of the abyss, and I could already feel the wind whipping up from within it and buffeting the hair around my face.

For the next few years, it was only through drinking that I could continue any sort of engagement in dating. Most of the experiences I had rarely became relationships; one was snuffed out pretty readily when I asked, with what I can now laugh about as trademark Autistic frankness, if he had never been taught to eat with his mouth closed.

Gradually, biology took charge of the situation: the older I got, the worse the hangovers became. The headache and nausea were manageable, but the existential anxiety was gripping. (Anecdotally, many of my Autistic friends report similar issues with alcohol.) Eventually I could no longer justify the social lubricant, knowing the nightmare that would follow it, so in 2014 I began to drink less, and then eventually in 2016, stopped completely. It helped, too, that I was uninterested in Australia's drinking culture, and so relished the opportunity to set myself against it, politically speaking. What's fascinating to me now, in retrospect, is that the less I drank, the more I began to wrestle with my identity. If I wasn't drunk, or even tipsy, I would sit at home, racked with fear about impending dates with men: I didn't particularly want to go on any of them, and even if I did, I knew that without the crutch of alcohol, I would struggle to understand the rules of engagement. It wasn't that alcohol helped me understand them, but in a way, it helped me forget that I didn't. When I stopped drinking, by extension, I also stopped having sex with men, then I stopped dating them. And when I stopped dating them, decades worth of realisation flooded in.

None of the men who have hurt me deserve to be immortalised in print in any great detail other than to serve as dot-point examples of the types of dangers that Autistic girls and women face. To those men, particularly the abusive ones, I say what the great Mae West said as Ruby Carter: His mother should have thrown him away and kept the stork.

Dr Michelle Garnett, one of Australia's leading Autism specialists and an incredible advocate for girls and women on the spectrum, sees Autistic women as experiencing a magnified version of the woes of many of their non-Autistic peers. 'Women, generally, have suffered and continue to suffer worldwide because they have been brought up to believe that they are inferior to men, that they are less worthy,' she wrote in 2018. 'Women with autism inherit this cultural idea as well as a neurology that is not prewired to understand people. As a result, they make social mistakes and pay high prices for these mistakes. They are judged, they lose friends, they attract the predators of life, the bullies and the sexual predators, [and] they are rejected and neglected.'

When a certain type of man discovers the flaws in your armour, he becomes a player in an eternal game of one-downmanship, the baton passed across years, decades from dodgy dude to deadbeat drongo to pantomime villain. At first, he will be at pains to tell you that he can't believe your ex treated you like that; he would never do that. Not only would he never do that, he's going to treat you better than anybody ever has. Your foibles, your triggers, your complexities all become the pieces of a complicated and intoxicating DIY project: he loves them, he loves you for them, he's going to be the first man in history who has truly appreciated you for Who You Are. And then, by some incredible coincidence, he begins to do exactly the same thing as his predecessor.

I was always so delighted that someone had 'chosen me', that I was 'loveable', that I very rarely stopped to consider what *I* wanted in relationships. As a result, dating me must have been a mystifying combination of unblinking dedication (that's what relationships are, right?) and arms-length mystery. Even when the relationship was unhappy, a break up was always somehow a surprise to me, and the cause for much distress. In *Aspergirls*, Simone points out that our emotional naiveté, when coupled with the unrealistic images of relationships instilled by books and films, means we frequently end up hurt.

The small handful of men *I* actively pursued, on the other hand, are the ones for whom I still have some fond feelings; they also, perhaps not coincidentally, were the ones whose grasp of gender and sexual identity were the most enlightened. Well, except for the one who did a burnout in his V8 after we broke up, but at least he was enthusiastic about cunnilingus, which is its own sort of enlightenment. I had a brief, beautiful affair in Los Angeles with a scientist who owned a single towel and gave me business cards from the Pentagon Comfort Inn for my birthday present. My uni boyfriend made me tapes of The Fall and The Teardrop Explodes and insisted on calling Mum 'Mrs B', even after my parents' divorce. All of it, of course, brought with it moments of 'good material', such as the time I found myself about to have sex with a man who had made it to twenty-eight without encountering a menstruating woman in the bedroom, and climbed aboard while asking him 'You like David Cronenberg movies, don't you?'

Even as I continued to date a parade of deeply average men, I quietly recognised my innate queerness had offered me a sanctuary. At twenty-seven, as I prepared to escape from that abusive relationship, I signed up for an e-newsletter from About.com, 'About Lesbian Life'. Every time it appeared in my inbox (I had marked it as 'junk', so that it was never visible in my main inbox, just in case someone was looking) I felt a whole-body sigh of relief. I always knew there was something else at play in my romantic life, it just took me a long time to fill in the gaps. For years I just told partners I had a low sex drive, even though on some level I knew that wasn't true.

Through my twenties I had allowed myself to inch towards an understanding of myself as bisexual, though it was only later that I came to realise what that meant to me: not, as the common understanding of bisexuality runs, attracted to 'women and men' (though that is a totally valid bisexual identity), but rather 'attracted to people who share my gender identity, and people who don't'. A few friends asked, while I was working things out, if I might be pansexual; attracted to people regardless of gender. The answer was no: gender *was* important to me. Beyond the occasional objectivities of pure fantasy, what I had come to realise was that I actually had no sexual attraction to straight cis men. (I'm only half joking when I describe myself as a 'gay bisexual'.) There was one last demon left to conquer.

Amanda Richards, a writer who came out at thirty-three, described something in an essay for *InStyle* that hit me like a bolt of lightning in my late thirties: 'I had been going through the motions, performing love and pleasure for my partners and myself, like some kind of elaborate act even I wasn't aware of. It felt good sometimes, but never great. I spent years letting myself be carried by a powerful current of misery.'

The strongest of my own powerful currents of misery, I now realise, used me as an emotional life-preserver over the course of nearly two decades, displaying behaviour so quietly appalling that my friend

Casey was moved to describe him as 'one of the worst examples of men in modern history'. For many years I referred to him as my 'Mr Big', since he was older, since I have often looked to *Sex and The City* to understand relationships, and since I knew about as much about him as Carrie did about Mr Big (which is to say, nearly nothing: not even his birthday). We met when I was eighteen, and for a time he was one of my early editors. We got together a few years after we stopped working together, and dated for about six months. Initially, as ever, I thought I was very happy; it was fun being part of a music critic 'power couple' (power is relative in the world of street press). Gradually, around the time the fire department woke us at 2 am in his condemnable share house because the chimney was on fire, I started to wonder if there might be something missing.

Towards the end of that time, in May 2002, Andrew W.K. was set to play the Hi-Fi Bar. Two of the tickets were ours, because Big was aware of the affection I'd had for W.K. ever since I'd heard 'Party Til You Puke' on one of those mix CDs stuck to the front cover of *Q Magazine* with the glue that looked like ovulation mucus. There was also, perhaps, an element of bargaining in the tickets. Big knew that I was starting to pull away from him; the tickets were a lure.

Despite W.K. being touted by *NME* et al. as one of the saviours of rock 'n' roll (at that point, one of many; poor rock 'n' roll was in a constant state of near death from around 2001 through to 2006), ticket sales were weak – weak enough for a promoter to be spotted outside on Swanston Street shortly before the show, handing out tickets to young skateboarders, who of course were up for literally anything that involved no exchange of money and the imminent possibility of severe hearing damage. The rest of the crowd comprised a few hundred music industry workers, wankers and freeloaders who shuffled in with free tickets to see if this *I Get Wet* fellow was really all he was cracked up to be. He certainly was: within a few songs, half the crowd was on stage. I saw Ben from Warped crying tears of ecstasy behind the guitarist from Obituary. I emerged from that gig having experienced a better life: joyful, loud, unburdened. A week later I broke up with Big in the Donut King at Daimaru.

A few years later I found myself at a dinner in one of those venerable (read: decrepit) weatherboard share houses in the inner north, populated with various people from The Scene, crowded around a giant pot of risotto that roughly a kilo of Savings brand bacon had been diced into by the host, my mate Tim. Tim returned, sodden, to the kitchen, having yanked some silverbeet out of the ground in the middle of a lightning storm and mentioned, offhand, that if Big got wind of the fact that we were hanging out – even as mates, which we were – he'd murder us both. Maybe it was this revelation, or maybe it was the kilo of bacon grease, but I suddenly felt as though everything around me had disintegrated into dust. I pushed Tim for more information: apparently it had 'destroyed' Big when we broke up. At that moment, a seed of doubt was installed in my head, where my Autistic brain would bury it deep. Had I made a mistake in breaking up with this guy?

The next eighteen years were criss-crossed with missed connections and meaningful looks, which – thanks to my triple doctorate-level engagement with romantic comedies – I took to mean we were Made For Each Other. He encouraged these thoughts by periodically returning to my life in order to create emotional chaos. Through the most tumultuous and painful periods of my twenties and thirties he would, he later admitted, surveil my social media, ostensibly to 'keep up to date' with my life. I wonder whether what he was really doing was keeping watch for any mentions of romantic misadventure so he could swoop in at a moment of vulnerability. Either way, he would regularly surface for a series of 'work lunches'. The reality was, of course, that in my naiveté and tender heart he saw an opportunity to give himself semi-regular ego boosts when his relationships (because he was *always* in one) had hit the doldrums; I was his emotional life raft in the storm. What I mistook for mysteriousness was, I now recognise, emotionally withholding behaviour. Despite it all, I allowed myself to be strung along, actively fostering this fantasy of fate having cruelly kept us apart all this time. (I had, like most people in Melbourne, forgotten all about Donut King at Daimaru.)

In 2019 he told me he had always loved me. Despite having nearly made it to the precipice of my own (re)coming out to myself, I was drawn back into his orbit: oh well, if I can't live an authentic life as my true queer self, at least I can get together with The One That Got Away. Over a series of breathless lunch dates and windswept park walks punctuated by clandestine kisses, he entertained the idea that we might, finally, be getting back together. At one lunch, he was so nervous he spilled tea all over the table, which I naturally took to mean that these 45-minute lunch specials were meaningful to him; at another, he cried when I suggested he could talk to me about his work stress. Then, of course, the mysteriousness returned: he'd take forever to reply to emails and texts, or would reply only with a 'just the facts' sentence about work, or that cursed 'jazz hands' emoji. Periodically he'd throw in something romantic, such as the 'CB-shaped hole' in his heart. A month later he told me there was something he couldn't explain via text or email. I wondered if he was dying, or gay, or something else that seemed profound. Over a terrible coffee, at a burner cafe I had never been to, because I knew I would never want to go there again, he choked on his own words: 'I can't leave my girlfriend.' I told him there was somewhere I needed to be, left the cafe, and never looked back.

The writer Armistead Maupin isn't Autistic, but he is gay. He knew he had been since childhood, and came out later in his twenties. In an interview at the height of *Tales of the City*'s success, he said, 'My writing didn't really flourish until I came out, because it's very impossible to keep a huge secret in your heart and be a good writer.'

The process of unlocking that huge secret in my heart was nearly complete, but had started years before, in Los Angeles.

I LOVE L.A.

'They're not fans of *you*, they're fans of the project that you've both worked on,' Kristen Stewart says of being part of a pop-cultural phenomenon as huge as the *Twilight* saga. 'You look up to people that you've shared something with, that you have a commonality with, so that's why whenever people go "How is it to be a role model?" I'm like ...' She rolls her eyes dramatically and waves a dismissive hand.

And how *is* it to be a role model, I asked only semi-satirically. 'Well, let me tell you!' she guffawed, leaning forward and stabbing at the air with her finger. 'I have lots to say!'

Having spent most of my life adrift in a nonstop daydream about icons of popular culture, it was a surprise (or 'a trip', as she might say) to find myself sitting in a room at the Four Seasons opposite Kristen Stewart as she pointed to my hairdo and said, in that way she does, 'I really like what you've got going on.' My hand reached up instinctively to the side of my head, where I'd pinned up half of my hair, like a fake asymmetrical undercut, as I bumbled some vague and immediately blushing thanks. After I was ushered out of the room by a press person, I rushed to the bathrooms and stared at my hairdo for ten minutes.

It was 2013 and this was my job now: determined to try my hand at what we might euphemistically call entertainment journalism, in

2012, at the age of twenty-nine and with $800 in my bank account and a foreign correspondent visa, I moved to Los Angeles, leaving my life behind (and walking away from my 'office' in Mum's back room as though I'd be back any minute). A lot of Autistic people I know thrive, somewhat ironically, in chaos, perhaps because in the maelstrom, our internal storm doesn't seem so different to the world around us. For me, this is particularly true of the chaos of international travel, which actually isn't really that chaotic: it's one of the few adult whirls where you are positively *encouraged* to carry an itemised itinerary, wear noise-cancelling headphones and consume full meals of highly processed food.

Spending time in L.A. was an opportunity to start afresh: to escape the 'grumpy music critic' persona I had constructed, and to flee the slow-moving car crash of trauma that had followed me since escaping that abusive relationship. In L.A. I could live the SoCal dream, staying positive, smoking weed instead of drinking, and eating well at the trough-like Whole Foods salad bar. More importantly, I could be whoever I wanted to be, and after reigniting my passion for the craft, I was pretty sure I wanted to be a screenwriter. Where better to go than the place where movies are made? The plan was to work on my screenplays while I paid my rent with entertainment journalism; by day, a mild-mannered stringer; by night, a glamorous screenwriter.

I had fallen in love with Los Angeles the first time I visited, in 2009, on a two-and-a-half day stopover on my way to New York. I caught a terrible sightseeing bus ('On your left is the El Pollo Loco store where Brad Pitt once worked!') to awful Hollywood Boulevard and wandered around in the rain, my flares soaked to the knees. I accompanied my sister's ex-boyfriend to a horrible slam poetry night that he had to attend because he was working as a casting agent. Ryan Gosling smiled at me in a hidden vodka bar, and the smell of the lemon-scented eucalypts on Fairfax and the wet concrete cast a spell on me. The town that had inspired so much of my favourite music, from Warren Zevon and Joni Mitchell to Tupac and Beck, had sunk its claws deep into my soul. When it was time to leave, I cried all the way to New York and then caught swine flu at a music festival: clearly this was nature's way of saying 'don't leave L.A.'

As it turned out, entertainment journalism was the perfect job for an Autistic person with a flair for performance. I had spent my whole life carefully studying how to move through the human world; here was a job where it was not just helpful to script like mad, but *essential*. I would scour old interviews with my upcoming subject and make a note of things – artistic ideals, political statements, philosophical assertions – to bring up casually during conversation, sometimes as though they were my own opinion ('You know, I've often thought that acting is a lot like ...') eliciting a relieved 'YES!' from the person sitting opposite me.

More than once, word filtered back through press reps and distributors that my interview subjects had greatly enjoyed chatting with me. This might seem like a weird flex, but for someone who had spent most of their life indulging in highly detailed daydreams about being friends with famous people, this was akin to having achieved Nirvana. Every celebrity interview was like a chance to rewrite history: after a lifetime of fudging social cues, struggling to maintain conversations and misreading emotions, here I was, having delightful tête-à-têtes with people I admired, and being paid for it, too.

The celebrity interview is a weird space in general, but it's weirder if, like me, you are neurologically geared towards misreading certain social interactions as being far more meaningful than they actually are. For the twenty or forty minutes assigned to us lower-tier stringers (what do you think this is, *Vanity Fair*?), with some careful research it is possible to enter a dream state where nobody, no journalist on earth, has ever fostered such a warm rapport with the actor or artist sitting opposite you. Not only are we getting along famously, it's possible we could be best friends.

I never asked 'hard questions', in part because I refused to (no, I will *not* ask Rachel Weisz about Daniel Craig) but also because I was too scared to; in fact, I barely asked questions at all. Questions become too much like routines, and routines are too likely to be shattered if the questions run out, or elicit only one-word answers. Instead, I would take in a sheet of 'talking points' and pray for a connection. The art of the entertainment interview is a delicate balancing act where for half an hour or so we are just two human beings existing on the same plane, conversing like old friends. It's a magic trick where childhood dreams come true, but there is, I now realise, an Autistic quality to this. Perhaps it also works because, like an actor, I have learned to bend myself to fit inside the mould of someone else. Sat opposite someone who plays other people for a living, we have a shared understanding; we're both chameleons.

I had done hundreds of interviews at *Inpress* and on air at Triple R, so I was well trained in how to get the most out of my time. The pecking order of Hollywood journalism dictated that I would usually be offered a roundtable interview, in which four or five journalists, each reporting for different territories, literally sit at a round table with one or two interviewees, for a short chat. This is a fraught interview approach by anyone's standards, because you run the risk of watching the sand empty out of the hourglass while a bossier (or, more commonly, extremely boring) fellow stringer monopolises the question time with lines of inquiry that draw stock responses from the interviewee. So, I perfected a method of procuring quotes that were absolutely unusable by everyone else at the table, and one that I now recognise was absolutely Autistic: swing straight for the subject's special interest.

Take, for example, Hollywood's most famous *Dungeons & Dragons* fan, Vin Diesel. At a roundtable for the release of *Riddick* in 2013, Diesel gamely answered all the usual questions. I bided my time, nodding at each response to someone else's not very interesting question. Even though the *Riddick* franchise had only clocked half as much big-screen time as the *Fast & Furious* saga at that point, it was well and truly a multi-platform phenomenon, taking in video games and graphic novels that have kept the 'IP' (that's intellectual property to the folks at home) ticking over. I saw my chance and asked Diesel if he would ever consider turning *Riddick* into a role-playing or tabletop game. He is, after all, one of *D&D*'s most high-profile adventurers.

'Very much so,' he said, only barely restraining his enthusiasm. 'Um ... I would love to do it.' A pause, testing the waters. 'You mean like classic role-playing?'

'Well yes,' I responded, 'I'm a *D&D* player myself.'

'Are you??' he said, before breaking into the cheesiest grin and double thumbs up this side of Wayne Campbell saying 'Zang!' Then he pulled himself back from the brink of deep nerd and squinted at me, reading me for tells. 'But you're probably a new generation *D&D* player.'

'No, actually,' I said, 'for years we played first edition *Advanced Dungeons & Dragons*, and our DM only recently decided to bring us into the 4E world.' Diesel's eyes widened, and it was clear we were about to get into it.

Vin: 'What's that like? I never made that transition.'

Me: 'It's a lot like *WoW*.'

Vin: 'So they modified it to *WoW*?? Undeniable references? Easier?'

Me: 'Yeah, a lot more area-of-effect spells ...'

Vin: 'Woooowww ...'

Me: '... and the rules are a little easier, so it's really straightforward for bringing in new players.'

Vin: 'Gotcha. But has it kind of defeated the old magic a little? The old lore?'

Me: 'A little bit. I miss the old lore.'

He shook his head slowly.

Vin: 'I haven't played recently, so I'm so old school in my playing, literally starting with the basic box set at twelve years old from my grandmother, and then actively collecting the first edition. But even going beyond that, and getting – did you ever use *Arcanum*, any of the third-party stuff?'

I nodded, he grinned.

Vin: 'Obviously! You create cool characters. I mean, my Witch-Hunter came from the *Arcanum*, and just to geek out, if you ever saw *xXx*, there's a Melkor tattoo on xXx's stomach. It's so goofy, it's such a dweeb thing.'

At that point, one of the other journos regained consciousness, asking rather urgently, 'Were you guys speaking English just then?', and it became clear things had to be brought back on topic. So, giving it one last hurrah, I told Diesel – just to make it totally clear that we were 'people' – I had my dice in my bag, and it wasn't a word of a lie. I kicked my bag under the table and the telltale clatter of Chessex against perspex rang out.

A beatific smile spread across his face and he scrunched up his eyes and said, 'Oh, *beautiful.*'

With minutes to go, the other journalists started to ask their questions again, and the magic faded; we were back at the roundtable, not the mom's basement of my dreams where Vin and I are adventuring again. Soon, the junket ended, and I wandered the streets of Beverly Hills, trying to find a bus stop.

Living in Los Angeles also afforded me the chance to pursue my own special interests with more gusto, just like my best friend Vin and his *D&D* adventures: from L.A, it was only a short train journey to San Diego, otherwise known as the heartland of cosplay, San Diego Comic-Con International.

SDCC is the biggest pop cultural expo in the world. Over its four-and-a-bit days, hundreds of thousands of people pour through the doors of the San Diego Convention Center to pay their respects to the pantheon of pop culture, be it comics, film, TV, video games or small-press publishing.

What strikes you about SDCC, aside from the sheer sensory overload of the whole thing, is the immensely good vibe. Remember in *Ghostbusters II*, when the guys play Howard Huntsberry's cover of 'Higher and Higher' out of Lady Liberty to 'really get the city's positive energy flowing'? That's what Comic-Con is like. (Minus the slime and the possibility of being crushed by a beloved landmark.) The incredible diversity of the crowd would make me weep tears of joy every year, and the collective enthusiasm in the room is always infectious. (I don't think it's unfair to suggest that neurodiverse people are probably overrepresented at Comic-Con and other similar conventions, either.) I have always liked to say that costume parties are a great social leveller: everyone turns up looking as silly as each other, and therefore the playing field is evened out. Comic-Con, and many other events like it, are costume parties on a grand scale.

Making costumes and props and dressing up had long been one of my most special interests; from the age of four I was always 'that guy' at the costume party. I've never been more profoundly depressed than during the two or so years I told myself, struggling beneath the pressures of neurotypical expectations of adulthood, that dressing up was 'for kids' and I should spend my time and money elsewhere. My time in L.A was the beginning of a new era, one in which I 'dressed up' four or five times a year. (I even managed to turn that special interest into paid work, teaching a short course at RMIT in costume fabrication techniques and thermoplastics. *Now* who's 'that guy'?)

Attending Comic-Con was usually both business *and* pleasure for me, with interview opportunities dotted throughout the weekend, which meant additional proximity to the firmament of stars that populated my daydreams. (Believe me when I say that eleven-year-old Clem was *very* pleased when thirty-year-old Clem found herself two steps behind Steven Spielberg on an escalator after a press conference.)

While my time spent on junkets and in the rarefied air of the celebrity interview was characterised by my tendency to fantasise that the interviewees were my new best friends, it was in Los Angeles that I met one of my *real* best friends, Ifer. We bonded when we were both ghosted by a mutual friend, a model who borrowed all of my high heels and never gave them back. Ifer and I would drive around in the sturdy blue van she used to ferry her nannying charges, singing along to classic hits on KRTH-101 and drinking too much Starbucks iced green tea. In the winter of 2013 she drove us all the way to Wyoming so I could attend a Sheridan-style leatherwork masterclass, pursuing my latest special interest. Whenever there was an earthquake (as there often are in L.A.) and I would start freaking out (as I often did), she would give me the nanny treatment: 'Drink your water, Clem.'

To this day Ifer is a port in the storm, a friend who has seen me for who I am, free of the baggage of my hometown. Even though we live a 14.5-hour flight from each other, we still text as though any minute we're about to grab her beloved dog, Anchovy, jump in the car and go to Glendale Target at 10.35 pm for some 'returns'.

The rest of my two years in Los Angeles loom in my memory like a dream: did I really do that, did I really live there? Did I *really* visit David Copperfield's subterranean magic museum in Las Vegas? Did I really attend Maroon-5's Halloween party at the Hollywood Forever mausoleum, dressed as Frank Henenlotter's Frankenhooker? I think, in a way, I did it to see if I could start fresh; to see who I really was if I wasn't busy trying to outrun the trauma of the previous five or so years. If music criticism had seen me construct an abrasive persona, which was equal parts occupational hazard and coping mechanism, the abusive relationships had calcified it into something deeply unpleasant: I was cynical, often drunk, and my inability to admit defeat and ask for help manifested in a know-it-all approach to life even as I was floundering.

But trauma has a way of catching up with you. While I lived in L.A. I lost a lot of weight; it was like my body was trying to shrink away from its edges. Sometimes I did this consciously, such as when I adopted a 'nutrient-dense raw vegan' lifestyle and started doing hour-long Hoopnotica workouts daily. Sometimes it was a side effect of being hard-up: there were months where Fairfax's new electronic invoice system was on the blink, and I lived on tortillas and eggs from the 99c Only store. The rest of the time I think it was just the unhappy side-effect of anxiety: if you're constantly ticking over at a low hum of existential terror, and walking everywhere in a big city where walking anywhere takes hours, it turns out you will begin to disappear. I discovered this when I went to Planned Parenthood to get my pill prescription refilled. 'Hmm,' said the nurse as she adjusted the slider on the scales I was standing on, 'one hundred twenty-seven pounds'. I avoided her gaze. She was right to say 'hmm', what was a tall person like me doing weighing in at 58 kilograms?

Though I enjoyed having conquered the challenge of travelling and living alone, I missed my family. Spending Christmas on Skype with Mum and Atti was one Christmas on Skype too many. Dad would send emails full of helpful pink crab emojis when I sent bleak missives from Starbucks. Blazey's kids were growing up, and Tash had a baby on the way. At the end of 2013, the Australian dollar had started to plunge, meaning that what had been very cheap rent when I arrived to an exchange rate of US$1.10 to my dollar had become eye-wateringly expensive now that it was hovering somewhere around US$0.70. That was the superficial (if perfectly pressing) reason to leave; more broadly, it was clear that it was time for me to return home and begin inching towards addressing the thing that had been gnawing away at me all this time: who was I? And why did life seem to be so difficult for me in a way that it wasn't for others?

Through it all, those forty or so minutes with Kristen Stewart – she liked my hair!! We're best friends!! – lingered as a sort of talisman. I observed that lots of other people found her cute, as I did, so, I reasoned, this was it: my chance to begin to slowly emerge from my chrysalis and test the waters. The first time I mentioned that I thought she was cute, the world didn't end: I wasn't summarily drummed out of town for verbalising the feelings that had followed me since my teens.

There were little moments along the way that said to me, 'Keep going'. Magical thinking, maybe, but when you're starting to reckon with your very being, those thoughts can provide a special sort of comfort. I took myself on a number of holidays to San Francisco, staying at a gay B&B in the Castro whose kitchen was always overrun by bears in terry towelling robes every time the free pastries arrived for breakfast. I was too terrified to actively do anything else – go to a queer club, for example – and I nearly had a heart attack when Aardvark Books' legendary store cat, Owen, 'saw' me browsing the queer shelves, but even this small step towards living authentically was a huge relief.

In 2013, I was standing on the platform, waiting for the Pacific Surfliner that would take me to Comic-Con along with a few hundred other nerds. As I struggled to lift my bag of costumes and my prop weapons, a beautiful woman wearing striped socks and elf ears smiled right at me, on her way to a different carriage, and it was like the sun coming out from behind the clouds. I can still see her face, though I don't know who she was.

A few years ago, after Kristen Stewart had begun to live as her authentic queer self, and as I was beginning to wrestle with my own identity, I returned to our interview to see if there were any 'signs'. I was struck by this moment in particular: 'Bella wears her heart on her sleeve completely; I only have mine to show,' she told me. 'Here's the thing: that's why I'm not ashamed of anything in this movie. Everything came from a very natural, explorative place. I could never have let myself down, because I was just trying to *find* something. Reaching for it is worth just as much. She is comfortable living in the fear of it all, because she knows that that's how worthwhile and truthful things are born.'

THEY GO TO BED WITH GILDA, THEY WAKE UP WITH RAIN MAN

All the 'good material' of my romantic misadventure, as fate would have it, led to my work as a lifestyle writer, first for Fairfax's *Sunday Life* and later for *Daily Life*, the digital 'women's' section. I had the perfect experience pool to draw upon: after all, the bread and butter of nominally feminist digital media is mostly men and how to date them. (Or, in some quarters, how to hate them, LADIES AMIRITE??). I was soon set to work writing countless pieces about dating: trends, my own experience, and everything in between. The irony, in retrospect, of someone who literally had no idea how to date *writing from a position of wisdom and authority* on the topic is, of course, hilarious.

What started as writing about dating soon extended to writing about the side effects of dating, which is to say, mistreatment and trauma at the hands of some of the men I'd had relationships with (or, more broadly, on similar topics). I have mixed feelings about much of the writing I did during this time as a nominally feminist voice. (In fact, there wasn't much that was nominal about it – in 2012 I was plucked to represent Australian feminism at a Sydney Opera House event alongside Germaine Greer and Naomi Wolf.)

The demand to perform trauma is a key tenet of contemporary feminism, and especially feminist media. The better that tales of abuse, rape, sex, dating, mental illness and eating disorders rated with readers, the more editors actively sought them out. I began to feel like I was churning through my own lived experience (whether traumatic, comedic, or the former disguised by the latter) in order to justify my position as a member of the 'feminist media'. The fact that this was my main source of income compounded my anxiety: it wasn't just 'who am I without all this trauma?' but 'how will I eat and pay my bills without writing about this trauma?' I was suddenly acutely aware of the precarity of my position: without this work, I had nothing. My lack of any concrete qualifications, my fear of The Office, and the gnawing void beneath my public persona beset me, like the ghosts of Christmas past, present and future all showing up on the one night.

Looking back at my work as a feminist commentator, I recall the time I spent in therapy, desperately scared that I would run out of 'material' and thus, lose my job (ironically, I was spending my 'food money' on therapy). I worried that my concern about monetising my own trauma for clicks somehow made me a 'bad feminist' who was letting the team down. And, I can now recognise that my issues with boundaries (lack thereof) meant that I said yes to many more assignments of this nature than I was capable, emotionally, of navigating; I was writing about trauma I hadn't even processed yet.

In the digital media content mines, it seemed much less possible, if not actively advised against, to engage in pop cultural criticism at arm's length than it was to constantly compare my own lived experience with that of celebrities and other public figures. Naturally, with the hindsight of diagnosis I now look at many of my first-person 'Why I ...' type essays (one pertinent example: 'A World Full of Annoying Sounds: What It's Like Living With "Misophonia"') and feel the need to add an asterisk to every headline: '*Because I'm Autistic'. It's difficult to read my previous writing about depression, anxiety, dating, gender and communication now that I know the real reason behind so many of my struggles.

In late 2016 I began my incremental 'retirement' (a recurring theme in my writing career) from feminist media, recovering with a few years' worth of blessedly uninflammatory real estate listicles ('Mad Max: Fury Road Home Decor Inspiration'), plus the occasional foray into cultural criticism disguised as lifestyle content ('Here's 7 Dystopian Future Landscapes with Better Childcare Facilities Than Apple's "Mothership"') and feminist film criticism. Abandoning 'professional' feminism also meant relaxing into my more transgressive cultural interests. Atti and I got into the local pro wrestling scene, and in 2017 created a documentary podcast with our new friend, hardcore wrestling legend KrackerJak. Every 'YOU'RE A JOKE, SEXTON!' I yelled from the sidelines of the Ukrainian Hall felt like it was undoing another thread of the preceding years of trauma and confusion.

It no longer mattered if I didn't have any 'material' about dating or trauma, so it was around this time, when I had stopped frantically treading water professionally and creatively, that I also pumped the brakes on dating. My dates with men became fewer and farther between, though that did increase the likelihood that my semi-annual Straight Date would bear the brunt of the previous six months' worth of questioning my identity.

Much like 'caustic music critic' and 'confident celebrity profiler', 'feminist media identity' was starting to itch at the back of my neck; without this professional persona I had adopted, who was I? It wasn't just that I felt like my public-facing persona didn't wash with the real me (I had no idea who the 'real me' was, or if it even existed!) but that so much of my work had become tied up in gender. My increasing discomfort in working as a Feminist Writer for Women's Websites was tied to the confusion and irritation I experienced any time I felt I was 'boxed in' as such. While I still identified as a woman (most of the time, at least), I resented that being the only thing I could be.

I am not the first Autistic person to feel this tension about gender. There is a considerable overlap between the Autistic community and gender diverse communities, with a higher proportion of gender diversity among Autistic people than in the broader non-Autistic or neurotypical population. Research appears stuck on the chicken or egg question of whether gender diverse people are more likely to be Autistic, as a large study[41] published in *Nature Communications* found, or vice versa, as suggested by a study presented in *Transgender Health*.[42] Many of the studies undertaken so far have focused on the clinical – such as drawing upon data gleaned from clinics specialising in gender dysphoria – and few have, for the most part, addressed qualitative accounts from Autistic adolescents and adults about their own experience of gender.

For those Autistic people who *do* later seek advice or counselling about gender identity, many find their concerns are dismissed as special interests or rigid thinking (indeed, one study of 'obsessional interests in children with gender dysphoria'[43] suggested as much): oh, the thinking goes, now they're obsessed about gender, just like they were crazy about One Direction or trains or dinosaurs. A recent qualitative study of twenty-two Autistic gender diverse young people[44] revealed the many additional barriers Autistic people faced when seeking to live authentically. One of the participants' responses spoke to me with particular clarity. 'I would like just [to finalise] gender identity so I can be more at ease,' they said. 'Everyone else knows who they are and what they would like to do. And just like any other teen or child I would like to know my identity and where I stand. But I don't know my identity. It's a bit more complicated than everyone else's.'

In 2016 a group of researchers called[45] for an agenda for research concerning Autistic LGBTIQ+ people. Their reasons included improving sexual and mental health support for Autistic LGBTIQ+ people, citing the fact that mental health professionals are limited in their ability to provide help due to a relative lack of literature on the topic. That same year, when I was starting to think about my own gender and sexuality in more concrete terms, my then-therapist made an off-colour remark about Safe Schools, and I knew not to bring that topic to the couch.

My notion of my own gender has always been fluid to me, so much so that it's only very recently that I've had any reason to think about it in such explicit terms; as it had always been a natural state, it never struck me that it was anything to discuss. My gender expression, like so many things about me, has often been either too much or not enough. There were the sexy years, all SUPRÉ miniskirts with Versace-esque built-in underwear (very handy) and fake tan and push-up bras and Miss V8 Supergirl contests. I prided myself on being able to run in high heels, and dyed my hair (and eyebrows) straw blonde. Then there'd be periods of neutrality; no hairstyle, no make-up, the same linen pinafore dress every day, like I was an extra in a durational performance of a dour dystopian-tone poem. *Then* there were the years where I refused to shop anywhere other than the 'men's' department and refused to remove my moustache or 'beard' hair.

I talk about these 'years' like they were discrete periods with an end and a beginning, but really they bleed into each other and overlap: during the dystopian-tone poem time I bought a bunch of hot 'after 5' gear from boohoo (including, yes, a gown with built-in undies), for example. When I was wearing sensible menswear, I would also overdraw my lip-liner like Kylie Jenner and dye my hair bright red. As soon as I started to settle into one type of gender expression, I'd run screaming from it.

This is amplified by any sense of the spectacle; if I feel myself becoming 'known' for a certain look, I will abandon it. As soon as people started asking me how I did my fluorescent green dyed underarm hair, I spent months assiduously removing all hair from my body. After wearing men's clothing for a solid year, I panicked that I didn't own many dresses, and emptied a Port Fairy op shop of its supply of 1970s nylon frocks. The longest running source of tension between Mum and me is her often strongly expressed belief that I do not 'celebrate' myself enough by wearing make-up and dressing up. God bless her; a nice outfit and a full face is her own form of both armour and self-expression, so it stands to reason that she thinks the same thing will lessen my depression and anxiety or help me get a date. (Ironically enough, one of our biggest arguments was over the Kylie Jenner look, a screaming battle that lasted an entire drive from Mt Dandenong to Collingwood; evidently, despite Mum regularly asking me to put on some nice make-up, that was *too much* make-up.)

The problem has always been that even though I'm perfectly capable of presenting myself in this manner, it has always felt like a facade, albeit an enjoyable one; whether I'm presenting more masculine or more feminine, they both feel, in a way, like drag. My approach to dating has always been troubled by this: the worry that anyone who takes me at face value in one form may recoil at the other sides of my expression once they emerge. If I 'snare' someone by dressing glamorously and with a full face of make-up, how will they feel when I look like a 1980s adult contemporary crooner, or a run-of-the-mill goblin? As I believe Rita Hayworth once said, they go to bed with Gilda, they wake up with Rain Man.

I first started consciously playing around with gender by getting involved in the cosplay community. Where better to expand your palette of gender expression than a world in which it is absolutely okay, nay, encouraged to dress as a giant robot or sexy cartoon mouse? Back in 2011, I went to Comic-Con as Dorothy Michaels from *Tootsie*, Sidney Pollack's masterpiece that stars Dustin Hoffman as an out-of-work actor who dresses as a woman to prove a point at an audition (hilarity, and complex critique of gender politics, ensues). Though my preference for subtlety meant I *wanted* to wear one of Dorothy's sensible 1982 day dresses, my eye for spectacle meant I settled upon the famous red sequinned dress from the 'Go, Tootsie, Go' sequence and the poster. It was a multilayered performance of gender, involving first binding my chest and packing, then building up Dorothy with padding and shapewear, but as I stared at my reflection in the Comfort Inn mirror I wondered what the hell I was doing. I was terrified that someone would think I was just a really ugly Jessica Rabbit; that everyone on earth had forgotten *Tootsie*. I wanted to get on a plane and go home immediately.

Happily, when I shyly entered the convention centre, someone screamed 'Hey, Tootsie!!' and ran over to take my photo; it turned out *everyone* remembered *Tootsie*. Later, I was delighted when the actor James Urbaniak wrote, in a Comic-Con wrap up, that his favourite costume was 'a young man dressed as Dorothy Michaels'. In 2013 I went back, dressed as Jon Snow; whenever someone called out 'Yeah, Jane Snow!' I burned with rage. *No, it's Jon Snow*. Gradually, I started to preference male characters over female ones – Gary King from *The World's End*, Will and Steve from *Stranger Things*, Michael from *E.T.* – and would still strafe against the notion that I was 'cross-playing' or 'gender bending' the characters. When planning a cosplay as Steve Harrington, *Stranger Things*' loveable himbo, I ordered my 'Steve' Scoops Ahoy name tag from a small engraving business, to go with my costume. I also ordered three sets of pronoun badges – 'she/her', 'he/him' and 'they/them' – just for safe keeping.

A couple of months after my diagnostic assessment, while still awaiting the results (pursuing an Autism diagnosis as a grown woman is a little bit like trying to get in at Berghain), I was on a date

date?????

        "'date'"

              ~~date~~

with a fellow who my dear friend Helen had insisted I meet. I can't recall if the phrase 'blind date' was expressly used, but what else do you call it when two human people who happen to be single and unlucky in love are given each other's phone number by a well-meaning mutual friend?

The date itself was *fine* – nothing to write home about, aside from his truly heroic consumption of red wine – and yet, once again, I felt that familiar sense of dread, as though even a mildly diverting date would necessarily have to be followed up with a relationship. Whether I was pursued or I did the pursuing, once the initial flush of excitement – a date! a second date!! – had passed, panic would set in: I don't want this. I didn't know *why*, but I had the distinct feeling of impending doom, like I was trying to outrun the boulder from *Raiders of the Lost Ark*.

Only, on some level, I *did* know why. Just as I knew why, for example, at twenty-four I had found myself, in tears, browsing the 'marital aids' shelf at the supermarket (horny goat weed!). I was there because I didn't want to have sex with my boyfriend, and on some level I believed I Had To because, after all, I agreed to go out with him in the first place and everyone thought he was very hot. I also knew why I had always been apprehensive about sharing a platonic bed with female friends, even though I appreciated the savings found in booking a single room together.

In late 2017 I got a haircut that gave me a gender crisis. Enthralled by *Stranger Things 2* since its release a few months earlier, I marched in to the salon and announced that I wanted to look like Billy Hargrove, the feral stud played by Dacre Montgomery (it was, alas, not his real hair). This was nothing new: for most of my life I had admired the reptilian masculinity of stars like David Lee Roth and Mick Jagger.

I was happy to dress (up) as a sexy woman from time to time, but I also wanted to look like I was about to spend three hours jogging up and down the stage at Wembley Arena. People talk about beautiful models 'giving' young girls a distorted sense of body image, but whenever I had the urge to starve myself it was so that I, too, might look great in a royal blue velour jumpsuit spangled with stars and stripes like Jagger in 1973. (If only I'd ever had an appetite for the sorts of party drugs that can really burn off calories.) So, when I watched Billy Hargrove's 1979 Chevrolet Camaro growl into the Hawkins High School car park to the tune of 'Rock You Like A Hurricane' and he stepped out in double denim, I was powerless to resist.

After a few hours in the chair, I had a bouffant mullet with bleached streaks we dubbed 'dad blonde': just like Billy. After the initial buzz wore off, I started to feel like I was in a mid-century horror movie about a transplanted organ taking over the host's body, only in this case it was the mullet that was controlling my sense of self. Preparing to fly to Sydney for a black-tie work event, I cried in every change room I entered: I looked too masculine for a gown, and too feminine for a suit; I barely knew myself. In the end I settled on the middle ground of a loose black crepe jumpsuit and managed to hit the red carpet without having a nervous breakdown. It wasn't that it was a bad haircut – it was *fantastic* – but it brought to the surface something that had always simmered inside me.

Half a year after the mullet crisis, I went with friends to see *RuPaul's Drag Race* Season 9 winner Sasha Velour perform at Chasers, where Mum had once modelled for Le Louvre. In the thirty or so seconds we were afforded by our purchase of a VIP ticket, I rushed to tell Sasha how much I appreciated her guidance, however distant, on matters of gender expression. She choked up as she thanked me for telling her.

In 2019, I grew all my facial hair out, just to see what it would be like. It turns out I have a beard. After a few months of stroking said beard like a pantomime villain (much to Mum's dismay), I shaved it all off and started wearing make-up again. I'm just as happy – delighted, in fact – when I am 'sir'-ed (most recently: by a nice young ADF member at a Covid-19 testing site) as when I am clocked as obviously, glamorously feminine. Most days I look like I'm in the middle phase of an *Animorphs* book cover, hovering somewhere between masculine ('men's' department jeans) and feminine ('women's' shirt). The rollercoaster ride continues.

When I think about my own gender, it is impossible for me to separate Autism from my sense of identity. The two are plaited together so tightly that sometimes it's hard to tell where one ends and the other begins. Was I having a meltdown about my hair being brushed because I'm Autistic and it was sensory overload, or because I resented the notion that my hair needed to be brushed because I was a girl and that's what girls do? Was it both? There's an interesting frisson when I think of myself As A Woman, even as an Autistic one; like thirty-year-old me hissing 'No, *Jon* Snow' at Comic-Con – I am happy to *live* as a woman until someone *perceives* me as one.

In truth, like many Autistic people I know, I swing wildly by wanting everything, and nothing, to have labels; it's the same for myself. Genderfluid? Gender non-conforming? Gender???? Woman???? Sometimes I make jokes about it – 'I'm gender chaotic' or 'I'm gender confused' – but it has only been since allowing myself to truly *be* Autistic that I've also relaxed about my gender identity and expression. I may never know how to describe my gender, but I know I have Autism to thank for its many facets.

HIGHER AND HIGHER

In July 2017 I received my Masters of Screenwriting. The last time I had graduated from anything educational I wore velcro 'hair jewels' and Green Day's 'Time Of Your Life' featured heavily in the ceremony. There was a part of me that half expected a vaudeville hook to emerge from the wings and yank me off the stage: this is an outrage! This woman is receiving a postgraduate degree despite having never graduated from university!!

The spectre of being a three-time university drop-out had haunted me throughout my life. Even as I was working, more or less full time, as a professional writer, the thought was never far from my mind: you'd know more if you'd got a degree.

Labels like 'dumb', 'remedial' or 'incompetent' have a habit of sticking; once we leave school, it may be that nobody calls us those things out loud, but the words burrow down into our minds and memories. I'm now a PhD candidate, having received my Masters with a high distinction in 2017. But prior to that, I dropped out of three different university and TAFE courses across a decade. There was always a part of me that remembered school, and the dreaded maths nightmare, and went 'yeah, you're probably not smart enough for uni'. Now, as one of only a handful of Vice Chancellor's Scholars at RMIT, I can see that it was precisely because of my unique and

Autistic approach to research and writing that my PhD proposal was received so warmly. But it took some time to get here.

After quitting fashion design, I studied professional writing at TAFE while working as a waitress, which, thanks to my chameleon tendencies (new persona: Best Waitress Ever), I was very good at. A semester into that course, I got my job at *Inpress* and never went back to TAFE. (I had planned to defer my TAFE course, just in case, but I took the admin very literally when she said 'we'll take care of it', and went on my merry way, and accidentally failed a whole semester due to absence.) With *Inpress* as the starting blocks, I had carved out continued work for myself as a freelance writer. In a way, I now see my fifteen or so years of freelancing as my own version of a bachelor's degree.

The move to L.A., and the excitement of both visiting movie sets and having some time away from the expectations of the 'personal brand' I had patched together in Melbourne, led me to rekindle the love for screenwriting that I had fostered in Media class at high school. When I moved back to Australia at the end of 2013, I decided to start taking it more seriously, and re-enrolled in TAFE, this time in an Advanced Diploma of Screenwriting, in 2015. A year into that course, a tutor suggested that I should consider applying for the Masters of Screenwriting at VCA rather than completing the second year of the Ad Dip. I also liked the idea of returning to 'mature-age' study, because I had watched Mum do it, eventually obtaining her PhD, and had so admired her for stepping outside the expectations placed upon her as a 'wife and mother'.

To say that undertaking my Masters was life-changing would be a huge understatement. It was the first time I felt like I had the brain space for further education, and I relished the act of *learning*. This was, in part, because I finally felt like I had found the right fit: at Masters level, there was less emphasis on (or, indeed, time for) the social whirl of an undergrad degree, and rather than working on countless scattershot assignments, the focus was largely on our projects. Taking a year and a half to write something felt luxurious.

Autistic people are uniquely likely to drop out of higher education, be it university or VET/TAFE. The change to routine post-school, the social difficulties that can arise (O-Week, going to the pub with fellow students, making friends), sensory and information processing, and issues with executive function (independent and unstructured study, getting to class on time, submitting assignments by the deadline) can all compound to create a hostile environment for Autistic people. From my own experience, I can say that while many universities have made admirable strides in supporting students with disability, Autism-specific support is still thin on the ground, or non-existent. I was bullied in one higher degree research lab by a fellow candidate; I was the one asked to move desks.

For Autistic people who may have struggled in school, tertiary education presents a new, if not entirely familiar, barrier to access. Research[46] presented by Australian Autism advocacy body Amaze in 2018 found that 35 per cent of Autistic students only achieve Year 10 or below, compared with 17 per cent of the general student population, and are 50 per cent less likely to obtain a bachelor's degree compared to students with other disabilities. A considerable number of Autistic students change schools multiple times, with rates jumping from 24 per cent in primary school to 44 per cent in secondary school.

Jack Howes, an Autistic man who co-authored a paper[47] following a qualitative study of Autistic people's experiences of university, has written about his own attempt to conquer higher education. 'In the autumn of 2011, as a hopelessly naïve 18-year-old whose life experiences extended to being miserable at school and playing Football Manager at home, I went to university to study History,' he wrote. 'After one term of crippling loneliness, reclusiveness and awkwardness, I left, never to return and receiving an autism diagnosis six months later.'

While others seemed to know from a young age that it was their destiny to become a lawyer, doctor, physical therapist or teacher, I was cursed with the sort of scattershot mind that jumped from job to job. The pressure to know what you wanted to be when you 'grew up' was ever present. You had to have an idea of your VCE subjects in Year 9, choose said subjects according to the university degree you'd study straight out of school, and then fly smoothly into your chosen career upon graduation. Getting my Masters was a case of fourth-time lucky, and I felt vindicated in my fierce belief that it's okay not to know what you want to be when you grow up until well after you've become a grown-up.

Ironically enough, screenwriting was what I'd put in my 'In 20 years time ...' section of the yearbook back in 1999, but it took me a long time to get back to that place, and to decipher that the wistful feeling I got in cinemas wasn't, in fact, about wanting to be a movie-star or SFX make-up artist (or costume designer, or key artist, or editor, or director ...). I was already a working screenwriter by the time I doffed my cap to the Chancellor on stage, having optioned my first feature script and done some 'gun for hire' work for TV, so the degree was more of a spiritual moment of recognition of that hard work than a ticket to work in 'the business'.

Since obtaining my Masters, I have been qualified to teach at undergraduate level, and have taught screenwriting and short-story writing. Teaching is the perfect gig for my Autism, since it combines two of my favourite things: performing for an audience, and 'sharing the taxonomic list'. My empathetic nature means I can also guide students through their writing and workshopping process in a way that makes them feel safe sharing their work. And because I'm imparting my love of screenwriting to them, it helps me feel energised about my own work when I get back to it, rather than drained.

I also, especially post-2018, have a unique understanding of the challenges that the classroom can present to neurodiverse students:

you won't catch any 'no phones, no screens' nonsense in my classroom. Need to wear sunglasses or have one earbud on in order to be able to filter out everything but what I'm telling you? Want to get up and march around as you work through your screenplay idea? Be my guest.

There is a cultural cringe in Australian creative writing academia that leads many students to believe they have to write 'serious' pieces; in screenwriting, this can lead to a panoply of dour family dramas, even when students would desperately love to write something more in line with their own passions. I start every semester by showing a video interview with Paul Thomas Anderson in which he, despite being a dour family-drama guy himself, recalls quitting film school after a lecturer told the assembled students they weren't allowed to even think about 'writing *Terminator 2*' in his class.

When my students realise that all bets are off in my classroom, it's deeply gratifying; they've written everything from satirical thrillers set in the world of amateur orienteering to postcolonial horror TV dramas. It's a special gift teaching a subject that many students take as a 'breadth' elective: it might be the only two hours of the week where an engineering or law student gets to indulge their creativity. It's on me to make those two hours everything they can be.

Because I've been a student so many times in my life (including quite recently), I like to think I have a unique insight into and empathy for the student experience. In other words, I've turned what was once a source of shame (my 'inability' to finish a degree or qualification) into a key skill: I'm aware of the barriers to engagement for certain students, be they Autistic, neurodivergent or otherwise. My role as a teacher is to find out what works for them, and help them achieve their goals and raise their voices.

For many years I lived the grind of striving towards greatness; no matter my achievements, I always stacked them against the fantasy achievements that would mean 'true success': I had done hundreds of interviews, but not for *Rolling Stone* or *Vanity Fair*; I had published many articles, but not a book; I had written screenplays, but not TV comedy. It was only once I felt the thrill of helping students to find their voices that I realised the 'great work' of my life might be helping others to achieve theirs.

I am extraordinarily lucky to be (at the time of writing) gainfully employed: I know this is not the case for many Autistic people, and indeed until recently I have spent plenty of time in my life either unemployed or underemployed. The unemployment rate for Autistic Australians[48] is 31.6 per cent; that's three times the rate of other people with disability, and almost six times the rate of people without disability.[49] Of unemployed Autistic Australians, 54 per cent had *never* held paid work, despite having both the desire to do so and the skills (and often qualifications) to match.

Many Autistic people (myself included) are world champions at feeling shame: we feel it when we have meltdowns or burnout, when we 'don't fit in' and when we 'can't' do certain things. For many of us, that shame can centre around employment. Barriers to work, whether they're structural (expectation of job interviews, workplace environments, stereotypical understanding of Autism) or practical (access issues, sensory issues), can make us feel like we are the problem.

I've experienced shame, both self-inflicted and societal, when I've been 'unable' to work in traditional office environments. The modern open-plan office (or as I like to call it, the hell forest) can be very difficult for some Autistic people: the lack of privacy (particularly audio), the unregulated temperatures and lighting, sometimes (in the case of 'hot-desking') even the lack of a secure workspace can be a nightmare.

In 2011, I took a short-term contract, working at *The Age* to help with the online entertainment content. Despite having the support of a great manager, and my editor being an old friend, the office environment was a sensory nightmare: temperatures fluctuated wildly, my 'smart casual' clothing was itchy and restrictive, and the smells from the open-plan kitchen would settle over the office like a pall.

We shared desk space with some breaking news journos, so I would often be trying to write 'Melbourne's Top 5 Pies' while overhearing a phone interview about a bloodcurdling plane crash. Towards the end of my time there, I could only cope by coming in early – 6 or 7 am – and burning through all my work before the floor became busy, then escaping home to recover in bed. When I resigned from that contract, I felt great shame at returning to freelancing: I was ashamed that, despite having positioned myself as a journalist all these years, I apparently 'couldn't handle' the 'fast-paced world' of journalism. I also worried it would look as though I 'didn't want' to work. I *did* want to work, just not in that environment!

I often wonder how much of my anxiety and depression was a normative response to existing as Autistic in a neurotypical environment, particularly as it intersected with work and the associated notions of 'functioning'. Do I feel anxious and panicked in the library at university because there's something wrong with me, or because the carpet is ridiculously patterned, the walls are glass, and the 'floating' stairs have huge gaps in them that make me feel like I'm going to fall through them and die? Am I 'incapable' of holding down a 'real' job, or does the modern open-plan office design create sensory overload?

When Autistic people talk about creating a world that is sensory friendly, some neurotypical people bristle at the notion, like we're suggesting we want everyone to be wrapped in cotton wool (which I admit would be very comfy). The irony is, a sensory-friendly world – like a more accessible world – is better for everybody, including neurotypical people. I have worked from home as a freelance journalist for the majority of my adult life, because there, I can control the environment around me. I know how much the noise and furnace-like thermostat of the open-plan office contributed to my reduced capacity to work and create in that environment – and I bet if those features were addressed, the general stress levels of the staff would be greatly lowered.

There are, of course, a number of admirable programs geared towards helping Autistic people find work; some of them were highlighted in the engaging ABC series, *Employable Me*. Unfortunately, these programs are often focused on a very specific understanding of Autism, and one that takes its cues from the male-skewed diagnostic criteria: that we all, necessarily, have high-level skills in STEM fields, or want to work in data, programming, banking or tech. These stereotypes are so widespread that some employers may not even know that women and gender diverse people 'can' be Autistic.

To the best of my knowledge, there aren't any initiatives geared towards other Autistic skills and talents – yet! But it's my hope that as a greater diversity of Autistic presentation is represented on screens, in print and in workforces everywhere, more opportunities will open up for Autistic people looking for work. Some Autistic people, for example, are well suited to work in industries like nursing, counselling, teaching or animal welfare. Others have great creative minds, or might be a great problem solver or crisis manager.

Our society is geared towards picking a niche for yourself before you're even allowed to vote, and then charging towards it at 100 km/h. This can make you feel like a failure if your path takes a different route, at a lower speed. Education is something young people are meant to do before they become workers (which is why we are all socialised to sneer at mature-age students); if you don't know what you want to be or do by, say, twenty, maybe there's just no hope for you. It's bullshit. The important part is just to keep learning, because that's – pause for huge groan from audience – how we learn who we really are.

I received my Masters in July 2017. Just over a year later, I would finally learn who I really was: Autistic.

YOU CAN GO HOME AGAIN

My friend and colleague Yenn Purkis, an Autistic advocate and author, recently described the experience of spending time with other Autistic people – their 'neurokin' – as 'like coming home after being in another country for a long time'.

A few months after I gave my address at the Yellow Ladybugs symposium, I spent a day in the city with Shadia Hancock, one of my fellow speakers. It was my first post-diagnosis experience of making a new Autistic connection: was it too late for me? Would years of attempting to pass as neurotypical mean that I would remain an outsider in the Autistic community as well as in the non-Autistic world? Within minutes of meeting up at Federation Square we had got on the wavelength ('sharing the taxonomic list') and I was quickly put at ease; by the time we'd spent an hour in Darren Sylvester's flashing dancefloor artwork, 'For You', laughing and stimming, my world had changed.

I suddenly realised how much of the pain I had felt my entire life had been a yearning for something I didn't know I needed: the ability to simply *be*, by which I mean, to be Autistic beyond the confines of my own safe spaces, and to be recognised as part of a community with its own unique culture.

Much of that community has been found online, through the #actuallyautistic hashtag and associated Autistic meme accounts. In being 'publicly' Autistic, I have both emboldened myself to engage with Autistic friends and colleagues on that level *and* found that other Autistic people have entered my orbit. The internet, with its lessened reliance on verbal speech and social cues, has been a refuge for Autistic people since time immemorial (which is to say, the days of dial-up).

In a *New York Times* feature in 1997, Harvey Blume described the possibilities of online interaction in fostering the nascent neurodiversity and Autism rights movements, envisaging Autistic people 'sailing to strange neurological shores on the Internet, and exchanging information about how to behave upon arrival'. With the 20/20 hindsight of diagnosis, I can look back on my own (considerable) time spent online and see that it was a space within which I could explore – sometimes to my detriment, and others' – new personas, learn (and be taught) about the world, and sink myriad hours into investigating my interests. It has, in both a literal and a spiritual sense, expanded the taxonomic list.

It is 'IRL', however, where I have most powerfully felt the impact of both Autistic culture and other Autistic people upon my own understanding of my place in the world (which, it could be argued, is Autistic culture in practice). I have experienced this, perhaps not surprisingly, in my areas of special interest, especially cosplay, and by extension the pop culture convention world; the best cons are both places where I am not just encouraged to dress as other characters but celebrated for doing so, and places where Autistic people (along with other neurodivergent people, and people with disability) are welcomed with chill-out spaces, medical lanyards and other accommodations. I will never forget the peace I felt when I was told I couldn't use one of the cosplay changing rooms because a person was chilling out in it, having experienced a meltdown on the convention floor; said person was wearing an absolutely enormous ensemble of fantasy armour.

Even though accommodations for Autistic people are a relief, there is something more affirming still about places, events and get-togethers that are *specifically* Autistic in nature. Jim Sinclair, the pioneering Autism rights activist, has written[50] about this contrast between places provided for Autistic people and inherently Autistic spaces, and the value of being Autistic together. 'In a shared autistic space,' Sinclair writes, 'autistic people are in charge. Autistic people determine what our needs are, and autistic people make the decisions about how to go about getting our needs met.'

Perhaps my most profound experience of Autistic space has been the one nurtured between my girlfriend Catherine and me: she is also Autistic. If queer love is inherently revolutionary, then queer *Autistic* love is positively utopian. Catherine does not care if I start 'quoting'; she will look at me beatifically as I reel off entire scenes of dialogue from my favourite films, TV shows and YouTube videos. Meltdowns and shutdowns are no longer shameful secrets hidden from partners, but things we can guide each other through. We foster our own echolalic idiolect, our engagement with the world boiled down to its purest form.

If I stretch out my leg and say 'that', Catherine knows I am referring to a meme, a variation on the 'razzle dazzle' template where a long-legged bird (captioned: 'me') on the beach ('people saying "stop doing/saying that!"') stretches its leg towards a wave breaking on the shore ('that'): it's a shared joke, but 'that' is also our true Autistic natures, squashed for many years under the expectation of non-Autistic niceties.

My internet dating profile made reference to neurodiversity and Autistic advocacy, and it was one of the first things we chatted about; she was diagnosed six months after I was (amusingly, my own article on the topic was sent to her while she was in the process of assessment), and together we navigate both the experience of late-life diagnosis and create our own Autistic universe. Our relationship is like returning home.

225

The experience of finally understanding my place in the world has been nothing short of life-changing. Though it might be tempting to frame this book as a 'recovery narrative', it is, in fact, quite the opposite. As I get older, and more comfortable with my (Autistic) place in the (non-Autistic) world, if anything I feel I become *more* Autistic. Not because my behaviours and symptoms are worsening, but because I am more comfortable existing as 'obviously' Autistic, and there are behaviours and experiences that I am only now coming to understand as inherent (and inherently Autistic). Instead of forging through periods of burnout or shutdown, I can now understand my body and mind's reaction to stress; early in COVID-19 lockdown, I used an AAC (augmentative and alternative communication) app – in simplest terms, an app that speaks when you can't – when anxiety started to scramble my brain and I found it difficult to speak. Years ago, I would have just pushed through, forcing myself to talk, and suffering the consequences.

After a lifetime of looking over my shoulder, I have gradually come to understand certain things I do as innate rather than 'odd'. This was at a macro level as much as it was micro. For years, in our share house, I felt self-conscious about little things, like my eating habits, or my tendency to watch the same movies again and again; 'Whoops, made too much of this again!' I'd say with a nervous laugh, or 'Just re-watching this for work!'

They may seem like little things, but by thirty-six I was carrying the heavy burden of three-and-a-half decades' worth of little things (and plenty of big ones), each of them adding another small weight to my back. The cost of internalising these moments and interactions and concerns and shames was at first a slow burn, then a rapid bushfire: I felt the pain of it every day.

Navigating other people's understanding of me as Autistic, on the other hand, has been … interesting. One or two people, upon hearing of my diagnosis, started to talk a little louder and slower when conversing with me, as though talking to a child. Others still tried to nitpick with the diagnosis, or question whether the specialists had 'got it right'; was I *sure* about that? Were they? I wondered: had I become *so* skilled in my masking that I'd actually managed to convince everyone around me that I was 'normal'? I couldn't possibly hope to fit what they understood as 'Autistic', given what they knew of it from popular media. After all, I could converse freely, and even look them in the eye. The truth, of course, is that every zippy conversation I had was paid for with an emotional hangover, and while I had trained myself to make polite eye contact with strangers, gazing into the eyes of those who really knew and loved me was often too much to bear.

I can now understand some of these initial reactions to my diagnosis as a manifestation, however subtle, of people's fear of Autism. The wool is pulled from your eyes, to a certain extent, upon learning that you are 'officially' Autistic. I had always been aware of certain prejudices against Autistic people – for example, when I was a waitress, my co-workers had refused to serve a family whose Autistic son's meltdowns meant he sometimes hit himself – but suddenly grasping the full extent to which society is geared against us was such an intense experience I can only illustrate it by way of movie references: Leeloo learning about 'War' in her encyclopedia, or Neo having *The Matrix* explained after awakening in a goo-filled pod and being rescued by Morpheus on the *Nebuchadnezzar*.

I had no idea, for example, that the drive to discover Autism's genetic marker – something that I had initially felt quite warmly towards, as a sort of 'official' acknowledgement of Autism as a family trait – was, in part, in danger of becoming a piece of the broader machinery of a 'cure'. The desire to cure Autism is nothing new – after all, it's difficult not to detect some aspect of the curative in Applied Behaviour Analysis, what with its 'extincting' of Autistic behaviours – but while it has, perhaps, become less explicit, it is no less sinister.

This is especially apparent in the subtle push towards eliminating certain conditions, either through in-utero genetic screening (such as the test for Down syndrome) or by the vetting of donors for reproductive technologies like IVF and IUI. Screening for heritable diseases is one thing; eliminating the possibility of a child with a disability or neurodivergence seems to be quite another.

Sometimes this is more explicit: in 2019, the *Washington Post* reported on the case of US Donor H898, a man whose donor sperm had led to 'an autism cluster': twelve children (possibly more) conceived using his sperm were diagnosed as Autistic, and some have significant support needs. Any family history of Autism had not been noted in the donor's profile. One mother, Danielle Rizzo, sued the sperm bank she had engaged, settling for US$250,000. Rizzo says she took legal action to encourage greater oversight in the largely unregulated donor sperm industry in the USA. 'I did not sue because my children are autistic. I was suing to right a wrong.'

Locally, it seems that regulation – at least in terms of avoiding a similar 'cluster' – is already in action. A close friend who had offered to provide donor sperm for a colleague was told – after the extensive pre-donation interview process – that his sperm would not be accepted by one particular fertility clinic, because of a 'genetic condition': his sibling is Autistic. This gave me pause: I would not have a problem raising an Autistic child (in fact, I would relish that opportunity), but if I were to ask an Autistic male friend to come on board as a 'BYO' donor at an IUI service, does this ad hoc screening process mean that we'd be turned away? Would bringing a 'perfect' donor to the table cancel out any administrative concerns about my own 'genetic condition'? Who is making these choices, and what are the implications of them?

This is one arm of what the bioethicist Rosemarie Garland-Thomson refers to as 'velvet eugenics'. In a 2020 investigation into the long-term implications of prenatal testing, *The Atlantic*'s Sarah Zhang observed the emergence of genomic testing companies that offered screening for a variety of conditions in embryos. 'The one test customers keep asking for,' the company's chief scientific officer told me,' Zhang wrote, 'is for autism. The science isn't there yet, but the demand is.'

The science may soon catch up with the demand. The spectre of elimination is seemingly so apparent that some of the guiding voices in Autism research have been moved to take a stand; in 2018, Simon Baron-Cohen wrote a position piece for *New Scientist* in which he implored genetic researchers to focus on work that would improve outcomes for Autistic people (such as early detection that could lead to therapeutic interventions). 'We at the Autism Research Centre have no desire to cure, prevent or eradicate autism,' he wrote. 'I hope the autism community will be willing to trust researchers who nail their colours to the mast in this way.'

The notion of Autism as a terrible burden to those around the Autistic person was memorably evoked by Jim Sinclair's 1993 address, 'Don't Mourn For Us',[51] at the International Conference on Autism in Toronto, delivered with an audience of parents in mind. In that groundbreaking speech, Sinclair tackled the notion that a child's diagnosis as Autistic is a cause for their parents to mourn. 'The tragedy is not that we're here, but that your world has no place for us to be. How can it be otherwise, as long as our own parents are still grieving over having brought us into the world?'

In a way, the few years immediately following my diagnosis have been an exercise in understanding the past.

To me, the past isn't a foreign country so much as it is a parallel dimension that exists alongside my current reality; the future (or at least, a vision of it, good or bad depending on the day) is equally alive. At any given moment I'm probably slipping between timelines in my mind: going for a walk on a sunny spring day while remembering, in real time, heading to the Royal Show on a similar day ten or twenty years ago, and thinking about what I'll make for the next Royal Show preserves contest. Sensory information – mostly smells and sounds, but sometimes textures or even temperatures – is the turnstile, nonlinear time the subway.

Or maybe it's more like how film critic Owen Gleiberman once described Bill S Preston, Esquire and Ted 'Theodore' Logan and their *Excellent Adventure*: as people who 'experience every moment of their lives as if they were watching it on television. Reality isn't real to them – it's a show they're living inside'. You have likely realised by now that it is hard for me to explain my place in the world without referring to popular culture and critical theory. That's because that is what I've used to make sense of my own experience in lieu of a diagnostic framework that explained it, but also because most people's understanding of a non-normative temporality is drawn from nonlinear movies about time travel. Hey, I guess it *was* me who stole my dad's keys!

These memories and fantasies aren't just the half-formed emotional detritus of life, they're vivid realities. One example I often think of is the first day of my Masters study. If I were to visually represent my experience of time on that day, it would probably look like this:

January 2004 (the past):	March 2016 (the present):	March 2019 (the future[52]):
I am watching The Darkness play their Big Day Out sideshow at the Corner Hotel. I rush to the front of the stage, and find myself standing next to my old school friend, Prentiss. I am wearing a black catsuit.	I am in a stuffy room in the Elizabeth Murdoch building at the VCA's Southbank campus, listening to our course coordinator discuss the screenwriting journey we are about to go on.	I start my PhD research, looking at the feminist implications of intergender hand-to-hand combat (when a man and a woman fight each other on equal terms) in action cinema.

So, then, what's it like to experience?

[overlapping, illegible superimposed text]

You might interpret this to mean that each of those timelines is obliterated by the others; slippage of information between temporalities leading to complete chaos, like having thirty-seven tabs open at the same time and cycling. See, they're all happening simultaneously, but in *Sliding Doors*, we only see one Gwyneth Paltrow at a time, because most people can't watch two simultaneous timelines concurrently without their heads exploding.

We 'know' a lot about Autistic perception of time if viewed through a filter of lack, which is to say that we're not very good at it. Autistic children have an 'impaired sense of time',[53] which explains, for example, their inability to show up for dinner promptly, or their tendency to sink hours into special interests while forgetting to eat, drink, bathe or sleep. Other research suggests a likelihood, in Autistic people, of mutations or anomalies in the clock genes.[54] Our 'duration judgement' may indicate 'perceptual idiosyncrasies'.[55] What if, instead, to fall back yet again on Professor Grandin's 'different, not less', we considered Autistic time not as a failure to adapt to neurotypical time, but instead as its own cultural concept? It is entirely possible: in te reo Māori, the word for Autism is *Takiwātanga*, 'in their own time and space'.

The process of understanding my Autism bleeds, naturally, into celebrating it; it is like stepping out of the shadows and into the daylight. I have travelled through time to write this book; to get to where I am now; to get to where I am going, to this moment in the sun. It's the first day of summer in 2020 as I write this, but it's also the winter of 1986.

It's an ordinary August afternoon, and my first complete memory is in the process of forming: we have come, along with my aunt, Mum's younger sister Catie, to see the re-release of Steven Spielberg's beloved *E.T. The Extra Terrestrial*, at the venerable Art Deco cinema, the Metro Theatre. On the screen that towers above me, Henry Thomas is carefully laying a trail of Reese's Pieces in a scrubby pine forest on the outskirts of suburban Los Angeles.

Though I would later come to base many of my mannerisms on mime artist Caprice Rothe's performance as E.T.'s hands, in this moment I am racked with fear as I watch E.T. move about the forest. I can feel my dress starting to stick to the back of my neck, my sweat fusing the damp cotton to the dark red velour of the seat. All around me, people's eyes are glued to the screen.

Perhaps, I think, they are as terrified as I am.

'Don't worry.'

Mum leans over from her seat in the cinema, taking my hand in hers, and whispers encouragingly, 'It's daytime now: nothing bad can happen.'

EPILOGUE: #ACTUALLYAUTISTIC

Though I've quoted lots of Autistic people throughout this book (to counter, in a way, the clinical view that is often the overwhelming tone of non-Autistic Autism discourse), and though this is technically my 'memoir', I also wanted to use this opportunity to share the voices of some of my Autistic friends and colleagues, all of whom – in their own way – have helped me understand my place in the world. Some I have known for quite some time; others have only recently entered my universe. Some of their experiences – particularly to do with later-life diagnosis – are similar to mine and others are vastly different. What unites us is our shared understanding of what it is to be an Autistic person in a non-Autistic world.

When I spoke to Yellow Ladybugs' symposium audience back in February 2019, I knew that I *wanted* to 'find my people', but I hadn't quite done that yet. There was still a part of me that felt a bit Johnny Come Lately about being diagnosed at thirty-six; did I really have a right to be part of the community? Fortunately, such fears of Autistic gatekeeping were unfounded. When I posted about my diagnosis on Instagram, a friend commented, 'Some of my favourite people are Autistic'. As I have learned, there is absolutely nothing better than surrounding yourself with as many Autistic people as possible. These are just some of their stories.

WHEN WERE YOU DIAGNOSED?

Shadia, 20, student and self-employed (they/them): I was diagnosed at three. Being formally identified at such a young age helped me access supports to educational and therapeutic opportunities. Particularly during high school, when I was experiencing bullying and became more self-conscious of being different, having a term to describe and understand how my brain works was incredibly important in fostering self-acceptance, pride and a positive Autistic identity.

Jae, 34, Autism advocate (she/her): I was diagnosed with Asperger's in 2000 when I was fourteen. In 2018, at thirty-two, I sought an updated diagnosis of 'level 2' Autism. As I grew older, I learnt – and continue to learn – more about myself and Autistic traits. Fluctuations in my capacity mean I am always learning new traits and coping strategies.

Jessie, 34, writer and Autism mentor (she/her): I was diagnosed in 2020 at age thirty-four. Diagnosis was really just a starting point for me. It forced me to really go through the backlog of my life and face up to my difficulties and traumas. As a person with complex trauma, OCD, bipolar disorder, and lots of delightful other things I'm overcoming, Autism was actually the piece I needed to start making some serious changes and to understand how and why these things have manifested.

Timothy, 26, student and Autism advocate (he/him): I was diagnosed at three years and three months. It gave the family a label and the incentive to invest heavily in intervention and other therapies to give me a head start to catch up in all delayed areas (everything).

Jessica, 36, artist and PhD candidate (she/they): I was diagnosed at twenty-eight. At the time there wasn't a huge amount of day-to-day difference, but reading about my diagnosis gave so much context to my life up to that point and made sense of a lot of comorbid mental health issues. Being diagnosed late means that there are many areas where you feel different from the way autism is presented in the media and larger culture.

Fleur, 32, university administrator (she/her): I was diagnosed the day after my thirty-second birthday with combined ADHD (inattentive and hyperactive ADHD). About six months later, I started being assessed for ASD and I am sure that it will be confirmed that I have both ADHD and ASD. I feel like when neurodivergent women talk about getting diagnosed there is a pressure to make it a feel-good story because we don't want to further stigmatise Autism or ADHD or scare other women and girls who may be wondering if they are neurodivergent. However, the truth is my diagnosis journey wasn't a feel-good story; there was an anger in me that was unleashed where I realised that I internalised a lot of rejection, abuse and hurt because I thought I was weird and I could do better. I am still working on my anger and how to manage these relationships as I do think some people just need better educations whereas others are just intolerant.

Mattie, 29, dry stone waller and carer (he/him): I tried to get a diagnosis when I was about twenty-one. I was told I was definitely Autistic after diagnostic [screening], but in the end they said they couldn't make a certain diagnosis because my upbringing was unusual, I was (in their words) 'too charismatic', and my being trans sort of messed up their diagnostic procedure. There isn't any proper standardised diagnostic process over here [in England] and where I live is pretty poor. The whole thing proper messed me up for a while; by now, I know myself and that I'm Autistic, and that a lot of my experience of getting diagnosed was malpractice. I wish it had gone differently, but it didn't.

Jo, 42, publisher and writer (she/her): I received a provisional diagnosis aged thirty-one, after my son was diagnosed as having Asperger syndrome aged seven. I did the first part of the process, with the same psychologist who diagnosed my son, and she told me that she believed I was Autistic but others might not because I present so well and had done so well professionally. Later, when I had a nervous breakdown aged forty, after my marriage ended, I saw a psychologist who didn't understand women and Autism, and who misdiagnosed me as bipolar; my GP agreed. I really freaked out, and forced myself to reassess everything. Four weeks later, I got in to see the psychiatrist I had been referred to. She assessed me and said I wasn't bipolar – that all the things that had made the other two medical professionals believe this were actually aspects of my Autism. I had told my original psychologist exactly this, based on my understanding of women and Autism, and she had argued that I was wrong. Because she was the professional, I believed her.

James, 38, software developer (he/him): I was twenty-nine years old. Through the help of family and friends, I had reached the opinion that I probably fit the diagnostic criteria for Asperger syndrome (this was in the *DSM-IV* era and therefore AS was a current diagnosis). I was fortunate enough to have the means to fund the diagnostic process, which many Autistic adults do not. It allowed me to understand the course of my life and various events in it as consequences of real, material differences in my brain's 'firmware' rather than necessarily a lack of effort or willpower on my part, or 'being a loser'. This acknowledgement of real differences also prompted me to consider more often the possible differences in the way my behaviour might be perceived by others and what I had intended. Often I will ask a trusted friend or colleague for their opinion on such matters, when before, it would not have occurred to me to do so, because for all I knew, I was 'normal'.

Catherine, 37, artist and teacher (she/her): I was diagnosed at thirty-five. At first I think I felt vindicated that I wasn't 'making up' my symptoms, that they were recognised by an authority figure (two, no less) with an official diagnosis. It was also a relief to be told that the difficulties I have had with executive function weren't merely a product of laziness or lack of good work ethic. [But] I also had an ambivalent relationship to diagnosis: if your identity in life since childhood has been that you're 'different', to suddenly be told that the things that make you unique and unusual are in fact what makes you part of a group can seem to diminish your individuality. There was a period of time post-diagnosis where I felt I had been given news that undermined my perception of myself as someone who is talented. Instead, the diagnosis seemed to imply I was defective. I don't think this feeling went away entirely until I was able to speak more with other Autistic people. On the whole, I would say that diagnosis has made me less hard on myself.

Tegan, 35, student (she/her): I was diagnosed late, at thirty-three. It was like finally being able to see myself for the first time, which sounds like a cliché, but the experience was actually deeply shocking, and took some getting used to. After my diagnosis my entire life had to be reorganised, re-examined and renamed. Mostly, I had to learn to be kinder to myself, and my past self. Living on the outside of all the usual avenues for gaining self-esteem, missing every expected milestone and constantly lagging behind my peers, are events that are no longer sources of deep pain for me, as they were before. I've had two years to settle into the diagnosis, and although I'm still working out the best way to live my life on a daily basis, I now realise that I'm not the problem.

HOW DO SENSORY ISSUES AFFECT YOU?

Shadia: I am extremely noise sensitive, which makes many environments incredibly painful and inaccessible. When I got my hearing tested by an audiologist, it revealed my hearing to be in the top 90th percentile of the population. My assistance dog trainee also helps me self-regulate and read my internal states. For example, when I am struggling with noisy environments, I will often pat her or put her on my lap for comfort, or she will alert me that I am anxious and I may leave the environment.

Jae: This can vary so much! I do not do loud, unexpected sounds well (like things banging). A lot of the time loud sounds and events are overwhelming, but if it's music I'm interested in and the rest of the environment is sensory friendly (not overcrowded for example) I can have lots of fun and not get overwhelmed! I love wearing noise cancelling headphones when the world is too overwhelming. Different types of light globes can be very glary and overwhelming too, especially old fluorescent ones. I have a galaxy projector lamp in my room, and the projection onto my roof is very calming.

Jessie: Up until recently, I was unaware my sensitivities were that different to anyone else's. I had no idea what a sensory overload was until recently, I just thought I 'felt bad' at times. I'm extremely sensitive to light and sound, and often touch. I do love movement, feeling like I'm moving, pushing myself, loud music, etc. I just can't take it all the time but I do love listening to music as it allows me to feel things I wouldn't otherwise. All up, my senses have become a glorious wonderland that I've been discovering for many months now. But, now that I understand them, I work with them.

Timothy: I am hypersensitive across all modalities, so incoming information is intense and uncomfortable in visual, auditory, tactile, olfactory and gustatory stimuli. I have sensory overload and anxiety issues surrounding sensory input as these can be very uncomfortable and at times distressing.

Jessica: I find it near impossible to follow conversations in loud environments. There is no definition for me between background noise and one person's voice and it is painful and exhausting to try and glean meaning in these situations. I also have trouble with harsh, bright lighting (I use only red lights at night and wear blue blocking orange glasses to watch TV in the evening), and I'm not able to wear scratchy or rough fabrics. I have a strong sense of smell and hearing which is a plus in my field but can also cause problems in day-to-day life with 'bad' smells or 'bad' sounds.

Fleur: My experiences of sensory stuff is like a lot of other late-diagnosis people where we start putting all the pieces together and be able to put names to things that we feel. I always needed to have my hair up in a ponytail and an extremely tight one too: I would sleep in a ponytail that was so tight, it needed two hair elastics to let me feel like I could function. I constantly have to moisturise my skin because if my skin feels dry I actually become unable to function or concentrate; same if my hair gets too greasy. I really struggle with clothes tags and I am noise sensitive, but it tends to be for yelling, kids being too loud and other people eating. I can sit in a bar or restaurant but if it's too loud, it just feels like a tidal wave and I just sink back into my chair and let everyone else speak.

Mattie: I startle pretty easily, but that's not always distressing; I don't mind my friends finding it funny. I find I prefer sound (having music or a podcast on) over what other people seem to think passes as 'silence'. I always have earphones in when I'm out and about.

Jo: I like to be able to control my auditory environment. I like to wear soft clothes – I am a little obsessed with finding second-hand silk and cashmere, for instance. And I can't wear clothes that irritate my skin, like pure wool that's itchy. I feel like my affinity for water, and for the sun on my skin, might have a sensory element. These things calm me in a big way, and my whole mood is different if I can feel sunshine and immerse myself in water.

James: Multiple people speaking at the same time, or one person speaking over a TV show, or music I am listening to is quite irritating; it feels like being stuck between two bands on two stages playing completely different songs. I avoid shopping centres with lots of hard, sound-reflective surfaces because they create the effect of even more voices than are actually there. My sensory issues are pretty mild compared to many other people on the spectrum.

Catherine: I certainly get confused about whether I am hot, cold, hungry or tired. I am very sensitive to the texture of fabrics and extremely bothered by some sounds in my environment. My sensory sensitivities make sleep very tricky. I essentially mummify my head before going to bed, much to the amusement of partners and my family.

Tegan: My sensory issues are numerous, and can be both a blessing and a curse. I can't seem to habituate to background noise, so I hear everything all at once and with equal volume, and this is pretty exhausting if I'm in the wrong environment, but exciting if I'm in the right one. Usually after I go out in public, or I spend too much time on my computer, I have to spend a long time in my bedroom afterwards, curtains closed, in order to recuperate. My room is a little oasis of calm, and I'm very happy in it. I also have a few strange synesthesias (which are common in those on the spectrum), one of which means I feel noise as physical sensations on my body. This adds a very beautiful dimension to listening to music, but can be a curse if I'm watching, for example, *The Nanny*.

WHAT WAS YOUR EXPERIENCE OF SCHOOL?

Shadia: Overall, I had a positive experience at primary and high school. At primary school, I had some incredible key integration aides who helped me with classroom tasks and helped me with skills related to organisation and communication. Not all aides were good; some would 'baby' me and take over tasks when I knew I was capable of doing them, which made me feel a bit stupid and shut down. Others would not give me enough support or believed that my mother was being 'overprotective' (not even kidding, I glanced at one of them texting this to their colleague), and would expect me to be able to push through tasks. The ones that had a positive impact knew the balance between acknowledging my strengths and giving me support when needed to truly empower me. My high school was structured differently to most schools; there were no year levels, every student had their own Individualised Learning Plan (ILP), and we were able to choose subjects we were genuinely interested in. Thankfully, my high school did not place emphasis on grades, but the learning experience.

Timothy: School can be very difficult for Autistic nonspeaking students, as it has been for me. I started Prep in Special School and it was not a good experience, too overwhelming, with teachers and aides having to attend to the other kids with different high support needs. Primary school (Years 2–6) was inclusive and mainly positive as I was accepted as a member of the class, and with a fantastic aide's support, participated in nearly all curricular and co-curricular programs. Secondary school was a nightmare, with active discrimination and exclusionary practices which rendered me unable to communicate using my preferred mode of Partner Assisted Typing (deemed by the school to be controversial). After strenuous negotiation from disability advocates and family, I was allowed to use PAT, but due to intense and extensive social isolation and alienation, I suffered clinical depression necessitating psychiatric intervention. I was only able to complete high school with more sympathetic school staff and an aide who became my friend, with more flexible timetabling arrangements and support from advocates, family and friends. To be in mainstream schools, Autistic nonspeakers invariably face an uphill battle, in obstacles from applying for enrolment, attendance and participation in programs as well as attaining social inclusion, a much too common story for us because we are seen as not good fits for the student mode. There was constant pressure from mainstream schools to our family and us to go into special education.

Jessica: I had a strange schooling that involved being put ahead one and a half years after moving to the UK and then being put back a half a year when we moved back to Melbourne. This meant that for the first half of high school I was [considered] remedial and difficult, and the second half I was 'gifted' in English and arts studies. What was consistent was my inability to grasp maths – even now my brain struggles to cope with simple addition. Numbers were never my thing.

Fleur: I was mercilessly bullied from preschool to Year 12. In primary school, I didn't play with any of the other kids until I was ten because I got so frustrated with them but also I just did not know how to relate to them. I felt a lot of the time I had to pretend I was interested in stuff to fit in but the other girls knew I was faking and just excluded me. I also wanted to talk a lot about the news (politics is one of my lifelong special interests) and this was so not cool, so I got bullied for being a square. One of my shorter term, memorable special interests were salmonella and the other girls wanted to talk about *Home & Away*.

Jessie: My experience of school was chequered. I was very shy, then the class clown, then entirely hyperactive, then dominant. I understand I was well-liked but I could be fiery at times (still can be) and I'd make a lot of blunders. Most teachers saw me as very smart, but there were subjects where I wasn't smart at all (maths, science, etc.). I spent a lot of time covering up my difficulties, not just from my teachers but from my family. Like most Autistic people, I was bullied throughout school and also throughout my adult life. But, I really loved learning; I was like a sponge.

Mattie: In school I was super bright, fairly bullied, fairly 'mature' and self-reliant. I think I worked out that other kids didn't mean ill but couldn't be trusted fairly early. That, along with other stuff in my life at the time, was pretty damaging. I very much retreated inwards while maintaining what I see now as an elaborate mask. I was very lonely and isolated, but didn't realise. I loved learning, though.

Jo: Primary school was fine, and I didn't think about social stuff much at all. I was very small and had very long hair, and when I was in junior primary, some of the girls liked to play with me because I was little and cute. Makes me cringe to say it, but that's what my mum tells me. I remember that it was when I was in Year 7 – one year out from high school in South Australia – that I started to very vaguely notice social stratification and that I was being teased for being a 'square' and for wearing my knee socks pulled up. Then in Year 8 and 9, I started to take the teasing about being a 'square' seriously, and started to deliberately fail and act up, so I would rid myself of that label. I was often a student of extremes – I worked really hard or I handed in nothing.

Catherine: On the whole, I have the privilege of being able to say that I had a fantastic experience of school. I went to the same very supportive, small private school from prep to year twelve, so other than the jump from year six to high school I never had to deal with the rupture of starting at a new school. I had teachers who paid attention to my strengths and weaknesses and a constant, supportive group of academically-inclined friends. I can see now that some of my behaviour was 'intervened' with by teachers early on, such as my rapid, sometimes erratic pattern of speech. The private school experience very much smoothed me out and polished me.

Tegan: I did very, very badly at school. I think I was the worst student in my class. I was a chronic daydreamer, I had undiagnosed dyscalculia, and I struggled to follow verbal instructions. I also went to a school that had no patience for students who were falling behind or disabled, so I was punished a lot for my failings. Nobody thought to have me assessed for learning difficulties; it was never mentioned, and there was no sympathy. The only class I did well in was art. By the time I finished school I was so humiliated by the experience that I didn't go on to University – and it took me another twelve years to gather up the courage to do so.

HOW DO YOU FEEL ABOUT 'FUNCTIONING' LABELS?

Shadia: My levels of functioning or support are very context dependent. Not only do they vary day to day, but certain environments and life events can also contribute to differences in functioning. For example, while I am on holidays and less 'cluttered' in my mind about anxiety surrounding university or work, I have more space in my executive functioning for cooking, cleaning, walking, and so forth. However, when I am overwhelmed or overloaded by a busy schedule, many of these basic daily tasks become very difficult. When there are too many disruptions to my routine, sensory issues, or other pressures, my anxiety will usually increase which affects my ability to read my internal states. These are times where I may go into overload, shutdown, or meltdown.

Timothy: Labels in general are stereotypes, and the so-called 'low' and 'high functioning' don't tell you much about the person, just the superficial aspects of speech and behaviours (etc.) that slot you into degrees of 'normal/neurotypical' performance and expectations.

Jessie: On a 'high functioning' day you'd see me as friendly, warm, thoughtful, on the ball, funny and relaxed. On a 'low functioning' day I'd struggle to get out of bed, look very pale, be very drained, or have a good old case of the irrits. Most people would be surprised to see me on a 'low functioning' day. I'm not the Jessie they know – I'm quite scattered, quiet and tired so I feel like I am a disappointment to people as they only ever really see me a certain way.

Jae: My psychologist actually didn't want to put a level down [with my diagnosis] because she knows how much I can fluctuate. Personal experiences (health and mental health, relationships, job security) as well as external effects (how accessible the world and other people are) definitely play a big part in fluctuations. I get Autistic burnout quite often, and it's hard to ensure I can take care of myself due to external demands like work.

Jessica: I can often 'pass' for neurotypical but in passing comes the toll of masking which leads to Autistic burnout and has most likely contributed to my chronic health problems.

Fleur: With my ADHD drugs, I do feel like there is a greater sense of consistency in how I function daily, and the constant waves of anxiety have disappeared. However, I still struggle a lot on some days, and if anything, my Autistic traits and behaviours are no longer drowned out by the ADHD so it's much more noticeable. I no longer drown myself in guilt whenever I have a meltdown; I had a really bad one when I thought my cat died in surgery and normally I'd feel sick with guilt the next day but instead I was like, 'Well, that sucked but this is me and today is a new day'.

Mattie: Functioning! Ha! It's hard to tell in some ways because I have lots of coping mechanisms (some mint, some maladaptive) that keep me going. Until very recently, functioning or not, I've had to make it work, so I've burned out a few times. Where I am now, I have a small but rich life, I spend almost no time around anyone I don't actively like, and I do work that is really good for me. In the past I have burned through a job every six months, had lots of panic and anxiety that were beyond the beyond. Basically, I think very strongly that my functioning is highly environmentally dependent.

Jo: My functioning definitely varies, but I feel it more in stages than day to day. It depends on what I am doing and what my environment is.

James: When my routines go undisturbed, people communicate with me clearly, give me instructions that are consistent and unambiguous, and I am in nice, quiet, safe, predictable environments, I 'function' pretty effectively, albeit still with an affect that could be read by careful observers as Autistic. Under stress, however, or in difficult environments, I feel as if my brain starts shutting down functions in ascending order of 'essentialness', much like the instruments in an aircraft that has lost power in an emergency.

Catherine: I can have periods in which I am tremendously productive and social, and then days in which the dishwasher needing to be unstacked and restacked makes me fall into an existential abyss. I don't think it's the dishwasher's fault.

Tegan: I don't think I feel like I'm ever 'functioning' and I'm not sure I ever will. Every day I'm burdened with the responsibility of having to manage myself as if I were a second job. No single task, no interaction feels automatic. Everything is a deliberate effort and takes its toll. I do have good days, or even good weeks where I seem to be on a roll, but it never lasts and I'll drop all the plates I've been spinning, and then I have to start again from scratch. Each day is its own new challenge. I think on the outside I can look like I'm functioning. I can get up, go for a run, see a friend and go grocery shopping, but internally there can be a war going on, an anxious pressure building up. I'm a little bit better at managing this anxiety, but sometimes it is simply unmanageable, and I have to let the collapse happen. In fact, the more I try to hold it in, the worse the meltdown will be. Part of learning about myself after the diagnosis was allowing myself time to fall to bits when it all gets too much, and to be patient and kind when it happens, instead of angry.

WHAT DOES BEING AUTISTIC MEAN TO YOU?

Shadia: To me, being Autistic is the way my brain is wired, how I process the world and things around me, and how I relate to others. Being Autistic comes with strengths, such as my attention to detail and dedication to specific areas of interest, as well as challenges like sensory issues, anxiety, and executive functioning difficulties. I am different, disabled, but not disordered or wrong. I cannot imagine not being Autistic and I wouldn't give it up even if it was possible, as then I would no longer be me.

Jessica: Among my close friends I feel acceptance, I feel 'normal', being Autistic doesn't necessarily mean anything aside from an ability to form tight, close bonds with my few very dear friends. Among strangers I can feel anything between a full-on *star* or totally inadequate depending on how well I am 'functioning' that day. With my family I can feel accepted and supported at times, broken and as a burden at others.

Timothy: I guess because I am extremely Autistic and a nonspeaker, most people find talking to me a trifle disconcerting. I don't really have the experience of anything but being Autistic, as I believe Autism affects me in numerous ways. Personally I feel that the differences in information processing, sensory issues and self-awareness (etc.) between neurotypicals and Autistics are a matter of degree rather than entirely separate categories altogether.

Jessie: When it was first confirmed to me that I could be on the spectrum, I actually thought it was really cool and interesting. It felt really badass! It was like I was suddenly part of a club that I didn't realise that I was eligible for – it was magnificent. I have a huge amount of respect for the spectrum itself and the people that are perched upon it. So, that was what it felt like in a bigger picture sense. But in a more intimate sense, being Autistic has given me a huge understanding of who I am and allowed me to softly inch closer to the person I have wanted to be in my life. She's been tucked away under there, and this diagnosis and self-understanding has allowed me to access her and breathe a bit of life into her.

Mattie: In terms of how I feel I 'fit' the idea of Autism ... I think class comes into it, and rurality. I grew up poor, living in the countryside. I didn't have to sit nicely, or do fancy family shit. I spent loads of my childhood alone; I didn't have to be hegemonically 'normal'. I have found as I've gotten older and people read me as a bloke more I'm socially read as a 'friendly, soft fella' and people are less surprised by me being Autistic than they were at me being an unintentionally gender non-conforming young woman. Big up the Autie lasses, women and enbies making it work. Respect.

Jo: Personally, I think I both embrace it and own it, and am ashamed of it. I wish I wasn't the latter, but if I am honest, I am. I embrace that it makes me who I am and I can't separate it from myself, or from the things I like best about myself. My sense of humour and fun, my creativity, my immersion in books and writing and the fact that all of my friends have come from that special interest that makes me who I am (and many of them are eccentric in their own ways, and I love this about them). I am ashamed of my poor executive functioning, which is also part of my Autism. It makes me feel like I'm not a proper grown-up and I worry that I'm going to really suffer when I get older as a result. I don't have significant savings (a few thousand dollars) or own property. I don't drive or own a car. I worry that I will age out of work and have no way of supporting myself.

Catherine: I'm still figuring it out. I have a deep suspicion of psychological discourses and categories as modes of interpolating and relating to the self. For a while after diagnosis I shied away from relating to myself too much through the category of Autism. I tried to identify more as 'eccentric' or 'weird' in a positive sense, as I might have when I was younger. I'm reassessing some of this scepticism now. I'm curious as to what positive understandings of Autism could be fashioned outside of the medical, lack-based definition that comes down to us from the *DSM* and its ilk. Neurodiversity movements are very interesting to me.

Tegan: Despite some of its difficulties, I don't mind being Autistic, because I like how I see, how I feel, and how I hear the world. I like who I am. The hardest part of being Autistic is actually how the world treats people who are different. Even the most caring person can have internalised ableism. It is the human condition to see things that are different as a social threat, and to push it away.

WHAT ARE THE MOST COMMON MISUNDERSTANDINGS ABOUT AUTISM?

Shadia: This is almost a book in and of itself. One that really upsets me is that Autistic individuals lack empathy or emotions. I am very sensitive to the emotions of others and often get overwhelmed by them. Similarly, I cringe when I read that Autistic people live in 'their own little world'. In my own experience, this was certainly not the case, and I was very sensitive to people's attitudes towards me. For instance, I often knew when someone didn't like me. Some of the misconceptions I have experienced is that I must have a milder, or 'less severe', form of Autism, which has caused me to feel dismissed about the struggles I face. Similarly, some people think that all Autistic people, particularly nonspeaking Autistics, have intellectual disabilities or that they aren't capable. This is also not taking into account the diversity of the Autism spectrum or presuming competence.

Timothy: I feel that the biggest misconceptions are we are either idiots or geniuses depending on situations and contexts, and we are very different in our make-up that marks us as Autistic, i.e., we can't read emotions, we can't do conversations, we have no concepts of social niceties, we have obsessive interests which are impractical or surreal.

Jae: There's lots of instances in the media where Autistic people's privacy and human rights aren't respected. But because we are all unique, it's hard to say how the media could do better in its portrayals.

Jessica: There were some great memes going around (shoutout to @aspiememes on Instagram) with a picture of an Autistic person from a TV show who were socially awkward and blunt but universally loved and supported, juxtaposed with a 'real life' version of someone who is struggling desperately to understand social situations and whether they are tolerated let alone supported. I've often watched depictions of Autistic people on TV and wished I hadn't spent my whole life masking. However, there's no guarantee I would have been met with the same (fictional) support these characters enjoy.

Fleur: I feel like there are people who think neurodivergent women are agents of chaos who enjoy attention and drama; that we somehow needed these diagnoses to get attention and be different when the reality is, most of us have spent our lives working our arses off to try and be normal and fit in. Every year I felt disappointed that I hadn't suddenly matured and grown out of my weirdness and become like everyone else. Every neurodivergent person I met was someone who just wanted to do their best and didn't want to be singled out. They just want to be accommodated, understood and for people to just be a little patient sometimes.

James: That we all have obvious spectacles of meltdowns. That we are all brilliant at one thing or another to 'make up for' the difficulties. That we desperately want to be neurotypical and that we want all of the same things they want but are tragically held back by our Autism (though that is not to say that never happens). That Autism necessarily has obvious physical manifestations, that there is an 'Autistic look'. On the other hand, I find that many 'Autism Parents' are so invested in the concept that 'if you've met one person with Autism, you've met one person with Autism' that they don't accept that the nature of Autism being a diagnosable condition means that there are common traits that Autistic people share.

Mattie: Mostly people seem unable to square in their heads that Autism is pervasive and always present. I am *always* Autistic, even when it's inconvenient, or embarrassing, or challenging. I think that is something that is very difficult for people to take.

Jo: Biggest misconception – that we lack empathy. That we feel less, when in fact it's the opposite. We feel more, but not always in response to the same triggers as neurotypical people. I feel like most representations of Autism are the cases that are obvious on the surface; I haven't really seen representation of cases like mine, that are more internal and subtle. That said, I feel like I see examples of Autistic women in books or on the screen who are not labelled as such, but feel deeply, genuinely Autistic to me. Particularly in books. I suspect there are a lot of women writers out there who are Autistic but don't know it.

Catherine: That we are all charmless bores. Or that we lack empathy.

Tegan: There seems to be this one, very popular and narrow idea of what Autism is, the 'rude and humourless savant', and whenever I see it represented in the media it's a little bit disappointing, and I do think that it might potentially do more damage than good in creating awareness. Although people with Autism do have a common set of traits, and yes some are rude, and some are savants, that is only one small subsection of an entire cosmos of personalities. In reality, Autistic people can be so vastly different from each other as to almost appear opposites.

HOW HAS AUTISM AFFECTED YOUR UNDERSTANDING OF YOUR GENDER AND SEXUALITY?

Shadia: I definitely think that being autistic has given me a different perception of social norms and helped me being true and authentic to myself. As a child I was a bit of a 'tomboy'; I wasn't affected much by society's binary views of male and female. When I worked out there was a name to describe my internal experience of gender, I realised that I do not view myself as gendered: I am just me. Gender is not a defining trait for me and others. I feel that this feeling of being different to others was exacerbated by the fact that my peers were quite difficult to relate to. I didn't understand why girls behaved the way they did, or why boys behaved the way they did towards me just because I was assigned female. Because of this, I feel my neurology and gender are linked, and I am unsure which one is the driving force. I like the term gendervague to describe this intersectionality. My sexuality has also been affected by the way I feel gender and how I connect to others as an Autistic person. I am pansexual, which means I am attracted to someone by their personalities and interests rather than their physical appearance and outer bodies. My ideal partner is someone who shares my love of nature and the environment, regardless of whether they identify as male, female, trans or non-binary.

Jae: I recently came out as a trans woman and started hormone replacement therapy. I have known for a long time that Autistic people were six times more likely to be gender/sexuality diverse, but I took a long road of discovery to reach the point of coming out, including fourteen months of being openly non-binary, and eight months of having changed my legal name. I'm hypersensitive to how society doesn't really support Autistic people, let alone Autistic trans/gender diverse folx, and that definitely played a part in how I explored my gender identity. I think this hypersensitivity has made it easier to come out and be who I am, rather than spend time thinking on new ways I can be judged by people.

Timothy: Haven't had time to explore this one yet, too busy with my numerous challenges like not having voluntary control of my body with a fragmented body map, huge info processing and sensory issues, and navigating a left-brain world with my right-brain modes of functioning.

Jessica: I have struggled with identity labels for my whole life. Even identifying as Autistic is still sometimes grating to me. I definitely know I am not straight, but labels feel confining and so I usually avoid them all together. This is inherently hypocritical of me as I understand the world easiest through categories and labels and so am always happy to have others label themselves. They are just not for me.

James: I suppose the 'outsider' perspective has led me to question a lot of stereotypical behaviour that tends to go along lines of gender and sexual orientation, especially since I have tended not to pick up the social cues that would have told me what behaviour was expected of me.

Mattie: I distinctly remember being considered and treated as gender neutral in school (this was long before I knew what transgender even was), sometimes as bullying – 'Are you a boy or a girl?' – but also just as a fact of life. I was just Mattie, and for better or worse I was accepted as my own separate social role.

Jessie: Discovering I am Autistic, and uncovering all those layers of built-up dust, has actually been the start of a process where I've discovered how exceptionally feminine I am. It has been lovely. I love dresses, make-up, looking and feeling beautiful. Like many Autistic women and people, I have a history of body dysmorphia. So for me, it's exceptionally important to me that I look and feel lovely after years of feeling pretty foul. Though I know that's not the case for everyone, being able to return to my more feminine self has been hugely important to me and actually instrumental in my healing.

Jo: I was a late developer in terms of actually having boyfriends (I'm hetero, so was always that) but was obsessed with romantic interests from around twelve. Like, I would choose a boy to have a crush on and then they would

(I now realise) become my special interest. I'd think and learn about them obsessively, would collect objects and knowledge around them, would hang around near them to observe them, analyse every piece of information or every interaction with them, but never had real relationships with them. What teen girls do, but to a far greater extent, I now realise.

Catherine: I'm gay and have never had a straightforward relationship to gender (was a tomboy when little, can only access femininity in a camp fashion as an adult, am somewhere between androgynous and what could be described as 'masc of centre' in my day-to-day life). I suspect there is much to be said about the way in which being Autistic has shaped my relationship to gender. But this is a topic that I have only just begun to think about.

Tegan: For as long as I can remember, I've felt half female, half male. I was a classic 'tomboy' kid, and was teased a lot for wearing my brother's clothing and being a bit rough around the edges. I'm also bisexual, which is a term I've only recently felt comfortable saying out loud. One pivotal moment after my diagnosis was learning that many people on the spectrum have a feeling of not belonging to a single sex. That was a massive relief, and has allowed me to exist in this state without tension and shame, and to embrace the ambiguity of who I am.

WHAT'S THE ONE THING YOU WISH PEOPLE KNEW ABOUT AUTISM?

Shadia: It is a neurological difference that encompasses a diverse range of experiences of the world. It is not a disorder, it is not something wrong, and not something that we need to mask over or fix to fit in with the 'normies'.

Timothy: That we are part of the human spectrum and have the same needs, desires, motivations and dreams as most people. It is very hard for the general public to be informed about AAC and speech-generating devices because mostly they don't have personal encounters with people who use diverse communication. I hope that with time and more aware-ness-raising on issues of non-speech communication, there will be more acceptance and understanding. Autism has been an intense and at times overwhelming experience. However, in facing up to my Autistic chal-lenges, of which there are many, I have developed and grown in resilience, determination and commitment to social justice and advocacy.

Jae: Sometimes we can't develop our true identities due to issues like living with transphobic family, lack of access to health and peer supports, or other reasons. I hope that future Jaes are able to get the supports they need, when needed – that one day we have an inclusive, accepting and supportive world.

Jessica: That it exists! That it affects your life in an ongoing way – both positively and negatively. That it is as 'normal' as any other neurotype. I wish neurotypical people would put in as much effort into their inter-personal skills, understanding and communication as most Autistic people do.

Fleur: I just want everyone to understand that neurodivergent people are all trying their best. Sometimes we can be frustrating, weird or inappro-priate but I hope people start understanding that we just really want to be good partners, colleagues, friends, children, siblings, parents, pet owners and that we just need to be allowed to do it our own way with perhaps some adjustments.

Mattie: I wish they understood more about themselves. Then they'd mind me less, and I'd mind them less.

Jo: That having it together on the surface doesn't mean you're not really Autistic. That it's about what's going on underneath, and how you pro-cess information and emotions, not how you manifest them for the world.

Jessie: I wish people would not view it as a disorder or an illness. To have your default wiring described that way is quite hurtful. I think, particu-larly for women who have likely been diagnosed with one disorder after another, it's nice to simply view yourself as something quite wonderful.

James: I wish people understood the core concept and not just superficial things that they picked up from specific Autistic people, real and fictional.

Catherine: That Autistic people are full, complex people worthy of dignity and inclusion in a human society that accommodates many ways of being in the world.

Tegan: That we crave love and friendship, just like everybody else does.

WHAT'S THE BEST THING ABOUT BEING AUTISTIC?

Shadia: One thing I love about being Autistic is that I appreciate the small details in life, which has helped me immensely with my artwork. It has also gifted me with an affinity with animals and nature. I often marvel at the intelligence of the animals I spend time with, and the intricacies of nature; a blade of grass, a bee pollinating a plant, the calls of birds in the trees.

Timothy: To be able to see the world with a different lens and to be able to understand about the underlying patterns and more visual aspects which neurotypicals may not be aware of because they are too engrossed with language-based processes.

Jessica: My favourite thing about being Autistic is the depth of my interest and excitement about the world around me! I am incredibly passionate and excitable. I am so saddened by jadedness and those who walk through the world with limited passion. I wouldn't give this part of myself up for anything!

Jo: My creative brain and sense of humour. I like who I essentially am, I think.

Catherine: This is very difficult to pin down as being Autistic is insepara-ble from my personality and entire suite of talents and weaknesses. That being said, I like my capacity for abstraction and analysis of conceptual patterns and structures. I like that this leads me to think deeply about the world from unusual perspectives.

James: The unique, somewhat detached outsider perspective we can have on many issues.

Jessie: I love my mind; it's creative and rich. Ridiculously analytical but also picks up on things others cannot. Despite many people thinking Autistics can't think out of the box, I find the opposite is true. I like my sensitivity toward others, I can tune in to how they are feeling and I genuinely care for others. And I choose to see great beauty everywhere I look nowadays which I enjoy.

Tegan: I think it's not feeling as much social pressure, and sticking to my own values even if this sometimes goes against what is popular. From what I can understand, neurotypical people are very socially motivated and malleable. They people please, and can be insincere, all in order to fit in. I don't feel the need to fit in, and I try to live my life as honestly and sincerely as possible. I like getting to decide what I like, and what I don't like, using myself as a guide, and nobody else. It feels very authentic.

Mattie: I love being Autistic. I love Autistics. I think fighting for the liberation and dignity and joy of all Autistics everywhere is a good mission to be getting on with, because we are everywhere. Justice for Autistics means justice for Indigenous peoples, justice for homeless people, incarcerated, trans and queer folk, survivors, Black, Asian, and on and on. That is what Autism brings and shapes in me: my freedom is everyone's freedom, 'cause I'm not sorted 'til we all are. Autism is a pathological need for justice, for me.

ENDNOTES

1   Puglisi, B, Ackerman, A, 2017, *The Emotional Wound Thesaurus: A Writer's Guide to Psychological Trauma*, Writers Helping Writers

2   Demazeux, S, Singy, P (Eds), 2015, *The DSM-5 in Perspective – Philosophical Reflections on the Psychiatric Babel*, New York: Springer, doi.org/10.1007/978-94-017-9765-8

3   Czech, H, 2018, 'Hans Asperger, National Socialism, and "Race Hygiene" in Nazi-era Vienna', *Molecular Autism 9*, Article Number 29, doi.org/10.1186/s13229-018-0208-6

4   Wing, L, 1981, 'Asperger's Syndrome: A Clinical Account', *Psychological Medicine*, Volume 11, Issue 1, pp. 115–29 doi.org/10.1017/s0033291700053332

5   Baron-Cohen, S, Leslie, A M & Frith, U, 1985, 'Does the Autistic Child Have a "Theory of Mind"?', *Cognition*, Volume 21, Issue 1, pp. 37–46

6   Happé, F & Frith, U, 2006, 'The Weak Coherence Account: Detail-focused Cognitive Style in Autism Spectrum Disorders', *Journal of Autism and Developmental Disorders*, Volume 36, Issue 1, pp. 5-25

7   White, R C & Remington, A, 2018, 'Object Personification in Autism: This Paper Will Be Very Sad if You Don't Read It', *Autism*, Volume 23, Issue 4, pp. 1042–5

8   Frazier, T W, Georgiades, S, Bishop, S L & Hardan, A Y, 2013, 'Behavioral and Cognitive Characteristics of Females and Males with Autism in the Simons Simplex Collection', *Journal of the American Academy of Child & Adolescent Psychiatry*, Volume 53, Issue 3, pp. 329–40

9   Dworzynski, K, Ronald, A, Bolton, P & Happé, F, 2012, 'How Different are Girls and Boys Above and Below the Diagnostic Threshold for Autism Spectrum Disorders?', *Journal of the American Academy of Child & Adolescent Psychiatry*, Volume 51, Issue 8, pp. 788–97

10   I wish this were a joke, but it is literally a formula devised by a group of mathematicians, commissioned by a lifestyle website, that claims to estimate a relationship's likelihood of success. And they say Autistic people are the weird ones.

11   Baxter, A J, Brugha, T S, Erskine, H E, Scheurer, R W, Vos, T & Scott, JG, 2015, 'The Epidemiology and Global Burden of Autism Spectrum Disorders', *Psychological Medicine*, Volume 45, Issue 3, pp. 601-13

12   Heilker, P & Yergeau, M, 2011, 'Autism and Rhetoric', *College English*, Volume 73, Issue 5 (May 2011), pp. 485–97

13   Castle, N, 1986, *The Boy Who Could Fly*, Lorimar Motion Pictures

14   Parsons, O E, Bayliss, A P & Remington, A, 2017, 'A Few of my Favorite Things: Circumscribed Interests in Autism are not Accompanied by Increased Attentional

Salience on a Personalized Selective Attention Task', *Molecular Autism* 8, Article 20, doi. org/10.1186/s13229-017-0132-1

15   South, M, Ozonoff, S & McMahon, W M, 2005 'Repetitive Behavior Profiles in Asperger Syndrome and High-functioning Autism', *Journal of Autism and Developmental Disorders*, Volume 35, pp. 145–58

16   Dickerson Mayes, S, Calhoun, S L, Aggarwal, R, Baker, C, Santosh, M, Molitoris, S & Mayes, R D, 2013, 'Unusual Fears in Children with Autism', *Research in Autism Spectrum Disorders*, Volume 7, Issue 1, pp. 151–8

17   Macari S L, Vernetti A, Chawarska K, 2020, 'Attend Less, Fear More: Elevated Distress to Social Threat in Toddlers with Autism Spectrum Disorder', *Autism Research*, doi: 10.1002/aur.2448

18   White, S W, Oswald, D, Ollendick, T & Scahill, L, 2009, 'Anxiety in Children and Adolescents with Autism Spectrum Disorders', *Clinical Psychology Review*, Volume 29, Issue 3, pp. 216–29

19   McDonnell, C G, Boan, A D, Bradley, C C, Seay, K D, Charles, J M & Carpenter, L A, 2019, 'Child Maltreatment in Autism Spectrum Disorder and Intellectual Disability: Results from a Population-based Sample', *The Journal of Child Psychology and Psychiatry*, Volume 60, Issue 5, pp. 576–84

20   Rumball, F, Happé, F & Grey, N, 2020, 'Experience of Trauma and PTSD Symptoms in Autistic Adults: Risk of PTSD Development Following DSM-5 and non-DSM-5 Traumatic Life Events', *Autism Research*, Volume 13, Issue 12, pp. 2122–32

21   Gravitz, L, 2018, 'Does Autism Raise the Risk of PTSD?', *Scientific American*, 1 October, viewed 25 March 2021, scientificamerican.com/article/does-autism-raise-the-risk-of-ptsd/

22   Reitman, I, 1984, *Ghostbusters*, Columbia-Delphi Productions/Black Rhino; Feig, P, 2016, *Ghostbusters*, Columbia Pictures/Village Roadshow Pictures

23   Kinnaird E, Norton C, Pimblett C, Stewart C & Tchanturia K, 2019, 'Eating as an Autistic Adult: An Exploratory Qualitative Study', *PLoS One*, Volume 14, Issue 8, doi:10.1371/journal.pone.0221937

24   Wilson, J M, 2019, 'My Autistic Son Is Having Chicken Nuggets for Thanksgiving – and That's OK', *The Mighty*, viewed on 25 March 2021, themighty.com/2019/11/autism-dietary-needs-thanksgiving/

25   Lovaas, O I, Koegel, R, Simmons, J Q & Stevens Long, J, 1973, 'Some Generalization and Follow-up Measures on Autistic Children in Behavior Therapy', *Journal of Applied Behaviour Analysis*, Volume 6, Issue 1, pp. 131–66

26   Kupferstein, H, 2018, 'Evidence of Increased PTSD Symptoms in Autistics Exposed to Applied Behavior Analysis', *Advances In Autism*, Volume 4, Issue 1, pp. 19–29

27   Leaf, J B, Ross, R K, Cihon, J H and Weiss, M J, 2018, 'Evaluating Kupferstein's Claims of the Relationship of Behavioral Intervention to PTSS for Individuals with Autism', *Advances In Autism*, Volume 4, Issue 3, pp. 122–9

28   By 'NeedsMoreTuba' (whose username I include if only to make a point about finding understanding in the strangest places)

29   Park I, Gong J, Lyons G L, Hirota T, Takahashi M, Kim B, Lee S Y, Kim Y S, Lee J & Leventhal B L, 2020, 'Prevalence of and Factors Associated with School Bullying in Students with Autism Spectrum Disorder: A Cross-cultural Meta-analysis', *Yonsei Medical Journal*, Volume 61, Issue 11, pp. 909–22

30   van Roekel, E, Scholte, R H J & Didden, R, 2010, 'Bullying Among Adolescents with Autism Spectrum Disorders: Prevalence and Perception', *Journal of Autism and Developmental Disorders*, Volume 40, Issue 1, pp. 63–73

31   Munkhaugen, E K, Gjevik, E, Pripp, A H, Sponheim, E & Diseth, T H, 2017, 'School Refusal Behaviour: Are Children and Adolescents with Autism Spectrum Disorder at a Higher Risk?', *Research in Autism Spectrum Disorders*, Volumes 41–42, pp. 31–8

32   Upthegrove, R, Abu-Akel, A, Chisholm, K, Lin, A, Zahid, S, Pelton, M, Apperly, I, Hansen, P C & Wood, S J, 2018, 'Autism and Psychosis: Clinical Implications for Depression and Suicide', *Schizophrenia Research*, Volume 195, pp. 80–5.

33   Hedley, D & Uljarević, M, 2018, 'Systematic Review of Suicide in Autism Spectrum Disorder: Current Trends and Implications', *Current Developmental Disorders Reports*, Volume 5, pp. 65–76

34   Simone, R, 2010, *Aspergirls – Empowering Females with Asperger Syndrome*, London: Jessica Kingsley Publishers

35   Pecora, L A, Hancock, G I, Hooley, M, Demmer, D H, Attwood, T, Mesibov, G B & Stokes, M A, 2020, 'Gender Identity, Sexual Orientation and Adverse Sexual Experiences in Autistic Females', *Molecular Autism* 11, Article Number 57, doi.org/10.1186/s13229-020-00363-0

36   Brede, J, Babb, C, Jones, C, Elliott, M, Zanker, C, Tchanturia, K, Serpell, L, Fox, J & Mandy, W, 2020, '"For Me, the Anorexia is Just a Symptom, and the Cause is the Autism": Investigating Restrictive Eating Disorders in Autistic Women', *Journal of Autism and Developmental Disorders*, Volume 50, Issue 12, pp. 4280–96

37   Butwicka, A, Långström, N, Larsson, H, Lundström, S, Serlachius, E, Almqvist, C, Frisén, L & Lichtenstein, P, 2017 'Increased Risk for Substance Use-related Problems in Autism Spectrum Disorders: A Population-based Cohort Study', *Journal of Autism and Developmental Disorders*, Volume 47, Issue 1, pp. 80–9

38   Kaplan, D, Elfont, H, 1998, *Can't Hardly Wait*, Columbia Pictures/Tall Trees Productions

39   Brown-Lavoie, S M, Viecili, M A & Weiss, J A, 2014, 'Sexual Knowledge and Victimization in Adults with Autism Spectrum Disorders', *Journal of Autism and Developmental Disorders*, Volume 44, Issue 9, pp. 2185–96

40   Ohlsson Gotby V, Lichtenstein P, Långström N & Pettersson E, 2018, 'Childhood Neurodevelopmental Disorders and Risk of Coercive Sexual Victimization in Childhood and Adolescence – A Population-based Prospective Twin Study', *Journal of Child Psychology and Psychiatry*, Volume 59, Issue 9, pp. 957–66

41   Warrier, V, Greenberg, D M, Weir, E, Buckingham, C, Smith, P, Lai, M-C, Allison, C & Baron-Cohen, S, 2020 'Elevated Rates of Autism, Other Neurodevelopmental and Psychiatric Diagnoses, and Autistic Traits in Transgender and Gender-diverse Individuals', *Nature Communications*, Volume 11, Article Number 3959, doi.org/10.1038/s41467-020-17794-1

42   Janssen, A, Huang, H & Duncan, C, 2016, 'Gender Variance Among Youth with Autism Spectrum Disorders: A Retrospective Chart Review', *Transgender Health*, Volume 1, Issue 1, pp. 63–8

43   Zucker, K J, Nabbihohn, A N, Santarossa, A, Wood, H, Bradley, S J, Matthews, J & VanderLaan, D P, 2017, 'Intense/obsessional Interests in Children with Gender Dysphoria: A Cross-validation Study Using the Teacher's Report Form', *Child and Adolescent Psychiatry and Mental Health*, Volume 11, Article Number 51, doi.org/10.1186/s13034-017-0189-9

44   Strang, J F, Powers, M D, Knauss, M, *et al.* 2018, '"They Thought It Was an Obsession": Trajectories and Perspectives of Autistic Transgender and Gender-diverse Adolescents', *Journal of Autism and Developmental Disorders*, Volume 48, Issue 12, pp. 4039–55

45   Bennett, M & Goodall, E, 2016, 'Towards an Agenda for Research for Lesbian, Gay, Bisexual, Transgendered and/or Intersexed People with an Autism Spectrum Diagnosis', *Journal of Autism and Developmental Disorders*, Volume 46, Issue 9, pp. 3190–2

46 AMAZE 2018, *Australia's Attitudes & Behaviours Towards Autism; and Experiences of Autistic People and Their Families | Research report for AMAZE*, AMAZE, Melbourne, Australia

47 Cage, E & Howes, J, 2020, 'Dropping Out and Moving On: A Qualitative Study of Autistic People's Experiences of University', *Autism*, Volume 24, Issue 7, pp. 1664–75

48 AMAZE 2018, *Australia's Attitudes & Behaviours Towards Autism; and Experiences of Autistic People and Their Families | Autism and Employment*, AMAZE, Melbourne, Australia

49 The study also found that, of those who were in employment, 45 per cent reported that they were overskilled for their current job.

50 Sinclair, J, 2010, 'Cultural Commentary: Being Autistic Together', *Disability Studies Quarterly*, Volume 30, Number 1, dsq-sds.org/article/view/1075/1248

51 Sinclair, J, 2012, 'Don't Mourn For Us', *Autonomy*, Volume 1, Issue 1, philosophy.ucsc.edu/SinclairDontMournForUs.pdf

52 I did end up starting my PhD in 2019, but I changed the topic.

53 Brenner, L A, Shih, V H, Colich, N L, Sugar, C A, Bearden, C E & Dapretto, M, 2015, 'Time Reproduction Performance is Associated with Age and Working Memory in High-functioning Youth with Autism Spectrum Disorder', *Autism Research*, Volume 8, Issue 1, pp. 29–37

54 Nicholas, B, Rudrasingham, V, Nash, S, Kirov, G, Owen, M J & Wimpory, D C, 2007, 'Association of Per1 and Npas2 with Autistic Disorder: Support for the Clock Genes/Social Timing Hypothesis', *Molecular Psychiatry*, Volume 12, doi.org/10.1038/sj.mp.4001953

55 Wallace, G L & Happé, F, 2008, 'Time Perception in Autism Spectrum Disorders', *Research In Autism Spectrum Disorders*, Volume 2, Issue 3, pp. 447–55

NOTES

Happy Meals
Parts of this chapter were originally published as 'Why Did the Sunnyboy Have to Die?' in *The Age*, 5 October 2016

The Undiscovered Country
Parts of this chapter were originally published as 'Farewelling Lane' in *Daily Life*, 4 July 2012

Dear Dolly Doctor …
Parts of this chapter were originally published as 'Back Issues' in *The Saturday Paper*, 10 August 2018

I Love L.A.
Parts of this chapter were originally published as 'Adult Dress-ups' in *Daily Life*, 18 July 2012

They Go to Bed With Gilda, They Wake Up With Rain Man
Parts of this chapter were originally published as 'Me Too, Myself and I' in *The Saturday Paper*, 28 October 2017

ACKNOWLEDGEMENTS

This existence of this book owes no small debt to Arwen Summers at Hardie Grant Books, whose clear-eyed critique, encouragement, and willingness to at times let me communicate solely in Psyduck GIFs took *Late Bloomer* from its embryonic stages to the book you hold in your hands. Arwen has long encouraged me to consider writing a book, and I'm thrilled it's finally happened under her watch; thanks to Leah Horsfall for having a twenty-first birthday party all those years ago so Arwen and I could have our meet cute. Vanessa Lanaway's and Anna Collett's guidance through the edits was like watching a close-up magic trick; thank you for working out what I was trying to say and helping my scrambled sentences come to life. (And Anna, thank you for the dinosaurs.) Thank you to Hannah Ludbrook for 'getting it', and getting it out there. Thanks to the whole team at Hardie Grant Books for your support and enthusiasm throughout the whole journey.

Late Bloomer would never have materialised were it not for the opportunity Yellow Ladybugs gave me when they invited me to speak at their 2018 Good Mental Health for Autistic Girls and Women symposium. Thank you to Katie Koullas, Natasha Staheli and the team at YLB for everything you do. Although one book could never hope to represent the full spectrum (sorry!!!) of Autistic experiences, it was important to me that *Late Bloomer* reflect some of that diversity, so thank you to Shadia, Jess, Timothy, Jessie, James, Fleur, Jae, Mattie, Jo and Tegan for trusting me with your stories. Extra special thanks to Dr Ali Schnable for your expert feedback (and for accompanying it with photos of Dawn, the greyhound).

One of my goals for Late Bloomer was for it to serve, in part, as a love letter to the Port Melbourne that lives on only in the memories of 'Port people'. I am particularly grateful to the volunteers of the Port Melbourne Historical and Preservation Society for helping to fill in the gaps in my reminiscence, and for everything they do.

My education as a writer has been largely thanks to the guidance and mentorship of the editors who have helped me hone my craft and find my voice across the course of two decades' worth of freelancing. To Andrew Mast, Larissa Dubecki, Sushi Das, Alan Attwood, Joel Gibson, Sarah Oakes, Steph Harmon and Stephanie Convery, Erik Jensen and Maddison Connaughton, I quite literally couldn't have done it without you. Thank you to Ani Baker for welcoming me into your writers group in L.A. back in 2013, and in doing so reminding me how much I enjoyed writing personal essays. To Victoria Hannan, Cath Moore and Nicola Redhouse, thanks for weathering my endless 'When your book came out, did you feel/think/worry …' texts. Thank you to Chris Anastassiades and Charlie Carman for fostering my nascent screenwriting practice and accidentally helping me write my way to a diagnosis. And though it would probably make her yell at me to use the term, thanks to my mentor Helen Razer for riding me on my cultural theory all these years.

Writing this book during Stage 4 lockdown felt a little like I was a stowaway on the mole-like drilling vehicle Virgil in the 2003 disaster movie *The Core*, burrowing ever deeper into the centre of the earth as chaos reigned and a turtleneck-wearing Stanley Tucci negged me. I couldn't have survived it without my confidantes and trusted early readers, whose every text and email kept me alive and typing as I shared tiny paragraphs and workshopped chapter titles: to Ifer Moore, Talia Cain, Luke Devine, James Wright, Adam Christou, Casey Freeman and Rachel Short, thank you. To Alex Doenau, thank you for keeping a steady stream of Moomin and Pokémon content coming during dark days. Thanks to my housemate Chris Tursi for all the Bunnings runs to facilitate gardening aka 'the drafting process'. To the digital *D&D* crew, Alex Mann, Jess Pinney, Michael Jenkins, Andy Hazel and Chris, thanks for bad pizza and good times during the depths of the draft. To Sahra Stolz, thank you for welcoming me into your family, fam. To Mike Skinner and Jenna Turner,

I treasure your friendship and your doggies, and I'm so happy we all met at Rose Street. Extra special thanks to my PhD supervisors, Dr Stayci Taylor and Dr Glen Donnar, for not exploding, Looney Tunes style, when I sheepishly revealed that I had also written a book during the second year of my candidature.

To my Superfluity comrades, Christos Tsiolkas and Casey Bennetto, thank you for your friendship, support and uplift; every Tuesday night with you is a blessing, but it was a particular gift during the writing process. Here's to our future in Smooth syndication!

My dog, Milly, unfortunately can't read, but hopefully someone will convey to her the depths of my gratitude for every cuddle, laugh and frisbee park visit she facilitated during this book's creation. She may never be a real service dog but I know I couldn't live without her.

To my love, Catherine, thank you for not running in the opposite direction when I revealed on our first date that I was writing a book while doing a PhD. Sorry that you sent me Frank O'Hara reading 'Having A Coke With You' as an act of love and I immediately started doing Frank O'Hara impressions; thank you for recognising that my love language is echolalia.

To my family, I would not be who I am today without your love and support. To Dad and Jane, thank you for every potato curry dinner party and lockdown FaceTime during this book's gestation, and thank you Dad for your unfailing support of pretty much every hare-brained creative endeavour I've ever undertaken, for your hand-drawn cards, and for instilling in me a love of a good story, well told. To Blazey, my life-long hero, I'm so proud to be your little sister and so grateful for our long talks; sit back and really see you guys, see ya. To Atticus, every fart, bottom-bunk terror session and party blower prank was worth it to be able to have a little brother and creative collaborator as cool and wise as you. And to Mum, whose own journey of reinvention and education inspired me to return to university and discover who I really was, thank you for everything: from reading me *Under Milk Wood* and singing me sea shanties to working together in the same department, everything I am I owe to you.

Finally, to Autistic people everywhere: your existence is a gift to the world. May the world finally rise up to meet you, on your terms.